BAD GIRLS

M. WILLIAM PHELPS

PINNACLE BOOKS
Kensington Publishing Corp.
http://www.kensingtonbooks.com

PINNACLE BOOKS are published by

Kensington Publishing Corp.
119 West 40th Street
New York, NY 10018

All Kensington Titles, Imprints, and Distributed Lines are available at special quantity discounts for bulk purchases for sales promotions, premiums, fund-raising, and educational or institutional use. Special book excerpts or customized printings can also be created to fit specific needs. For details, write or phone the office of the Kensington special sales manager: Kensington Publishing Corp., 119 West 40th Street, New York, NY 10018, attn: Special Sales Department, Phone: 1-800-221-2647.

Pinnacle and the P logo Reg. U.S. Pat. & TM Off.

ISBN-13: 978-0-7860-3244-0
ISBN-10: 0-7860-3244-8
First Kensington Mass Marked Edition: September 2013

eISBN-13: 978-0-7860-3245-7
eISBN-10: 0-7860-3245-6
First Kensington Electronic Edition: September 2013

10 9 8 7 6 5 4 3 2 1

Printed in the United States of America

HIGHEST PRAISE FOR M. WILLIAM PHELPS

NEVER SEE THEM AGAIN

"This riveting book examines one of the most horrific murders in recent American history."

—*New York Post*

"Phelps clearly shows how the ugliest crimes can take place in the quietest of suburbs."

—*Library Journal*

"Thoroughly reported . . . The book is primarily a police procedural, but it is also a tribute to the four murder victims."

—*Kirkus Reviews*

TOO YOUNG TO KILL

"Phelps is the Harlan Coben of real-life thrillers."

—**Allison Brennan**

LOVE HER TO DEATH

"Reading anything by Phelps is always an eye opening experience. His writing reads like a fiction mystery novel. The characters are well researched and well written. We have murder, adultery, obsession, lies and so much more."

—*Suspense Magazine*

"You don't want to miss *Love Her To Death* by M. William Phelps, a book destined to be one of 2011's top true crimes!"

—*True Crime Book Reviews*

"A chilling crime . . . award-winning author Phelps goes into lustrous and painstaking detail, bringing all the players vividly to life."

—*Crime Magazine*

KILL FOR ME

"Pelps gets into the blood and guts of the story."

—**Gregg Olsen,** *New York Times* best-selling author of *Fear Collector*

"Phelps infuses his investigative journalism with plenty of energized descriptions."

—*Publishers Weekly*

DEATH TRAP

"A chilling tale of a sociopathic wife and mother willing to sacrifice all those around her to satisfy her boundless narcissism . . . a compelling journey from the inside of this woman's mind to final justice in a court of law. Fair warning: for three days I did little else but read this book."

—**Harry N. MacLean,** *New York Times* best-selling author of *In Broad Daylight*

I'LL BE WATCHING YOU

"Skillfully balances a victim's story against that of an arrogant killer as it reveals a deviant mind intent on topping the world's most dangerous criminals. Phelps has an unrelenting sense for detail that affirms his place, book by book, as one of our most engaging crime journalists."

—**Katherine Ramsland**

IF LOOKS COULD KILL

"M. William Phelps, one of America's finest true-crime writers, has written a compelling and gripping book about an intriguing murder mystery. Readers of this genre will thoroughly enjoy this book."

—**Vincent Bugliosi**

"Starts quickly and doesn't slow down. . . . Phelps consistently ratchets up the dramatic tension, hooking readers before they even know they've been hooked. His thorough research and interviews give the book a sense of growing complexity, richness of character, and urgency."

—**Stephen Singular**

MURDER IN THE HEARTLAND

"Drawing on interviews with law officers and relatives, the author has done significant research and—demonstrating how modern forensics and the Internet played critical, even unexpected roles in the investigation—his facile writing pulls the reader along."

—*St. Louis Post-Dispatch*

"Phelps expertly reminds us that when the darkest form of evil invades the quiet and safe outposts of rural America, the tragedy is greatly magnified. Get ready for some sleepless nights."

—**Carlton Stowers**

"This is the most disturbing and moving look at murder in rural America since Capote's *In Cold Blood*."

—**Gregg Olsen**

SLEEP IN HEAVENLY PEACE

"An exceptional book by an exceptional true crime writer. Phelps exposes long-hidden secrets and reveals disquieting truths."

—**Kathryn Casey**

EVERY MOVE YOU MAKE

"An insightful and fast-paced examination of the inner workings of a good cop and his bad informant, culminating in an unforgettable truth-is-stranger-than-fiction climax."

—**Michael M. Baden, M.D.**

"M. William Phelps is the rising star of the nonfiction crime genre, and his true tales of murderers and mayhem are scary-as-hell thrill rides into the dark heart of the inhuman condition."

—**Douglas Clegg**

LETHAL GUARDIAN

"An intense roller-coaster of a crime story . . . complex, with a plethora of twists and turns worthy of any great detective mystery, and yet so well-laid out, so crisply written with such detail to character and place that it reads more like a novel than your standard non-fiction crime book."

—**Steve Jackson**

PERFECT POISON

"True crime at its best—compelling, gripping, an edge-of-the-seat thriller. Phelps packs wallops of delight with his skillful ability to narrate a suspenseful story and his encyclopedic knowledge of police procedures."

—**Harvey Rachlin**

"A compelling account of terror . . . the author dedicates himself to unmasking the psychopath with facts, insight and the other proven methods of journalistic leg work."

—**Lowell Cauffiel**

Also By M. William Phelps

Perfect Poison

Lethal Guardian

Every Move You Make

Sleep in Heavenly Peace

Murder in the Heartland

Because You Loved Me

If Looks Could Kill

I'll Be Watching You

Deadly Secrets

Cruel Death

Death Trap

Kill For Me

Failures of the Presidents (coauthor)

Nathan Hale: The Life and Death of America's First Spy

The Devil's Rooming House: The True Story of America's Deadliest Female Serial Killer

The Devil's Right Hand: The Tragic Story of the Colt Family Curse

Love Her to Death

Too Young to Kill

Never See Them Again

The Dead Soul: A Thriller (available as e-book only)

Murder, New England

Jane Doe No More

Kiss of the She-Devil

This book is dedicated to any child who has been abused and not allowed the grace of growing up in a loving, caring, healthy environment.

AUTHOR'S NOTE

On the surface, this might seem like any other sensational true-crime tale. Girl meets girl. Girl falls head over heels. Drugs and sex and staying up partying for days at a time ensue. With that narrative playing as a background theme, fantasy and role-playing "fun," along with a bit of amateur porn filmmaking tossed in, become the norm. When the rush of the drugs and living on the edge subsides, darkness settles; their lives go from petty shoplifting (zero) to—finally—murder (one hundred). Add to that a *Thelma & Louise* jaunt through the southwestern countryside, packing booze and drugs and guns and gusto. Along the way, there is some frolicking, and even a mock wedding. A confrontation with police happens. A few courtroom dramas. Betrayal. Then a she said/she said moment of derision—or, rather, division—occurs. And, for the hell of it, toss in a bit of what some described as black magic and witchcraft.

Okay, so maybe it's not your *typical* true-crime story.

Beyond that scandalous, drama-inviting headline, however, this book is the story of two young women caught in a whirlwind of dysfunction and chronic drug use, drifting closer together, until one day they collide in an avalanche of lust, craziness, and murder. What starts out as an unexpected affair—one of the girls was dating males at the time; the other had a child with a man—turns into a case of who killed whom, why, and how an overly aggressive sexual appetite is sometimes confused with love. More important, it is a cautionary tale of teens growing up in a world brimming with very little adult supervision and chaos. Their lives were on a crash course, with no one there to direct or steer them away from imminent disaster. It doesn't excuse the behavior or the terrible crimes committed along the way, but it does explain that all-important, ubiquitous question I get asked more than any other: "Why does someone commit murder?" Here, in this case, you're going to hear from one of the girls involved—and her story will eventually produce answers you likely did not expect.

I would ask that, as you read this book and become familiar with the wild and crazy lives these girls led, try to keep from judging Bobbi, especially, on what she has done and where her addictions have brought her. It's going to be easy not to like Bobbi Jo Smith. Be mindful of that. Because we cannot convict someone of murder based on feelings. A guilty verdict has to be about the evidence against the accused.

So there you have it: Two girls on separate paths meet and realize life is full of surprises. The decisions these girls make after hooking up change their lives forever. The decisions they make on their own, however, will change the way in which the truth is exposed and how "justice" prevails.

For God made not death: neither hath he pleasure in the destruction of the living.

For he created all things, that they might have their being: and the generations of the world were healthful; and there is no poison of destruction in them, nor the kingdom of death upon the earth:

(For righteousness is immortal:)

For God created man to be immortal, and made him to be an image of his own eternity.

Nevertheless through envy of the devil came death into the world: and they that do hold of his side do find it.

Wisdom of Solomon: 1:13-15; 2:23-24

PROLOGUE

THERE ARE MILES upon miles of unpaved, gravel-packed roads all over Texas. There's also a litany of tarred surfaces in great need of repair and repaving, rickety barns ready to fall over from just the right gust of wind, and old homes far beyond the fixable improvements of a Home Depot makeover. In many ways, all of this adds to the bucolic beauty of rural Texas. And when you think about it, especially while watching a dust cloud kick up behind an old Chevy heading out into an open field on a sunny, dry day, it becomes a metaphor for life, not only in the Lone Star State, but everywhere else, too. Because life in the real world—for most people, I think—does not consist of a white picket fence, a family dog, a pair of healthy kids, two vehicles (or, rather, one SUV and a minivan) sitting on a plush blacktop driveway, a golf course lawn cut every Saturday on a John Deere, some manageable debt, colorful, blight-free perennials, perhaps a boat, barbecues on the weekends, Christmas bonuses, vacations, family photos developed at the local Walmart hanging along the banister. Sometimes life throws daggers. And if you end up on the receiving end of one, well, watch out.

You're dead.

Or certainly maimed for life.

No more soccer-mom minivan trips across town with your neighbors' kids, arguments over white or wheat PB&J school lunches, walks in the park with the ladies from church while taking in all of the town gossip, PTA meetings, Little League games, ice cream running down the filthy arms of whining kids. No. If you happen to be on the receiving end of one of those daggers, you'll find yourself staring down the tunnel at that white light—if you're lucky—and buckets of tears, along with a lifetime of melancholy chiseling away the days. Unemployment checks (while they last). Food stamps. And, after waiting in the church line, bricks of sour orange-colored block cheese.

This will be your life.

Bobbi Jo Smith was not one of those "lucky" kids, her parents jumping for joy on the sidelines while she scored the winning goal. She never played Barbies with the popular neighborhood girls. Nor had she become part of what is the new, twenty-first-century "working class" searching for the next meal and a government handout. Somewhere in between, Bobbi was just a girl, essentially, when she realized her mother didn't give two shakes about her. And Dad? Well, who the hell was he, anyway? *Where* was he? By the time Bobbi was old enough to look around and not only put into context, but truly understand, where she was being raised, she found herself in the sleepy, shanty little Texas town of Graford, of which many in the state had never even heard. For those kids like Bobbi, in certain sections of this rather pleasant town boasting a mere 578 residents (2000 census), they looked around and met the despondent gazes— distant and stoic—on the faces of everyone surrounding them. They eventually realized they were staring into a mirror. The young gawked at their futures; while the old shook their heads at their past. There weren't too many moms and dads around to take their babies for walks, or to share their days watching *Sesame Street* and *The Electric Company*. If you were fortunate enough (and so very few were), you saw your parents long enough during the day to get yelled at and maybe stung by the slap of a whipping belt. Not for what you did. That was too easy. But for the shitty life your parents had to deal with every day. Aggression, the experts call it. Repressed anger misdirected at the human beings you could hurt the most and, largely, get away with. Not everyone in Graford lived this way, of course. That is not what I mean here. But for Bobbi, this was her life.

And it was one of the many reasons why Bobbi relied on her grandmother. The old woman—and

Bobbi's son, the child Bobbi had before she was old enough to work legally, or have the guts to come out and live the lifestyle she wanted—meant everything to Bobbi.

My mother was never in my life, Bobbi told me as our conversations began in early 2012. *My grandmother raised me.*

Bobbi had learned from her upbringing, adding, *I'm a great mother.*

Yet she wrote this to me from a jail cell.

Go figure. The value this young woman put on things. The bar she now lived under set fairly high. At first, it didn't make sense. But then, later on, it did, once I understood the framework of Bobbi's life and how she ended up behind bars, facing five decades of never feeling the warmth of the sun's glow on her back as a free woman.

I'm nothing like I was raised. And I'm thankful to God for that.

Again, a strange comment coming from a woman who had been in prison for eight years already at the time she wrote it.

And she was only in her twenties.

Still, prison was four walls and a lock. Bobbi could never get used to this life. On the day one of her best friends left prison, out on parole, Bobbi turned to her as she walked away.

"I don't want to die in here," Bobbi said. "Please don't let me die in here."

* * *

It had been years since Bobbi saw her son. But in January 2012, the boy was brought into Gatesville Prison for a visit with a woman he really didn't know. To the child, perhaps, Bobbi was some sort of a folk hero, locked away behind bars for a crime, according to Bobbi, she had not committed. A vicious murder, in fact, that Bobbi claimed a casual bed partner of hers at the time committed—a cute girl Bobbi had known for nearly a month or so before the man Bobbi considered a father figure was shot repeatedly in the head at point-blank range.

"It's like we've never been apart," Bobbi said after the visit with her boy, now eleven years old. "I love him so much. He's my motivation."

The boy became Bobbi's light. A constant beacon of hope and clarity she sees on a horizon beyond the concrete prison walls surrounding (maybe engulfing) her. It's that love she has for her child that drives Bobbi today, helping her to, she noted, *push through this place . . . [that] at times . . . is almost too much to consume.*

Odd word choice there, I thought: "consume." As if Bobbi is being force-fed a system she doesn't have a taste for.

Bobbi claimed to have not spoken to a man in eight years—even the male guards inside the prison. This was one of the reasons why Bobbi had developed a bit of anxiety about meeting with me while I was in Texas (March 2012). Thus, a prison

visit I so much looked forward to wasn't meant
to be.

I think Bobbi was happy with this outcome. I do
not feel she wanted a face-to-face with me—not
then, anyway. She could have made the visit
happen if she wanted. But she didn't trust me.
And I, to be clear, didn't believe she was innocent
at that time. I didn't trust *her.* I thought she was just
one more guilty, incarcerated female murderer,
begging me to listen to her story in hopes I would
believe what was now hindsight tethered with carefully chosen lies.

Writing to me, however, became the perfect way
for Bobbi to explain (and express) herself in what
was a nonthreatening environment; her way of
telling me how things actually happened. Facing
me, allowing me to question her and put things
into perspective, might have been too much, too
soon. In the end, what we worked out turned into
the ideal circumstance. I could e-mail Bobbi. Yes,
e-mail. I was able to send the e-mail to a site run by
the prison system, and Bobbi, after receiving the
e-mail that day or the following morning, would respond by a phone call to a friend, or a letter (she
cannot e-mail me back). It kept our conversations
moving fluidly. What impressed me right away was
Bobbi's willingness to answer *any* question. In
many passages of this book, Bobbi's conversation
with me will be styled as though it had occurred in
a spoken situation—not a written reply or passed-

along response. Our give-and-take was such that we were speaking on a personal level.

Along this journey, Bobbi and I had arguments; she angrily accused me of the most egregious exploitations, as others have before her and still others will in the days to come. Then she apologized. She condemned my work (in general) and apologized again. Our relationship over the course of telling this story changed remarkably. Yet within it all, I got to know this woman. And, more important, as I pushed through the evidence in this case and interviewed Bobbi extensively (often asking the same questions in different ways), I began to believe she was convicted of a crime she did not commit.

Those early letters between us were the first in what would become a host of correspondences over the course of a year. Each detailed a specific portion of the life and times of a young girl who had moved in with a considerably older man after she got pregnant as a young teen (knowing she was a lesbian). She wound up in prison a few years later, doing what amounted to life for a murder she has repeatedly and steadfastly denied having any part in—a murder, I should point out, I believed Bobbi had committed when I began this project.

This book is going to explore the entire case in great depth. With all of the resources available to me—trial transcripts, police reports, letters and journals, autopsy reports, recorded interviews by law enforcement, interviews with all of the key players, along with a modest amount of additional resources—I believe I was able to get to the bottom of who murdered forty-nine-year-old Robert "Bob" Dow. And this conclusion, for certain, will shock some, infuriate others, and hopefully give some understanding of why Bob was murdered.

PART ONE

LOVE IS BLIND

CHAPTER 1

"SOMETHING BAD MAY have happened."
It was the only fact she was certain of.
Beyond that, the woman thought the victim might
be "a friend of her niece's." His name "might have
been" Bob, but that was all she knew. She feared
the worst, however: "Bob Something" was dead.
She didn't know the exact address—where the
police could find him—but she could explain to
someone how to get there, and would escort cops
to the house if they wanted to meet her somewhere in the neighborhood.

On a quiet evening, May 5, 2004, forty-eight-
year-old Richard "Rick" Cruz called the Mineral
Wells Police Department (MWPD) and explained
what his wife, Kathy, had just told him. Both Kathy
and Rick were in somewhat of a panicked state.
Not freaked out. But their feelings were more of

a puzzled, what's-going-on–type thing they didn't quite understand.

"Have you heard anything about someone being shot on Eighteenth Street?" Rick asked the 911 dispatcher.

Rick had the street wrong. It was actually Twentieth Street. Still, dispatch wasn't in the business of sharing information with worried callers phoning in to report gunshots fired at people.

"What other information do you have?" the 911 operator asked.

Rick explained the layout of the neighborhood best he could. He said he and Kathy weren't all that familiar with Mineral Wells and this particular neighborhood where Bob supposedly lived. They had only heard about it.

The operator said they'd send an officer out to Eighteenth Street to check things out.

Rick and Kathy Cruz lived in Graford, Texas, directly next door to Kathy's mother and father, Dorothy and Fred Smith. Graford is about fifteen miles from Mineral Wells, where the shooting was said to have occurred. Kathy and Rick had arrived home at about 4:30 P.M. Rick was driving. As they exited the vehicle after Rick parked, Kathy's mother, Dorothy, standing on her porch next door, waved them over.

"Come here," Dorothy shouted. She seemed frazzled and agitated, as if in a hurry to get them over there so she could speak her mind about something.

"What is it?" Kathy asked.

Dorothy was "very upset," Kathy later explained to police. Kathy and Rick noticed Dorothy was on the telephone. Apparently, after walking over and assessing the situation, Kathy found out that Dorothy was talking to her other daughter, Kathy's sister.

Something terrible was going on.

"What is it?" Rick and Kathy asked.

A pause. Then a bombshell: Somebody shot Bob.

Dorothy got off the phone and clarified what she knew. As the story went thus far, somehow, Dorothy explained, Kathy's niece (Dorothy's grandchild)—who had been living with Dorothy intermittently throughout the past year—might be involved in the shooting. Nobody really knew how or why, or any of the circumstances surrounding the story. Just that it was urgent someone get over there to this Bob Something's house immediately.

Rick walked into Dorothy's house. According to what he later told police, without explaining what he was doing, he headed into his niece's room to have a look around.

"You stay here," Rick told Kathy, who was becoming more upset by the moment. Kathy's niece had lived with the Cruzes for a while as well. Kathy had been close to her.

The idea Rick had in mind was to see if he could find something in the house that might clarify just what the hell was going on.

A note.

An e-mail.

Anything.

There was probably a simple answer. Usually, there was. People overreact. Perhaps Dorothy, in all of her excitement, had totally misinterpreted the situation and blew it out of proportion. Drama. Every family, in some form or fashion, had certain members that thrived on it.

Upon immediately entering the young girl's room, Rick found an empty gun holster. Exactly what he did not expect.

Where is the weapon?

Then he found an unloaded pistol in a second holster.

This alarmed Rick. The report of a shooting. A gun missing from a holster. Another weapon on the bed *in* a holster. Rick wasn't Magnum, P.I., but then again, he didn't need to be a private investigator to figure out that something was up. And it didn't look good.

Rick ran out of the room, then out of the house. While outside in the front yard, Rick called the MWPD back on his cell phone.

"Have you found anything?" Rick asked the operator. He sounded more serious.

"No. The officers out at Eighteenth Street haven't located anything suspicious." The dispatcher wondered what was going on. Was this guy—Rick—playing games with the MWPD?

Rick hung up. Then grabbed Kathy's attention. "Listen, we have to head out to Mineral Wells ourselves and find out what's going on."

Kathy thought about it.

Good idea.

They took off.

On the way to Mineral Wells—having no clue, really, where in that town they were headed—Rick phoned Kathy's sister, her niece's mother, Tamey Hurley. She asked for directions to a house in Mineral Wells where Kathy's niece had been hanging out at, and living in, lately. There was even some indication that the niece was working with the guy who lived there. Bob Something.

Tamey had been to the house.

After getting more detailed directions, Rick decided that he'd better stop first at the MWPD and relay what he had uncovered.

"I have the gun," Rick explained, referring to the pistol he had taken out of the room in Dorothy's house. "Do you want it?"

The cop was a bit taken aback. "We need to find that house first, Mr. Cruz. And we need to see if anything happened—then we can take it from there."

Kathy's niece was young, just nineteen. According to Kathy and Rick, she liked to "get on drugs and exaggerate things." She came across as a tough, gangsta-type chick, but friends who intimately knew her said she was terribly misunderstood, and that she was kindhearted and always erred on the side of her humility. But the bug of drug addiction had bitten her hard. Drugs had become her life. And although she had been in a relationship with a man, engaged to be married, and had had a baby, she was an open and admitted lesbian. She had been struggling to come out and live that lifestyle, carefree, suffering from the ill effects of suppressing who she was.

They left together, the cop following Rick and Kathy.

Rick pulled onto Eighteenth Street first and didn't seem to know where he was going. He was driving slowly past each house, checking to see if he recognized any of them. In back of him, the cop became impatient as each block passed. The officer threw up his hands, beckoning Rick to tell him what in the hell was going on here. Was this some sort of a joke?

After some time of Rick's stop-and-go game, the cop got on the telephone with Kathy's sister and she talked him directly over to Twentieth Street.

Finally they arrived at the right house.

Bob's home.

Patrol Corporal Randy Hunter then got out of his cruiser and told Rick, "You stay here by your truck and wait." Hunter said he needed to approach the door by himself.

Procedure.

Hunter knocked on the front door as Rick and Kathy looked on.

No answer.

"I'm going around back," Hunter said. "Stay where you are." He held up his hand as to indicate stop. The plan was, Hunter later said, "to check and see if anybody may have been in the backyard, look around. . . ." He wanted to see what he could find out.

Nobody seemed to be home, but Officer Hunter noticed something peculiar as he focused on the back door of the home.

One of the windowpanes had been smashed.

"Something may have happened inside," Hunter recalled later, speaking about that moment he spied the broken back window, "that we needed to investigate a little further [and] check the welfare of the people inside."

Several additional officers arrived. Hunter approached the house slowly, his weapon drawn, reached for the knob and opened the door.

"Mineral Wells Police Department!" the veteran cop yelled as he slowly walked in. "We're here with Richard and Kathy Cruz. We're coming in."

Not a peep.

Hunter announced himself "four or five times" before heading into the kitchen.

As he made his way through that area of the house stealthily, as if expecting to be ambushed at any moment, Hunter heard music. A radio or television was on.

Coming out of the hallway from the kitchen, Hunter spied a "subject," as he described the person, "somebody lying on [a] bed. . . ."

He pointed his weapon toward the subject and shouted: "Mineral Wells Police Department!"

No response.

"The size of the body . . . it appeared to be a male," Hunter recalled.

But Randy Hunter couldn't be 100 percent certain, because the bottom half of the subject was covered with a blanket. And from his neck up, the subject's face was covered with a pillow or bag of some sort.

Hunter carefully approached the subject, bent down, and placed two fingers on the man's carotid artery to check for a pulse.

No sign of life.

As Hunter grabbed his radio to call in additional backup, he saw blood.

"We're going to need an ambulance over here . . . ," Hunter said into his handheld. "Send Captain [Mike] McAllester and Sergeant [Brian] Boetz, too."

They were homicide investigators.

Hunter worked his way around the corner from that small bedroom and located in the back of the house a second bedroom, which he also approached with caution.

The door was slightly ajar. Hunter pried it open gently and saw a "hospital-type bed . . . with all kinds of stuff piled on it." As he walked toward the bed to check the other side, "an arm fell out from underneath a blanket. . . ."

Oh, boy . . .

CHAPTER 2

SHE BELIEVED IT TO BE some sort of celestial "sign." Those incredibly vivid dreams invading her sleep were coming "for a reason." They were fuzzy images, certainly, filled with metaphors of "which path to take," she later explained. In one, Jennifer "Jen" Jones believed she was setting herself up for failure simply because she had been born (as they might say in Texas) "kin" to Clyde Barrow, half of the infamous Bonnie and Clyde murderous duo. Indeed, according to Jen's grandmother, who was said to have made a shrine in her house dedicated to the old murderer and bank robber, Jen had that bad blood of the Barrows coursing through her veins. As such, there was nothing she could do about it. Jen's mother before her, Kathy Jones, had set herself on that same path. Kathy was tough as rawhide, a bar bruiser and career criminal, in and out of jail. Kathy had even come close to death a number of times, stabbed and beaten. Jen never saw herself in that same manner. However, coming from that sort of pedigree, she developed a thick exterior and a disastrously unhealthy inner dialogue. She began to convince herself that she could do anything. And all of those dreams she was having lately—those demons speaking to her at night—they fit right into the madness that had become her life. In other words, she felt doomed.

To fail, that is.

"I found a list once," one of Jen's sisters explained to me. "Jennifer was, like, just about fourteen. It was a list of all the guys she had slept with. She stopped at one hundred. I asked why [the list abruptly ended]. She said she lost count. The list started with names. As it continued, she dropped the names. I asked why. She said she didn't even know some of the names of the guys she'd had sex with."

One hundred was likely an exaggeration, but the sister's point was clearly made.

Because of the Clyde Barrow connection and a mother she viewed as destructive, unavailable, and quite caught up in a world of drugs and crimes to support bad habits, Jennifer Jones obsessed over the self-prophesized fact in her head that her life had been paved by a road already chosen for her. No matter what she did, no matter how hard she tried, Jen believed nothing could get in the way of this tragic evolution that was her fate.

So why fight it? Jen decided. Why not embrace

its ambiguity and dark side? Years ago, Jen wrote about her chosen future in a journal, which had become her best friend at the time. On December 28, 2000, just five days after her fifteenth birthday, Jen sat down and confirmed the inevitable: *These dreams are coming to me for a reason. . . .*

The fifteen-year-old Jennifer Jones had no idea how visionary—call it wishful thinking, a self-fulfilling prophesy, creating her own reality, whatever—those dreams of her future were to become. The baby-faced, clear-skinned, attractive Texas teen, with long brown hair and a Colgate smile, had set herself on a dangerous and deadly course, indeed. She didn't know it, but in front of Jen was a carefully chosen path, which her mother, likewise, had tried to manage before her. It was one that Jen had predicted for herself years before. It occurred in tandem with a new "love" of her life— a deceivingly pretty, petite unnatural blonde blinded by the power and curse of addiction— which would end up becoming Jen's proverbial scapegoat.

CHAPTER 3

IT WAS 7:30 P.M. ON MAY 5, 2004. By most accounts, it had been a quite night in Mineral Wells, Texas. Mineral Wells is a mostly white, bedroom community of about sixteen thousand, located in the northern central portion of the state pushing up toward the Oklahoma border. Fort Worth is the closest major city; Dallas and Irving are not too far east from there.

Before Rick and Kathy Cruz had telephoned the MWPD and reported what appeared to be a murder, the town had enjoyed a near-nonexistent homicide rate: Between 1999 and 2004, for example, there had been three murders. So residents killing one another was not what Mineral Wells worried all that much about. If you asked the locals, the major problems in Mineral Wells dated back to 1973, when the military installation known as Fort Wolters transferred its last remaining helicopters out of the popular base. This action began the economically devastating process of closing. At one time, Fort Wolters kept Mineral Wells bustling with plenty of military money floating around in bars and petrol stations and every other type of financial mainstay holding up a small community.

During what are often called the financial heydays of World War II, some say nearly 250,000 soldiers filed their way through the Fort Wolters Base, with another forty thousand during the Vietnam War. After that last copter and soldier left, however, Mineral Wells felt the hit immediately. All of that military money vanished seemingly overnight. Add to that the collapse of the cottage industry of the Baker Hotel, an icon in Mineral Wells since the 1940s and 1950s.

The Baker Hotel was a resort, a bona fide destination for many tourists and Hollywood celebrities and curiosity seekers from all over the world. The likes of Marilyn Monroe to FDR made visits there. Everyone came in search of some of that old "crazy water" said be tapped in Mineral Wells springs. The town had been founded on a certain type of mineral water that had sprung up and was thought to have some sort of a therapeutic value. It was said to be the cure for everything from arthritis to insanity, hence the "crazy water" name. As a result, the town became somewhat of a miracle cure destination. Everybody wanted what was in that water. The Baker Hotel, a rather huge landmark in town—now run-down and about to fall in on its own building blocks—

became the go-to hot spot. There in the center of town stood a high-rise establishment with mineral baths on the top floor.

"People came from all over to soak in the baths and then profess it was a cure for anything they had," said one local. "So, back in the fifties and early sixties, this was a booming town."

Throughout that time, the economy was great; the military was rocking and rolling. The Baker Hotel became similar to a little Las Vegas, and all was copacetic in town. But then the military base closed and the bottom fell out. No sooner had that happened than the Baker Hotel imploded as well.

As the years have progressed, Mineral Wells has fallen more in line with the familiar poverty-stricken, jobless brand that has become small-town America. It became ravaged by the horrors of what meth and ice can do, robberies, burglaries, auto thefts, and rapes. Not a trade-off, necessarily, for a low murder rate; but a fact the locals—many of whom were born and raised in Mineral Wells—could not and would not ever deny.

"Still," one local told me, "Mineral Wells sometimes gets thrown that way"—being a bad place to live—"but it's really not. Probably just like anywhere else, we have the same problems other communities have. We're average people."

Yes, the one fact that MWPD officers and the locals will acknowledge all day long is that, despite the downturns throughout the years, Mineral

Wells has "one of the lowest, if not the lowest, murder rates in the state."

Indeed, murder is not a call the MWPD gets all that frequently.

Randy Hunter and several other MWPD officers, who arrived on the scene to back him up, weren't in the house all that long. When Hunter and the other police officers emerged, Rick Cruz heard additional sirens—other cops and an ambulance. Now it all seemed real to the Cruzes. Something had happened—something terrible, something sinister, and maybe even deadly.

Officer Hunter must have found something inside the house, Rick Cruz surmised, looking on.

Hunter came out and walked over to Rick and Kathy as additional cops and the emergency medical technician (EMT) van pulled up. "I'll need that gun, Mr. Cruz."

Rick handed it over. "What's going on?"

The officer didn't say anything.

"What is it?" Rick asked.

The cop said nothing.

Then again, he didn't have to. The look on his face, the arriving officers and EMTs, said it all. What had started hours earlier as a "maybe" was now something much more serious. Someone had been shot. No doubt about it. And by the look of it, Rick and Kathy Cruz knew while standing there in Bob's driveway, sizing up the scene as it unfolded in front of them, that the cop was in no hurry to help the victim out. And that could mean only one thing.

By now, the MWPD believed there were possibly two victims inside what was an absolute garbage dump of a house on Twentieth Street. Police found a male and a female. Or a mother and her son, as it turned out. That first responding officer, Randy Hunter, knew the man was dead. But the woman, she was alive—just barely. The MWPD had no idea what happened: how, why, when, or by whom. They only inferred that a gun was somehow involved. Hunter and his team of responding officers did a cursory search of the house, where they had found the one man, presumably Bob— unresponsive, lying on a bed, cold to the touch, dead as road kill.

As Hunter walked into that second bedroom and the arm fell off the bed, he heard a groan. And it scared him.

What in the hell? Hunter thought.

Not *another DB*.

There was an elderly woman awake in her bed in that adjacent room, buried under a mound of covers. The room was a complete mess, "junked out," said one law enforcement source. There were empty Happy Meal boxes all over the place. The old woman had been watching television, actually. And when Hunter approached, weapon drawn, ready and expecting to find her dead, too, she looked at him quizzically and wondered what in the world was going on. It was obvious that she had been underfed and was perhaps suffering from malnutrition and some form of dementia.

"Out of it," one cop told me later. She was totally oblivious to the fact that the man—her son—in the room next to her was dead. "Once she got some fluids in her, though, she bounced back quickly and was, she let us know, totally surprised that the cops were in her house."

One report had her sitting up in bed at one point, saying, "Is there anything wrong, Officer?" Meanwhile, Hunter was digging her out of the covers she was buried under when he realized she was alive.

The responding officers were smart not to touch or meddle with the crime scene. It's amazing how many first responders muck up what can be a slippery slope when walking into a crime scene involving a potential homicide victim. It's those first responders, most forensic scientists will agree, that can make or break a case depending on how they go about closing off and securing a scene. In this case, the MWPD had trained its officers properly—apparently. There was a protocol and it had seemed to be followed.

* * *

Thirty-five-year-old MWPD Detective Brian
Boetz was at home, already done for the day, enjoying his life outside work, when the call came.

"We have what appears to be a double homicide . . . out on Twentieth Street," dispatch said.

"Got it. On my way."

One murder in Mineral Wells on a Wednesday
evening was beyond rare. But *two*? That got Boetz's
attention mighty quick. He didn't waste much
time hopping up out of his chair, grabbing his
weapon and radio, firing up his black Yukon SUV,
and kicking stone and dust from his driveway as
the siren blared, the lights flashed, and Boetz
found himself heading toward a possible double
homicide.

Inside the house, Randy Hunter made sure the
old woman was taken out by EMTs and brought directly to a hospital.

It took Detective Boetz about fifteen minutes to
get to the scene. He stepped out of his Yukon, saw
Richard and Kathy Cruz standing and looking
rather puzzled, and then headed into the house.
No sooner had Boetz arrived, than his captain,
Mike McAllester, pulled up.

Boetz was a Texas transplant. His mother, grandfather, grandmother, and he had moved to Mineral Wells from Denver, Colorado, when Boetz was
twelve.

"My dad lives somewhere in Oregon, I think,"
the detective told me. "I don't know for sure. I
don't keep in touch with him."

Taking a look at the house from outside as they headed in, Boetz and McAllester easily determined that no one had been taking care of the place. They'd seen worse, sure. Nonetheless, this house was nothing more than a run-down, dirty, substandard, ranch-style box of decaying wood, nearly overcome by aggressive, vinelike vegetation, with paint peeling off like confetti.

The EMTs were gone by the time Boetz and McAllester arrived. A cursory look at the neighborhood and it was clear that they were looking at a cookie-cutter series of similar single-family ranch homes on postage-stamp sects of land. This was part of suburban Mineral Wells. Most homes were kept up best they could be under the conditions of the economic times and not much drive to fix up a community that had been falling to the ills of the drug culture for years. Drugs have a way of working themselves into the nicer communities, once the suburban partyers move on from weed and booze and into the heavier stuff, such as heroin, crack, and meth. There is no defining line much anymore, separating the "hood" from the "burbs," unless a Realtor is talking exclusive areas of the town. Drugs are everywhere.

"The town of Mineral Wells is definitely in decay," one visitor to the neighborhood told me, "and none of the homes in that neighborhood will be in *Better Homes and Gardens*."

An understatement.

"We entered through a back door"—after

reaching in through what was a windowpane of smashed-out glass, with a bit of blood surrounding it, and unlatching the lock—"and found a victim deceased and an elderly female subject still alive in her bed," Randy Hunter explained to Boetz as they got together inside and talked.

"No kidding."

"Yeah."

"So it's not a double?" Boetz asked. He was confused. Dispatch had called in potentially two homicides. Could there be another victim, besides the old woman who had been taken to the hospital?

"No, just the one," Hunter said. He pointed to the room where the body had been discovered.

"Thanks."

The old woman, Hunter further explained to Boetz, was unmindful of what had happened inside the home. She had no idea someone had shot and killed her son.

"There's one deceased person inside and one being attended to [at the hospital]," Boetz explained to his boss, Mike McAllester.

It was 8:23 P.M. Boetz had a look around the house before heading into the bedroom to examine the DB. It appeared that the old woman had lived inside her room and was being *kept*—for lack of a better term—by someone, probably her son, Boetz surmised.

The victim was naked, lying on a bed, half his body covered with blankets (as if he had been sleeping). A pillow or some sort of laundry bag

covered what was left of his face. He had been
shot, apparently point-blank, several times; the
right side of his jaw had been blown nearly off his
face, his cheek nothing more than ripped, torn,
and bloodied flesh.

"Looks like the elderly lady has been neglected," Boetz said. Interestingly enough, there was
a lock on the outside of the old woman's door.
Whoever was supposedly taking care of her had essentially locked her inside the room. It was clear
she hardly—if ever—left that room.

Boetz asked Sergeant Brad Belz, who had just
arrived, to position himself at the front door,
saying, "Keep a log of anybody coming and going
from the crime scene."

"Will do," Belz said.

Boetz asked Officer Gary Lively to do the same
at the back door. "Don't let anyone in."

"No problem, Detective."

Boetz and McAllester took a moment to look
around the house. A basic ranch, the front door
opened into a small living room, which was "just
messy . . . in somewhat disarray," Boetz recalled.
There were mattresses on the floor, pillows and
blankets and garbage strewn all over, as if several
people had been living in the house and sleeping
anywhere they could find an open space. There
was a desk, with a computer and a chair. "Stacked
up on top of a stand, where the TV was on, was a
bunch of videotapes. . . ." There was some other
furniture spread throughout the room, sparse as it

was, but it was old and decrepit, like the inside of the home itself. And there was a lone fan, Boetz took note of, "noisy and running," sitting on a table. This gave the inside of the house a rather creepy feel, as if the fan were the only living thing left.

Taking a right out of the living room, Boetz stared down a short hallway, which went into the kitchen on the right and a sitting room (bedroom) on the left. In the kitchen, dishes and pots and pans were stacked everywhere: on counters, in the sink, on the table.

Disgusting. No other way to put it.

Heading toward the rear of the house inside the kitchen, Boetz studied the door. One of the panes had been smashed and there was blood on the glass and door itself. Not a lot, but enough to get a sample. On the floor below were several bits and pieces of broken glass.

Boetz and McAllester walked into the bedroom with the DB. A pillow—or, as Boetz realized now, a laundry bag—was covering the man's face. The idea, Boetz knew, was to "back up for a moment and look at the big picture of what could have happened." Any good cop will explain: The scene will speak to you if you don't interrupt the process.

Looking around, Boetz pointed to the wall. There seemed to be a few pictures missing. The corners of the photos or pictures were still attached to the wall by tape and staples, but the body of the pictures was gone. Boetz could tell by the grime and dust marking an outline of where the pictures had hung that someone had removed them recently. The walls were a putrid tan color, like coffee ice cream, smudged with filth and dirt and grease. There was a bureau to the left of the victim, a stereo on top of it. The bed itself was a mattress on the floor. The striped laundry bag covered the victim's face and upper chest area; a floral blanket with flowery patterns of pink and green and white and yellow covered the man from his belly button down.

"Gunshot wound on his left bicep," Boetz said out loud, noticing the wound.

"Have you looked underneath the pillow?"

"I haven't removed it, no," Boetz responded.

Both investigators had been told that the entire area had been searched, around and inside the house, and "no other persons had been found." The only wound visible to Boetz and McAllester was on the victim's left bicep. He had been shot in the arm.

Boetz had Detective Penny Judd come into the room and photograph the wound on the man's bicep.

Looking closer, Boetz noticed a hole through the laundry bag/pillowcase. He could see gunpowder residue.

Judd snapped a photo, and continued the take photos of the entire room, the victim, and anything else Boetz pointed out.

"That gunpowder residue," Boetz said, "means he was shot at close range."

Someone had placed the laundry bag over the man's face and fired—almost like an execution. Organized crime figures do this: They sneak up on someone while he sleeps, place a pillow over his face, and fire a few shots into the head. Just like in the movies.

But that wound on the bicep?

Didn't add up.

There was a pair of men's jeans on the floor by the side of the bed. McAllester walked over and, carefully, being certain not to disturb what could be an important piece of evidence, he reached inside the back pocket and took out what appeared to be a wallet.

He looked for a license.

The Cruz family had it right. The guy's name was Bob. He was Robert "Bob" Dow. He was forty-nine, his fiftieth birthday about a month away. Bob had a potbelly stomach, but he was otherwise in what was average shape for an American by today's standards. He was butt naked underneath the covers. Either he had been getting himself ready for bed when someone shot him, was already sleeping, or his killer had surprised him.

As Boetz stood near Bob Dow, he looked closer at the walls, where he had seen those missing pictures earlier.

There was blood on the wall.

"Vic's?"

Was it blood spatter from the gunshot wounds?
Boetz and McAllester didn't think so.

It appeared to Boetz that whoever removed the
pictures had cut himself or herself during that
process, or was bleeding before doing so.

Over near the northeast corner of the room was
a green chest—like a pirate's—sitting on the floor,
BOBBY'S was written on it. Boetz bent down and
had a look. It seemed that someone had popped
the chest open. Wearing latex gloves, Boetz had a
look inside.

Later, Boetz said, "We found some ammunition
and a gun."

CHAPTER 4

JENNIFER JONES WAS three years old when her mother, Kathy Jones, moved out of the house she kept with Jen, her three daughters, and her husband, Jerry Jones. It was 1988. Jen didn't see Kathy all that much, to begin with. As it happened, Kathy had begrudgingly turned (according to an article published many years later in the *Texas Monthly,* several police reports, and Kathy herself, testifying in court and admitting in an interview with me) to "cleaning other peoples' homes and working as a prostitute" for cash to feed a growing and ferociously intensifying crack cocaine habit.

In January 2001, several weeks before Jen turned sixteen, she was sitting and thinking about her mother and the times they never had together. Yet the stories Jen had heard about her mother throughout the years—and the fact that most of the time when Jen ever saw her mother, the visits took place inside a local prison on Sunday afternoons—were grating on her young psyche, trying to convince her that she was that same person she didn't want to become.

In a rather open and adolescently honest journal entry as a sixteen-year-old, Jen talked about spending the night with a boy, saying: *But we didn't do anything.*

Why hadn't she slept with him?

Because . . . I didn't want to, she wrote.

Without truly understanding the situation, Jen was trying to convince herself that she would never be like her mother—a woman she had mostly heard wild stories about while growing up. She *could* say no. She was trying desperately to ward off—even fight—what she viewed as a demon plaguing her: that dreaded cycle of dysfunction. Jen had been hardwired since the time she could walk to live life on terms she saw fit. But here she was, denying herself, and trying to turn a new leaf.

When she got home the next morning after being with the boy, one of Jen's sisters approached her.

"You're turning out just like Mom," Jen's older and more experienced half sister, Audrey Sawyer, the offspring from a different father, said.

"What?"

"You go out and you don't tell anyone where you're going."

Audrey explained later that she was genuinely worried about her little sister. Audrey claimed she had been a mother to Jen for a lot of years, being

the older sibling and watching over her, but Jen
didn't want to hear it anymore. There was no way,
she told herself, she was going to wind up like
Kathy Jones, the mother she never had. Jen was
determined not to allow that to happen. Sure,
Mineral Wells wasn't Dallas or Forth Worth, and
there wasn't much to offer a girl with no grades
to speak of and no real skills. Still, Jen had
dreams of leaving town someday. Maybe moving
to Washington State. Maybe meeting someone
and enjoying a middle-class life. She had once said
she liked reading *Better Homes and Gardens* magazine. She'd browse through the magazines and
picture herself in one of those plush homes that
had a lawn like carpet. Maybe a husband. A dog.
Some kids, too. That perfect life set up in the
magazine wasn't a pipe dream or a fairy tale to
Jen; it was doable. She believed all she had to do to
get it was to *want* it bad enough.

I'm not going to turn out like my mom, Jennifer
wrote in her journal on January 22, 2001.

As each day passed and the prison kept that
revolving door well greased for Kathy—with
charges ranging from shoplifting to driving without and/or with an invalid license (several times),
registration and insurance, possession of a controlled substance, unlawfully carrying a weapon,
assault on a family member, theft, DUI (several
times), prostitution, and on and on—Jen was
determined not to turn out like the woman who
never raised her.

When Jen's father, Jerry Jones, would try to persuade Kathy to return to the house after another round of ripping and running (hanging out with the crowd, drugging and drinking), which took her away for weeks or months at a time, Jen wondered why her father would go to such desperate lengths. Did they really need Kathy in order to live their lives? Jerry wasn't a candidate for Father of the Year, by any means. However, he was doing the best he could with what were four children—all girls—and an absent wife. As the story went (and we should take these anecdotes here with the Jones family as just that: their version of the truth), in order to watch the children whenever Kathy decided to end up in jail or head off on a bender, Jerry had to quit his job as an oilman. He took on being a local handyman, Jen told a reporter, where he would fix doors and windows and do odd jobs for locals. He even started to clear rocks from fields for neighbors and businesses to earn extra money. He supposedly hunted for family food (deer and other game) and brought home produce from his parents' garden.

Family looked on from the sidelines, helping where they could—worried, of course, about the children. But it wasn't easy.

"Everyone *except* Jerry tried to keep Kathy away," said one family source.

None of this was quite enough to replace for Jen what she lacked most: a female figure to give her that maternal advice and guidance as she needed it, someone to discipline her the way she needed punishing. Jerry had his hands full with these kids (two of whom weren't his by blood). He couldn't keep tabs on all of them all of the time; and the older they got, the more freedom they wanted and were allowed. So before Jen had even celebrated her seventeenth birthday, she'd given in and tried dope—the same poison that had buried its claws deep into her mother. On February 5, 2001, Jen wrote about the experience and how much she enjoyed it, calling the night out "a blast." She said she had "tried weed" for the "first time" and "got high." It "felt OK." It took her out of the moment, allowed her to forget about her shitty life. She even joked about how high she got: *I couldn't stand. Then I couldn't hold my eyelids up.*

There was a touch of uncertainty in this particular entry, as if Jen felt guilty about giving in and stepping over to the other side, which she had sometimes claimed she wanted no part of. It was a strong feeling, a magnetic pull. Not so much experiencing shame, but Jen was "disappointed" in her behavior and ultimately for being so weak. She expected more out of herself in one respect; yet, in another entry, she wrote how she reasoned: *As long as I feel good, I don't care.* She talked about how one boy wanted her "for the sex." She wrote, *I care, but then I don't.*

On February 5, 2001, Jen did not come home. But (like her mom might have done) she did return the following day. Jerry Jones was furious at his daughter for staying out all night without calling. He felt Jen slipping from his grasp. In all of Jerry's anger and frustration to control a child who was well on her way to becoming uncontrollable, Jerry—without realizing it or wanting to—said the wrong thing.

It started as Jerry gave Jen the silent treatment on the day she returned. This was his way of showing Jennifer how upset he was.

Jen's response (in her journal) was rather emphatic: *I don't want to hear his voice anyway.*

She then wrote how disgusted she felt after finding pictures in her father's high-school diploma, which she had come upon by mistake inside Jerry's nightstand. *And he doesn't want to lose me,* she added, not going into detail about what had made her think so differently about her father.

Finally Jerry broke his silence that day and spoke to Jen, preaching perhaps the wrong message, at the wrong time: "I'm about to not care if you come back anymore!"

CHAPTER 5

BRIAN BOETZ WAS not the typical small-town detective you'd expect to find in a relatively unknown Texas town like Mineral Wells. When he was a boy, Boetz did not necessarily receive a "calling" to become a cop. His uncle had been a sheriff in Deming, New Mexico. Anytime Boetz heard his uncle talk about "the job," Boetz's ears perked up.

"I'm not saying he talked me into becoming a police officer," Boetz told me, "but anytime he talked about it, the stories piqued my interest."

It sounded thrilling and adventurous, which is one reason why lots of young boys are attracted to the game of cops and robbers. There's a certain hubristic sense of self in heeding what is a call at a young age to become a lawman. You want to do good in the world, sure; but you also feel the need to feed a certain part of the ego that thrives on outdoing yourself or having the spotlight on you.

For Brian Boetz, though, that was never part of it. He wasn't so much interested in the limelight as he was with figuring out puzzles.

There was no doubt, he said, that once he decided to take the test and become a cop, "From day one, I knew I wanted to be involved with criminal investigations. When I started in Mineral Wells in 1995, I knew that I wanted to be an investigator."

It took Boetz five years of patrol work, learning the ropes, paying his dues, before he took the detective's test and earned a position as an investigator in the Criminal Investigation Division (CID) of the MWPD. It's fair to say this is a coveted spot—that is, considering there are only four investigatory positions to go around in the MWPD, within a force of twenty-eight sworn officers, including the chief.

The worst cases to get handed, Boetz said, were "sexual assaults involving children. And we have our fair share of them."

One of the most gruesome murders Boetz ever investigated took place inside a small convenience store.

"We get there and the female clerk was nearly decapitated. The killer used a machete. And you know, all for a little over a hundred dollars out of the cash register."

Cops like Boetz will agree that it's those types of brutally senseless cases that have become the norm in police work. On average, about two-thirds of murders are easily solvable. In 2004, for example, there were approximately sixteen thousand murders in the United States, about one-third of which went cold, or unsolved. For a police department the size of Mineral Wells, however, there was rarely ever an actual "caper" to dig into as an investigator.

But here it was, May 5, 2004, and Detective Boetz found himself involved in what appeared to be a whodunit. It was that blood on the wall that bothered Boetz most as he and Captain Mike McAllester surveyed the homestead of Bob Dow's mother—plus, the idea that Bob Dow was killed at such close range.

He knew his killer, Boetz thought. "That was clear to us almost immediately."

The scene screamed of such a personal crime.

Before long, realizing there wasn't much to do inside the bedroom where Bob Dow had been slain, Boetz, who was now the supervising officer at the scene, looked on as crime scene investigators (CSIs) tagged evidence inside the home with little yellow placards (markers). It wasn't about looking for that one hair or cigarette butt, maybe a bullet casing left behind by the killer. Evidence like that would help, obviously. However, most homicide scenes did not reveal that sort of Hollywood-type evidence, at least not at first blush. The job was not like *CSI* or *Law & Order*. Those TV dramas tried hard to get it right, and sometimes they did. But investigating the type of homicide the MWPD was looking at on this night was more about putting the pieces together, step-by-step, analyzing what evidence they uncovered, putting boots to the ground, and taking the case to the street.

"It's whatever evidence inside the house we thought, as we looked around and studied the crime scene," Boetz explained, "that was pertinent (or maybe not) to the crime."

Boetz and his team walked around and studied the place, especially inside the room where the murder, clearly, had occurred. They looked for subtle hints of what happened. Was it a home invasion? Was the murder a consequence of a burglary gone wrong? Revenge? A love affair? An unpaid debt? A bad drug deal? All of those were possibilities, Boetz knew; each of these would have to be explored on some level. Then again, the evidence, as each piece was collected and analyzed, would determine if the murder actually had occurred in the bedroom, and if the shooter left behind anything to place him or her at the scene.

A smart, well-schooled investigator did two things in this situation: He left every option open and investigated the case until he was absolutely certain he had his man.

McAllester called the district attorney (DA), Ira Mercer, and asked him if he could get over to the scene ASAP.

"I'll be there in a few," Mercer said.

It was smart to have the theoretical prosecuting

DA at the scene, directing traffic, so to speak, watching over the processing of the scene. It was a good way to head off any future problems. This type of murder was not common in Mineral Wells, and policies and procedures were in place to make certain a thorough, flawless investigation ensued.

Not long after Ira Mercer arrived, Judge Bobby Hart walked through the door. A passerby would think there was a party going on at the house, for every law enforcement official in town wanted in on what was sure to be the town's most sensational murder case in some years. But that wasn't the purpose of the judge's visit. Hart was there to pronounce the victim dead and order an immediate autopsy or not.

Again, procedure. Dotting the i's and crossing the t's.

After McAllester brought the DA and judge up to speed, he told Boetz he was taking off. Richard and Kathy Cruz were still outside, waiting. McAllester had spoken to them briefly and gotten some information, but he needed to get the couple down to the MWPD so they could be officially interviewed.

"I'm told," McAllester explained to Boetz, "that they have something." Richard and Kathy Cruz thought they knew who the potential shooter might be.

"All right, I'll finish up here and get down there as soon as I can," Boetz said.

With McAllester gone, Detective Boetz focused

on the computer desk and PC in the living room. Computers, cell phones, BlackBerries, iPads—electronic devices of all kinds that people use on a daily basis—are what detectives seek first and foremost beyond the most obvious clues. Those electronic gadgets and machines can tell a lot about a person and the final movements of their lives, and often leave behind a trail to follow.

Boetz first focused on several photos of females he found on the computer. After studying them closely and going back into the bedroom where the murder had occurred, he saw that there might be a connection.

The corners of the photos that were torn off the walls inside the suspected murder room displayed partial images that seemed to match the corners of the photos on the computer. The setting was certainly the same. The context of each photo taken from the wall matched some of the photos of several girls on the computer.

"It was obvious," Boetz said. And the more he studied this, "[I] realized the pictures were of the same people."

They had faces now to those missing pictures ripped from the walls in the bedroom. And yet, was it significant, or just another dead end? Did the person who killed Bob Dow remove the pictures? Were they photos of the murderer? There could be, after all, a simple explanation to the missing photos, or a thousand different reasons why they had been ripped off the wall.

"These [images on the computer] were certainly people of interest that we wanted to find and interview," Boetz said.

In the photos that Boetz found on the PC in the living room, most of the girls were young. They were partying in a lot of the shots. What was also clear was that they were willing participants. It looked as though they were having fun mucking around, kissing each other, and kissing an older man, who appeared to be partying *with* them.

Bob Dow?

It was.

There was booze and weed and harder drugs being used in the photos. One photo depicted one female having oral sex with another female, one of her breasts exposed. Boetz couldn't really make out the faces. Digging deeper into the computer, Boetz discovered girls who appeared to range in age from their young teens (minors) to adults in their forties, drinking alcohol, popping pills, smoking weed, meth, and even crack cocaine. As he searched deeper into the PC, he uncovered videos. Shocking, raunchy videos. Triple X. Lots of the girls were having sex and showing off their naked bodies. Some were giving oral sex to an older man and to each other. There were mock snuff films of girls pretending to kill one another with knives and guns. Some were extremely graphic. Some were tame. Others were obviously made under drunken circumstances, which the parties involved would probably like to forget. Still, the films were certainly made inside the house, with what appeared to be a dozen or more different girls—some of whom seemed to be underage.

In total, Boetz and the MWPD would uncover some six hundred photos and videotapes of young girls and women doing all sorts of *Girls Gone Wild* antics, including illegal things—some sexual, some not. A number that later came out was in the thousands. Clear throughout was that only one man showed up in the photos and videos and appeared to be behind the camera most of the time, directing the girls.

Bob Dow.

"He was the one filming, and he was the one calling the shots," said a law enforcement source. "He was the man behind the camera and sometimes not just behind the camera."

Best thing here for Brian Boetz was to get all of these photos and videotapes tagged and bagged. Then Boetz needed to head over to the MWPD and see how McAllester was making out with the Cruzes. Maybe begin there. Get some of these photos (the more respectable ones, anyway) out into the community and start asking around to see if anyone knew the girls. The Cruzes had led the MWPD to the crime scene. There was a good chance Kathy Cruz and her husband knew a lot more—and maybe even knew some of the girls in the photos.

CHAPTER 6

SHE STOOD WITH her arms by her side. She wore a black tank top. A tattoo of a sad sun dotted the side of her bicep, a way for the world to see and understand how she felt inside. The first time Audrey Sawyer saw Bobbi Jo Smith, Audrey thought the tank top–wearing, tattooed young girl was a "little boy." Bobbi had cropped hair, cut in a crew cut of sorts, dyed white gold, streaks of brown and black shaved tight into the sides. Bobbi sported one of those genetically lean, petite bodies. She sometimes wore baggy jeans, a chain wallet, black boots, a spiked leather wristband, and a belt to match. Bobbi had a bump in her step. She cared about the way she looked and carried herself. Bobbi was a lesbian and damn proud of it. Not in a GLAAD-like way, marching in parades and waving rainbow flags, but rather flaunting herself in front of other women and putting the package out there on the market. One friend later recalled

Bobbi's eyes and how charming and yet gloomy they seemed, as if she'd had her share of bad luck, rough times, and had managed to survive by will alone. Several people, one prosecutor, and the murder victim, Bob Dow, called Bobbi "a chick magnet." One of Bobbi's strengths, which she didn't have to work hard at, was a penchant for making friends with girls, regardless of their sexuality. Bobbi was likeable in so many ways: easygoing and easy to get along with. Yet, if you didn't know Bobbi and didn't take the time to *get* to know Bobbi, you might misunderstand this young woman and make snap judgments about her.

"Once I got to know her, I realized that she wasn't at all like people had tried to make her out to be," a good friend of Bobbi's told me, recalling the moment they became friends, which was months after they first met. "Bobbi never tried to clear up what people said about her, because in her mind she felt like she didn't have to defend lies. I used to tell her that I saw greatness in her, and that she had the potential to *be* great. When I told her that, it was hard for Bobbi to see what I did, because she lacked the self-esteem to understand that she had that greatness within. I would remind her of this all the time. Not everyone has it, but Bobbi does. And anyone being honest with themselves that truly knows Bobbi will agree."

Holding Bobbi back during that period when she first met Audrey was a voracious appetite she'd developed for drinking and drugging. Beyond anything else, partying was Bobbi's life, her true passion. She hadn't known anything different for quite a while. Getting high, Bobbi was hooked on that feeling of slipping away from all of the pain of the past. The drugs and booze deadened that emotional ache she felt, like nothing else ever had.

Still, that same friend explained, "Even when she was at her worst, I'd witness Bobbi give her last, whatever it was—even when she didn't have her last to give. And the thing is, Bobbi would give it to the *very* person that talked about her behind her back—her enemies. She used to always tell me how she never wanted to become like the people who cursed her and made fun of her and hated on her."

Bobbi had an uncanny knack for turning "nothing into something, or a bad situation into something positive and good," added her friend. "For example, someone I once knew wanted to have cards made. You know, like thank-you cards." Bobbi was known for her artwork. She had the touch. "And there was this girl who originally made up the cards, but she charged an arm and a leg for what looked like what a grade-school kid might have done. I told Bobbi about it. How this girl was overcharged for crappy work. Bobbi redid all of my friend's artwork for free. And you see, *that's* who Bobbi is. She's loyal. She's real. She'll say things how they are. She'll speak the truth even if it hurts *her.* She won't ever argue. She'll always try to defuse a bad situation. And *that's* what some people don't like about her."

There are other aspects of Bobbi's character that alienated people in her circle. It's hard for some to be around a strong personality, like Bobbi: someone unafraid of standing by her truth.

"Bobbi doesn't kiss ass," that friend concluded. "That's not what I mean. But she will not hesitate to make a situation right, even if she wasn't in the wrong. And that's just her. She will respect and value your beliefs and opinions without coming down on you. The loyalty that I have seen her exhibit blows my mind. Once she's your friend, watch out—that loyalty will be there until the very end. I could go on and on about the things that make Bobbi special. Look, I'm so not saying she's flawless, because she has her days, like most anyone else, and she's done things she's not proud of. But her good far outweighs any of that."

The one characteristic Bobbi's friend said she displayed more than any other?

"If Bobbi does something wrong, she'll *own* it. And regardless of the consequence, she'll admit her flaws. That's who she is. And *that's* what I love about her."

It was late February/early March 2004. There was a party in the middle of the courtyard in the center of the Spanish Trace Apartments. Audrey Sawyer lived at the Spanish Trace complex with her half sister Jennifer Jones, Jen's father, Jerry, and another sister. Bobbi was standing with some friends, drinking. Audrey spotted her, but she didn't think too much of this rather interesting-looking girl with the sun tattoo.

Audrey had been with guys, but she was a bona fide lesbian—that much she had never denied herself. But this girl, Bobbi, Audrey never thought for a moment on that day she would ever find herself falling for. And yet that was Bobbi: As soon as you got to know her, you realized how genuine and sincere and likeable she was, not to mention how much she cared about people in general.

A few days after Audrey saw Bobbi standing, partying at Spanish Trace that first time, a friend called. "Hey, I want you to meet someone."

"Yeah," Audrey said, "who?"

Audrey was skeptical. In Mineral Wells, everyone knew everyone. And in the lesbian community around town, the circle was very small. Audrey probably knew the girl already.

"Name's Bobbi Jo Smith," her friend said.

Audrey thought about it. She went back to that day she saw Bobbi in the courtyard. A chick like Bobbi might be just what the doctor had ordered for Audrey, who had gone through a bit of a rough patch lately.

"Come on over," Audrey told her friend.

* * *

Jennifer Jones and Audrey Sawyer grew up in the same house with two other siblings. Jen and her sister, Stephanie, have the same father, Jerry; Audrey and their other sister, Emily, Jen's two half sisters, have different fathers. The girls were all born to the same mother, Kathy Jones.

They were reared in Lone Camp, a relatively nice area in central Palo Pinto County. Life was good, Audrey explained, adding how there were fine memories etched in the walls of that old house they called home. And yet, Audrey was quick to point out, those warm family recollections came with a price.

And didn't last long.

"My mom left when I was six," Audrey said.

"Jennifer was almost four and Stephanie was almost two when I left the house," Kathy Jones told me during an interview.

"We moved around a lot," Jen later said.

Before the bottom of the family unit fell out, Audrey stated, their mother was a "traditional" mom. Kathy taught Sunday school at the local church. The entire family attended church services every weekend and helped out where they could. Kathy worked at a church day care. It was Kathy, Jerry, Jennifer, Audrey, and their two siblings. The family thing was working. Jerry was employed by a local oil company. The kids attended school regularly. They all got along and did things together.

"My mom took us places," Audrey said. "The

park. The zoo. Normal things. We had a huge area where we lived. There were acres and acres surrounding the house."

The kids went about their early childhoods with carefree spirits, doing what it is kids between the ages of two and nine do: playing and hanging out with neighbors, watching cartoons, having fun. Kathy wasn't Betty Crocker, but she wasn't *Mommie Dearest,* either. She loved her children, arguably loved her husband, and wanted what was best for everyone. But the devil soon found his way into their lives and began wreaking havoc quickly, once Kathy had a taste of his poison.

"My mom and Jerry got into it because my mom wanted to get a 'real job,'" Audrey explained.

The door had opened. In church, the family learned that you don't allow an entryway for evil, or the master of lies will find his way into the home and destroy it. And once he's allowed in, no matter how, he'll spread his wrath so subtly, no one will ever see it coming.

"Jerry didn't want her to work like that," Audrey insisted. Jerry was old-school: The husband worked, and the wife stayed home with the kids.

Kathy wanted to get out there and labor fulltime. She felt the pull of the street. Back then, Kathy had the body and the looks to go with it. She felt she could make money with those assets.

"I went to work at Sinbad's in Fort Worth," Kathy explained to me. "A strip club."

She and Jerry started to argue. Those in-house

quarrels soon turned into Kathy leaving with the kids.

Things went on like that for a while: a seesaw of getting along and not getting along. Kathy was making money and taking care of the kids. And then, as the tale goes, Kathy met a woman at the strip club and sparked up a close friendship. This new friend had just gotten out of jail. One thing led to another and . . . we've all heard the story.

"My mom was introduced to drugs," Audrey said, "and them two started partying."

Kathy told me there was one thing driving her to take off her clothes: "Getting the money."

From there, Kathy explained, her life spiraled out of control. Fast. She hit the streets full throttle with her new friend and found an easy way to forget her troubles.

"I've been dealing with the devil since I been about fifteen," Kathy told me. "Taking pills and stuff from the time I was fifteen. . . . I lived in Fort Worth with my dad and mom, and I was leaving home all the time, starting when I was thirteen. Lived on the street till I was seventeen."

Soon after Kathy hit the brick, running full steam, Jennifer and Stephanie went back to Jerry. Kathy couldn't handle them any longer. She'd pop over during the week to visit with the kids. But Jerry, Kathy said, "always threatened that if I didn't come back to him, I would *never* see the girls."

Then Kathy found she couldn't handle her

other two kids, Audrey and Emily, so they wound up with Jerry, too.

"She couldn't take care of all of us," Audrey said.

Kathy Jones, however, had no trouble taking care of herself.

"She was always in bar fights . . . even with men," Audrey said with a strange, boastful pulse of envy. "She never backed down. She was *tough*. She's been airlifted to hospitals several times for fighting, overdosing. And one time she fell and hit her head. . . . When she wasn't on drugs, my ma was into family stuff. She liked to sew, make all of our dresses. . . . She was loving." Yet, when Kathy was on Satan's venom, Audrey added, she "just didn't want to be around anybody."

She withdrew from life.

"The girls have seen a lot," Kathy said of her children. "They've lived a *hard* life."

A majority of Jennifer Jones's formative years, Audrey claimed, were spent watching her father, Jerry, along with her little sister, head over to, as Audrey put it, "the hood," in search of Kathy. Jennifer and her sister tagged along with Jerry as he'd scour the projects and mean streets of whatever town they lived in then, looking for their mother, so he could drag her back home. There were times, Audrey explained, when he'd even give Kathy money, knowing what she was going to do with it.

Kathy told me this was around the same time

when she started waking up in the morning with a drink in one hand and going to bed that same night with a crack pipe in the other. A typical night for Kathy in those days involved scenes she'd only, up until then, seen on television.

"Once, my boyfriend brought me over to the dealer's place," Kathy recalled, "and he pulled a gun and put it to my head—all because my boyfriend had brought this 'white girl'—me—over to the house."

This was how Jennifer grew up—watching her mother fall, time after time, and all of them trying to lift her up from the depths of what had turned into a relentless addiction.

Soon the girls were split up. One of the sisters went out to find her father in California. Audrey took off and ran away with a boyfriend, only to be found and brought back. It was Jennifer who stayed behind with Jerry and moved into a trailer in Strawn, Texas, a little town south of Graford, off the I-20.

By now, Jen was into her "I'm not going to end up like Mom" stage of heading out at night with boys, running around, smoking weed, and thus beginning to develop a street mentality that sneaks up and kicks a person's ass if she's not able to thwart it. The fact was, Jen was turning into her mother, however slow and progressive and stealthy the process seemed. On February 18, 2001, Jen confided once again in her trusted journal, writing how "so much has happened" in her life that she could hardly wrap her adolescent mind around it all. She had gone to Bluff Dale the previous night, a small town of about two thousand, about an hour's drive from where she lived in Strawn. There was a boy there whom Jen had been eyeing.

Went . . . to make a promise to stay sexually pure till [I'm] married, she wrote, almost mocking herself, finishing the sentence in a sarcastic laugh, *I already broke it.*

It was then that Jen first began hurting herself for the hell of it. Her sister and a friend dared Jen one night to burn herself. "Use the cigarette lighter," her sister's friend encouraged. "Go ahead, Jen. . . ." The idea was to keep it lit and heat up the metal tip so it was hot enough to leave a burn mark on her skin, like a cattle brand.

Jen took a look at everyone, fired the thing up, got it red hot, and pushed the tip into her arm, singeing herself with a hiss, melting her skin like wax, leaving behind a mark. She'd succumbed to peer pressure, it seemed, with not so much as thinking twice about it. Her friends had pushed her to do something and she did it. And the strange thing about that day was, Audrey later clarified, Jen realized how much she actually *liked* the pain. She had found a release. A way not only to allow herself to feel alive, but to gain attention while doing so; and, all at once, she had begun to carve out the "badass" reputation she had been desperately chasing (same as her mother).

"She wanted people to talk about her in that way," Audrey said.

Same as they talked about Kathy, who had a reputation as someone to be feared, a woman who did not mess around and took no bull from anyone. Kathy kicked ass first and never asked questions. Jen had heard these stories. As Jen was growing up, Kathy had become a legend in Jen's fragile, inexperienced, immature mind. Those shoes of Kathy's, Jen realized as time went on, were going to be hard to fill, but she *could* do it.

During this chaos, Jen and her sister had, at times, lived with an aunt and uncle, experiencing bouts of normalcy. That aunt and uncle—the Brownriggs—watched Jen and her sister, bought them things, and had a positive effect on their lives. They lived in Granbury, a fairly good-sized town of about eight thousand in Hood County, south of Mineral Wells and Fort Worth. For intervals, Jen would stop her bad behavior as her aunt and uncle influenced her and her sister with routine, parental discipline, and showed them love. Jen felt a sense of being involved in a family unit; she had everything a child on the cusp of going completely bad needed to turn things around. Audrey later explained that Jen had even gone so far as to call her aunt "Mom" once in a while and appreciated the structured atmosphere of having to answer to an adult, an authority figure. Jen felt that someone cared about her and what she did. She even started to do well in school. She stopped drinking alcohol and gave up cigarettes. She wanted to prove to her aunt and uncle there was good inside her. She could do the right thing under the right circumstances. All she needed was a chance.

"They even took her and [her sister]," Audrey said, "on several vacations, cruises, and things."

Rewards. Every kid needs a carrot—needs to chase *something*. Jen was no different. She saw a rainbow. She felt there was some good that could come out of a life she had not discarded entirely. She *could* turn things around.

While living with her aunt and uncle in late 2003, Jen met a boy, whom she referred to in her journal as "my wish come true." As Jen saw him, this kid was a straight arrow; he was the perfect counterpart to Jen's wiry, wild side. He played piano. He sang. He was an honor student. *He is so sweet and talkative,* Jen wrote. They had gone "parking" one night. Jen wrote: *He is only 18, but he would be smart and sexy for me.* What she meant by "only 18" was that she liked much older men. When she met this boy, she was just seventeen; so they were just about the same age. This was different for her. He went to Texas Tech. She called him her "dream man."

In this journal entry, it's clear Jen knew what was good for her. She felt it with this boy. The entire relationship gave her a warm and fuzzy feeling. *We [talk] about everything,* she wrote, *except drugs and drinking.* He wanted nothing to do with either, and Jen respected him for it.

"I'd rather have a boy first," Jen's new friend told her one night as they discussed marriage and children.

"Oh yeah?" Jen responded, smiling.

"Then a girl," he followed up. "Girls are hard to raise."

Jen thought about that comment. Boy, did she ever know what he was talking about.

And he is right, she wrote, describing the conversation.

CHAPTER 7

IT WAS ONE THING for Captain Mike McAllester to get the gist of the Cruz story outside, in front of victim Bob Dow's mother's house. However, it was quite another to lock them down to a statement that they would sign.

Richard Cruz was a forklift operator at a rather large employer in Mineral Wells. Cruz was a workingman's man. He was a blue-collar guy who, he said later, was just trying to be a good citizen in coming forward to report what he had heard. What he wanted to make clear to McAllester was that his statement was absolute hearsay. He was talking about things that his mother-in-law had told him and his wife.

McAllester said he understood. The MWPD was in the information-gathering stage of its investigation. Nothing more.

Both Kathy and Richard Cruz seemed nervous. Rightly so, perhaps. Murder was serious business.

The Cruzes knew they had potentially devastating information about a suspect. Someone they actually knew. A family member.

Kathy Cruz's niece.

Richard Cruz explained that he and his wife valued the close-knit family atmosphere he believed he could characterize when talking about the Smith family. Dorothy Smith, his mother-in-law, was a good woman. She had great instincts and didn't mind helping family members in need.

"Well, what happened to lead you to call us?" McAllester asked.

Cruz explained how he and Kathy had arrived home from work at about four-thirty that day, which seemed like so long ago now. "And as we got out of our vehicle," Cruz explained, "Kathy's mother waved us over to her house."

McAllester took notes and listened, saying, "Continue. . . ."

"Well, Dorothy was very upset. She was talking to Kathy's sister on the phone."

As Richard Cruz spoke, McAllester got a sense that Richard was confident in what he was saying—that he believed Dorothy. Continuing, Cruz explained, "[Dorothy] said Kathy's niece shot Bob."

"Her name?"

"Bobbi Jo Smith," Cruz answered. "She's nineteen. Bob is an acquaintance of Bobbi Jo's."

"Did she say what happened? *Why* she shot him?"

"Dorothy said Bobbi Jo came over to her house and was 'very upset.' She said she had shot Bob. . . .

I told Dorothy after she told us that maybe it didn't happen that way because Bobbi Jo likes to exaggerate, especially when she's on drugs."

It was hard to believe that a nineteen-year-old girl the size of little boy, as Cruz described Bobbi, could manage to shoot a much bigger, older, and stronger man like Bob Dow. McAllester thought about the crime scene he had examined and how Bob was lying on his back with some sort of laundry bag over his head. Maybe his killer had surprised him? Maybe Bob Dow's killer snuck up on him, tossed the laundry bag over his head, and unloaded those rounds into his face without him ever knowing what hit him?

"What else did Dorothy tell you?"

"She said, 'No way.' Bobbi Jo wasn't making it up."

"How'd she know that?"

"Dorothy said she spoke to Bobbi Jo's girlfriend"— who was apparently with Bobbi when she showed up at Dorothy's, both freaking out, talking about shooting Bob Dow—"Her name is Jennifer . . . and *she* said, 'Bobbi Jo shot Bob. . . .'"

Richard Cruz explained how he'd searched Bobbi's room inside Dorothy's house and uncovered a holster with a missing weapon and an unloaded second weapon. Then he told McAllester how he called the MWPD and got Bobbi Jo's mother on the phone; she helped coach the cop following him toward Bob Dow's house.

McAllester knew the rest.

Obviously, the MWPD needed to corroborate both secondhand and thirdhand statements by finding Bobbi's girlfriend—this Jennifer—and also getting over to Dorothy's and obtaining a statement from her. Still, according to these two witnesses, Bobbi Jo had admitted to murder.

This thing was coming together rather quickly for the MWPD—just as they were accustomed and used to. In this town, when applying effort, the solving of murders seemed easy. But there had to be a catch somewhere. And what about the old woman found nearly unresponsive and literally starving to death inside a second bedroom in the house? How did she play into this scenario? Was she even coherent enough to speak?

McAllester cut Richard and Kathy Cruz loose. Then he called Dorothy Smith, who sounded unnerved. McAllester asked about Bobbi Jo Smith. Did Dorothy's granddaughter admit to shooting Bob Dow in the head?

"Yes," Dorothy said, speaking through tears. "Bobbi Jo told me that she shot and killed Bob."

"Thank you, ma'am. A detective will stop by tomorrow morning to take your statement. Is that okay?"

"Yes, I'll be here. But please . . . please . . . be careful and don't hurt my granddaughter," Dorothy insisted. Dorothy pictured some sort of task force out and about, searching for Bobbi Jo.

She didn't want police to manhandle Bobbi and get into some shoot out. Dorothy loved Bobbi, knew she was a good kid, and couldn't believe what was happening. There had to be more to this. Bobbi Jo had never been in trouble with the law—ever. Maybe it was all some sort of misunderstanding?

"Okay, ma'am, we understand," McAllester said. "But if your granddaughter contacts you again, you need to call us right away."

"Yes, I understand," Dorothy answered.

"Do you know where she is now?"

"She was here with her girlfriend, Jennifer. She left with Jennifer and at least two other females."

Four women, Dorothy explained, all together.

She was wrong. It was actually five women. All lesbians.

"Do you know who they are, ma'am?"

"No. I don't know their names. Only Jennifer."

"Do you know what type of vehicle they were driving?"

Dorothy thought about it. "A truck," she said. "They were all in a truck."

Bob Dow, McAllester knew, owned a 1989 Chevy pickup.

Which was also missing.

Mike McAllester took a ride over to the hospital to see if he could get a few moments with the woman, Bob Dow's mother, who had been brought

in after Dow's body had been discovered. McAllester was told Mrs. Dow was in the emergency room.
Her status was considered "weak, but mostly okay."
She was getting her strength back. But whoever
had been caring for the old woman wasn't ful-
filling his or her role, certainly. It had taken
some time and lots of fluids to get Mrs. Dow's
electrolytes back in check, but she was coming
along well.

McAllester also found out since heading over to
the hospital that Bob Dow didn't actually live in
the house where his body had been found. At
least, that is, on paper. Bob had his own trailer in
Weatherford, about twenty miles east of Mineral
Wells, where one would suspect he spent most of
his time. Through the impression the MWPD was
getting, Bob's mother's house was his personal
party house.

"For an eighty-six-year-old woman," the doctor
told McAllester as the detective walked toward the
emergency room to speak with Mrs. Dow, "she is
doing reasonably all right. She suffered a stroke a
few years back. So all considering, she's okay."

"Any indication that she has been neglected in
any way?" McAllester asked.

The ER doctor looked at her chart. "I don't
think so. No."

"Can she talk? Can she communicate with me?"

"Ah, no, not really. And listen, I'm not sure she's
even aware of anything that happened inside the
house, anyway."

"I may need to speak with her at a later time when she's able."

The doctor said that would be fine. Just not right now.

McAllester drove back to the crime scene. He wanted the exact information on Bob Dow's truck, so he could forward it to dispatch.

After finding the info, McAllester called dispatch, saying, "Get that out to TLETS. . . ."

TLETS is the Texas Law Enforcement Telecommunications System. There were over one hundred thousand law enforcement personnel with access to TLETS. "The core component of TLETS is a store-and-forward-message brokering system that ensures safe, secure delivery of content being transmitted throughout the system," according to the Texas Department of Public Safety (DPS).

As the night wore down and McAllester headed home, an all-points bulletin (APB) went out on Bob Dow's truck, which the MWPD believed was carrying *four* young females—one of whom was now wanted for questioning in the murder of the man who owned the vehicle.

CHAPTER 8

WHEN LATER ASKED ABOUT her childhood, Jennifer Jones's simplified analysis was straightforward and concise: "It wasn't good." After Kathy Jones left the home, Jerry Jones had a tough job of raising the girls. The older they got, the harder it became to keep a leash on them and provide. "My father," Jen added to her recollection of those years, "he wasn't able to support me."

After quitting high school, Jen said, she "tried to get a job." But the nearly eighteen-year-old girl found out quickly that she wasn't "very good" at working. So each job that came along—and they were limited, at best—became a chore. She'd end up quitting. She never said whether she made the jobs out to be more than they were, or she had a run of bad bosses. Either way, there aren't too many kids in the world who get up every morning with smiles and burning desires to rush out to their jobs. But they do it to support themselves, as emerging, responsible adults, who live healthy lives, often do.

Apparently, Jennifer wasn't interested in growing up.

It was just a few weeks before her eighteenth birthday when Jen, now out of school, found she had much more free time on her hands than was good for her. If she would have just stuck it out, Jennifer Jones could have likely graduated within a year's time. However, she wanted to get out on her own and fend for herself. School, Jen felt, was holding her back. So she moved to Santo, Texas, about a half-hour drive from Mineral Wells, explaining in court later, "I went to Santo and it's just . . . it's just the peak of my life where, you know, I felt like everything was falling apart."

Jennifer did that sometimes: She would use the wrong word. "Peak," at least here, would lead one to believe her life was running full speed, heading somewhere.

It was not.

This move to Santo culminated in what was a long list of homes Jennifer had set her boots down in over a period of about a dozen years. All of the shuffling around had taken its toll on her, or so she later claimed. Not so much physically, although she was rather tired and stressed from frequently moving and changing schools. Psychologically and emotionally, Jen was feeling the effects. She was a wreck. Always waking up, wondering where or when her next home would be. Leaving

behind friends she had made. There seemed to be
constant change in her life.

"It hasn't been very easy," Jen said of her childhood as a whole. "Not only moving from place to
place, making new friends, the relationships that
I've had with guys in my past, losing my virginity at
the age of fourteen, trying drugs at fourteen, my
parents separated, my grandmother dying. It's
been very testing."

This statement clarifies the fact that Jen suffered from not having enough direction or discipline. She had very little support when it came
time to begin living outside of the nest on her
own. She had hardly any social skills to survive on
her own and fend for herself as an adult. All Jen
knew, one could argue, was disappointment, loss,
and instability. On the other hand, one could also
contend that Jennifer had completely given up on
not only herself, but on life in general—because
she did have a support staff to lean on when she
needed to, a loving and caring aunt and uncle.

"As the girls [Jennifer and Stephanie] grew up,"
Jen's uncle told me, "we did things like buying
them an entire roomful of furniture, clothing that
was appropriate, and whatever else they really
needed to 'fit in' with other kids. Most of the time,
Kathy was in jail (thankfully)."

Jennifer's uncle (not by blood) and his wife,
Jerry's sister, said they believed in and practiced "a
simple 'rewards' system. When the girls achieved
milestones, we offered damn nice rewards—

several cruises (Jamaica, Bahamas, et cetera), ski trip to Vail. . . . After we had purchased the girls' furniture, and painted and fixed up their rooms, hung curtains to make them proud to have guests at their rented trailer home, we learned that Jerry was being evicted."

It was a great disappointment to Jennifer's aunt and uncle. They had worked so hard showing the girls how life became about the choices one made. Time and again, they had given the kids a fresh start.

"All the . . . work we put in [went] down the drain, and the furniture [was] put out on the curb as trash," Jennifer's uncle explained. "That was the last straw for us, and we took the girls into our home."

If her aunt and uncle couldn't save Jennifer and her sister from a distance, they thought, their influence on a daily basis, inside their own home, and the overall inspiration and example they could set daily, would achieve far better results.

"We had clear rules, simple to follow, easily understood," Jennifer's uncle said, recalling the time the girls moved in. "No drugs. No pregnancies. No drinking. Other than that, it was pretty much just 'Don't be stupid.'"

Practical, sage advice. Or maybe just common sense.

The girls' aunt and uncle started construction on a 6,200-square-foot home and lived in a mobile home behind that massive, growing structure. The girls had to share a room in the trailer, but they were each assigned a room upstairs in the main house. They were both allowed to give their input on its design and decoration.

"It was truly *their* home," said the uncle. "[We had four] acres on the Brazos River. [It was] beautiful, peaceful, serene, and [a] healthy environment. When Jennifer was old enough to get her driver's license, we worked with her, teaching her driving skills . . . and then went over to Dallas and purchased a cute little used Honda Civic, red with spoiler, perfect for a teen driver. We made improvements to the car, keyed remote for safety, alarm for security, and bought both girls cell phones." (This was when a cell phone was a relatively new thing.) "I helped her with her homework and school projects, just like any parent should do for their own child. Her grades were improved, she seemed happy," Jen's uncle observed.

Stephanie stepped up and took to it all like a child growing into a responsible adult might. Jen's sister made the right choices and carved out the best life she could for herself. She took great advantage of this wonderfully blessed opportunity. Yet, there was something inside Jen that couldn't make heads or tails of it. Maybe she had seen too much? Jennifer was older than Stephanie. Perhaps the damage had been done and Jennifer didn't know *how* to accept love?

"Jennifer has always had this extreme self-destructive streak," her uncle said. "We talked of college, jobs, education, and a future. All we asked in return was respect and adherence to the rules. . . ."

Jennifer couldn't do it.

Regarding her mother, Jen later summed up Kathy's role rather convincingly and sharply: "She's been in and out of jail, in and out of prison, in and out of my life."

Never there for more than a whisper of a promise and a hug on the way out the door. And when Jen did see her mother, Kathy was generally always asking for something, or showing her daughter the proper way to smoke weed or drink alcohol.

"I used to buy them beer," Kathy laughingly told me.

It was that constant state of not having a solid, consistent female role model in her life to bond with and rely on, Jen later claimed, that set her on a path of destruction—one she could never turn away from, no matter how much love her aunt and uncle gave her. She needed encouragement, love, and praise as much as any other teenager— especially during those ultraimportant and imperative years, when the impurities and immoral behaviors of society flow past the teen's eyes, begging for her to take part, reaching out sometimes through peer pressure to grab hold. The wrong type of influence was all around Jen. At a time when the child needed a female to talk things over with, she was alone, having to make decisions by herself. One could argue her aunt and uncle were always willing to listen and stand in for the parent, but Jennifer didn't obviously bond with them or take to that "rewards system," which they offered.

"No, I really didn't," Jen said when asked about receiving love from her mother, or any of the adults in her life while growing up. "Every now and then, you know, someone would give me a pat on the back. But it's just . . . it wasn't really enough for me. You know, it's really hard when your family is not really there for you. And it's just as"—and she cried here while continuing—"a kid, well, you want that. You know, you want to feel loved and you want that approval from everyone without having to try that hard."

Near this time in her life, Jen later confided to her journal, when that path of good and evil split, Jen found herself facing a choice. For a kid in this position, the easiest way is the most likely way. Jen chose the path of least resistance. She chose the road lined with various ways in which to forget about that life she desperately wanted to leave behind. On this path, she could numb any pain she felt with drugs, sex, crime, and a crowd of kids just like her to cheer her on. As soon as Jen found someone she could relate to on an intimate, personal level of emotion, she jumped at the chance to prove herself to that person. Despite an earlier promise she made to herself not to be like her mother, life for Jen now was about chaos and not feeling comfortable within a stable environment. Jen felt good when there was a storm brewing or happening. Stability had never been what she was used to. Being bad made her comfortable.

After a time of moving around from place to place, getting kicked out of her aunt and uncle's, moving back in, getting kicked out again, Jennifer Jones found herself living with her father, Jerry. It was March 2004. She was eighteen and now living at the Spanish Trace Apartments on Second Street in Mineral Wells. Meth and the dopers who sought it out surrounded Jen. ("They would make that stuff and ship it by truckload from Mexico into Mineral Wells and other Texas communities," one law enforcement official told me.)

Spanish Trace is a two-story, post–WWII tenement showing its age. It's located on a U-shaped street off Second Street, with apartment buildings on each side. Residents were known to hang out in back and around the building when the weather cooperated. It seemed to Jen that when she looked around, there were scores of kids her age feeling the same way: aimless, directionless, looking for the next big gig, the next party, the next good time.

On March 25, 2004, sometime in the afternoon (according to one version of this event Jennifer would later tell), she stood in the kitchen of her father's Spanish Trace apartment, staring out the screen door. It was one of those warm spring days in Texas: nearly 80 degrees Fahrenheit, the sun burning down, drying out the dirt patches of dead yellowed grass. The parking lot was full of vehicles just about ready to cough one last time and be put up on blocks. Jennifer was bored. A job she'd just quit at the Chicken Express turned out to be just one more negative in a life that did not measure up. Each failure seemed to feed the next. Jennifer was vulnerable and weak. A "poor me" syndrome had settled on her. She had quit school and ended up at Chicken Express. And she couldn't even make that work!

Dressed in her pajamas, Jen lit a cigarette and sat on the back steps of the apartment. (Again, this is *her* version—which no one else involved later agreed with.) She stared off into the distance and thought about things. This run of bad luck and disappointment had to come to an end at some point. She was sure of it. Things could not be this bad for this long. Jen knew she had created the latest mess (same as most of the others), but it did not make it any easier to swallow. She'd even written about it in her journal the previous night, noting, *I [screwed] up again, like always.* She sometimes liked to start out an entry by blaming herself and pouring on the self-pity, which allowed an escape clause to feel good about what came next: getting high. Here we go again. Screw it. Life sucks. It's too damn hard. Fire up the pipe.

One of the major regrets Jen had was totally letting her aunt and uncle down just recently. Late the previous year, Jen had been living in their house again with Stephanie. It was near the time they had been busy designing and building that new property. Things were going along well. Jen had hit a hot streak. She felt loved and needed. Alive. A productive member of society. There was someone in her life to answer to. Her aunt or uncle would not let Jen get away with things. Jen welcomed the limitations put on her.

"And then they found a pipe she was using to smoke dope, which Jen had made out of a lightbulb," Audrey explained.

"We found drug paraphernalia in Jennifer's room in our trailer," Jen's uncle corroborated. "I spent five and a half years with the Tarrant County District Attorney's Office, and have *zero* tolerance."

Jen's uncle and aunt packed her things and called Jerry. "Come and get her. She'll be waiting outside the front gate."

They weren't about to allow Jen to explain her way out of this one. No way. Rules were rules. She had broken one of the central tenets of the house. It was as if she had spit in her aunt and uncle's faces.

"She took the home we gave her and flushed it down the toilet," her uncle continued. "Not to mention putting us at risk. A very fine thank-you, indeed."

Jen brought hard-core drugs into her aunt and uncle's house. A big, huge no-no. So Jen moved into a motel room that her dad, Jerry, was renting in Mineral Wells. Jerry had been booted from an apartment weeks back for not keeping up with the rent. Jen and Jerry and Audrey stayed in the motel for a few more months; then Jerry found an opening at Spanish Trace and moved in. Jen went to Santo for a quick spell, but she moved back to Mineral Wells with Audrey and Jerry.

So here she was now, sitting on that back stoop of the Spanish Trace Apartments, shaking her head, exhaling cigarette smoke, thinking about the mistakes she'd made, pondering the people she'd let down, the family members she loved, and all of the missed opportunities. She considered the way she had tossed the good things in her life aside for a pipe, took the easy road, and had nothing left.

I had everything going really good for me and I started on that shit again, Jen wrote. *This is where I always [screw] up.*

It was as if Jen never gave herself the chance to be good; somehow she'd always manage to sabotage her life.

There were trees facing the back of the Spanish Trace Apartments. Jen could see them from where she sat on the stoop. According to one version of her story she later told, Jen found herself lost in thought, gazing into those woods, wondering what life had in store next.

Everything my heart desired, she wrote, talking about her time with her aunt and uncle. *Car . . . cell . . . I had a boyfriend. . . . Life was great.*

Stubbing out her cigarette, Jen stood.

[My boyfriend] broke up with me. . . . I am going to Fort Worth in the morning.

Audrey was supposed to show up at Spanish Trace that morning. She had taken off for a few days. She'd called Jen the night before and told her she'd be by. After speaking with her, Jen sat down and wrote how she was looking forward to seeing her sister, but hoped Audrey arrived without her "dike [sic] girlfriend."

The dyke Jennifer referred to was Bobbi Jo Smith. And wouldn't you know, just as Jen flicked her cigarette butt, turned to open the door and go back inside, Audrey pulled up, in fact, with Bobbi Jo.

Great, Jen thought.

Audrey needed to pick up a few things. She had been basically living with Bobbi Jo, who was staying with an older guy, Bob Dow, at his mother's house not far away. It was one party after another at Bob Dow's mother's place, Audrey told Jen. Bobbi had a mattress on the floor in the living room she sometimes slept on, but she also slept in Bob's room, which had two beds. Bob's mother lived in a room by herself, and he supposedly took care of her. "But [Bob] more or less just collected her checks and tossed her a McDonald's hamburger and some water every few days," one girl who frequented the house later told me. Bob had a trailer he lived in on the edge of town; he used his mother's house for sex and drug parties with women and young girls. Bob liked to film and take photographs of the girls who came over to the house. If a female walked into that party house, in other words, she was essentially signing up to be filmed. Most of the girls knew this.

"Every time I showed up," said one woman, who had gone over there quite often, "it seemed like Bob had a camera hanging from around his neck."

Before stepping into the apartment, Jen saw that Bobbi Jo was sitting next to Audrey inside the car. There were "two other people," according to Jen, in the backseat.

"Stay here," Audrey told everyone inside the car. "I'll be right back."

Audrey walked into the apartment. Jen sat back down on the porch steps.

Jennifer knew of Bobbi Jo. Not a lot about her personally, but enough to know that Bobbi was a chick who liked to party with other girls, and get down and dirty. Jen had never heard anything bad about Bobbi Jo, and there really wasn't much to say in that regard. Bobbi readily admitted she liked to drink, drug, and have sex with women. Life was about working, drinking, sexing, and drugging. Bobbi was young. Audrey had said Bobbi was fun to be with, although she also knew that this thing with Bobbi was probably not a long-term relationship. Bobbi was too free-spirited. She liked to be around a lot of people. Bobbi also worked for Bob Dow. Not just doing handyman types of jobs for him, but there was talk that Bobbi was the lure for Bob Dow—that she got paid for bringing young girls (some just teens) home to Bob so he could have sex with them and/or film the girls. The bait Bobbi waved in front of the girls was the free drugs and booze, along with a safe place to do it.

"Ever kiss a girl?" Bobbi Jo allegedly asked Jen.

Jen later testified that she was sitting in her dad's apartment, watching television, when this conversation occurred, but then she also said it took place on the front stoop as she sat there, staring into the woods that day. A third version of this day was then changed to Bobbi popping over to pick up Audrey and hanging around while Audrey got ready. While waiting, Jen claimed, Bobbi would jokingly harass her. Hit on her. Tease her.

"No!" Jennifer supposedly snapped in response to the question about kissing a girl. She was taken aback by Bobbi's frankness.

"Ever been with a girl?" Bobbi pressed (according to one recollection of Jen's). Then she gave Jen a wink. Bobbi wanted Jen—no doubt about it. Jen was a beautiful girl. She was young and pretty. Bobbi had heard that Jen had never been with a girl. And Jen carried herself like a fine-heeled, much older twentysomething, not the teenager she was. Bobbi was attracted to that. Jen was a quest, a "thing" for Bobbi to conquer.

"Can't say I have, Bobbi," Jen responded.

"How 'bout a relationship with a girl?" Bobbi asked, laughing. "Ever have that?"

Jen had gotten used to the comments. She shrugged it off. "Nope."

On this day, reportedly, Jen was sitting on the back porch and Audrey pulled up with the gang; the way Jennifer told it another time, Bobbi had yelled from the car window: "You ever kiss a girl?"

Bobbi wore a white-colored wife-beater T-shirt. That sad and angry sun tattoo on her arm was in full view as it hung out the open window, a cigarette hanging from her mouth. The smoke billowed up, stinging her squinting eyes.

"No!" Jennifer yelled as she prepared to walk back into the apartment.

"You want to?" Bobbi asked.

Jen thought about it. "Ah . . . no."

Bobbi took a pull from her cigarette, blew the smoke out the window, and then yelled, "Well, Jen, I could change your mind!"

Audrey was just getting back into the car. "Leave her alone."

Audrey had not heard the conversation and told me it never took place.

Jennifer told this story to a reporter in the weeks and months after she was arrested.

Bobbi Jo Smith told me this scene, born from the imagination of Jennifer Jones, never happened.

CHAPTER 9

BRIAN BOETZ WAS TIRED. It had been a long, late evening. Boetz could think of a thousand other things that he would have rather done the previous night than try to make sense of what seemed to be a senseless, brutal homicide. But here was the seasoned cop on his way back to the MWPD to see what his captain, Mike McAllester, had come up with during his interviews with Richard and Kathy Cruz. In ways that most non–law enforcement civilians wouldn't understand, it can be exciting, actually, for a detective to wake up to a mystery—a case that needed his immediate attention. Homicides in Mineral Wells were not a normal course of business, and to have one like this made the days go by a bit faster. For a cop, nothing could replace the satisfactory feeling of putting a kid toucher or child abuser behind bars. But on some days, an officer welcomed the change. There were only so many pedophiles and dopers and people neglecting their kids that a police officer could take down without going out of his mind.

On the morning of May 6, 2004, which was already shaping up to be another gorgeous Texas Thursday, as Boetz rolled into the precinct, baseball fans in Texas were celebrating and, at the same time, in a state of mourning. Controversial Houston Astros pitcher Roger "the Dodger" Clemens had recorded his 4,137th strikeout the night before, putting Clemens in second place, a hairbreadth behind Texas Ranger great Nolan Ryan, an icon of Texas sports.

The good news this morning, Boetz soon found out, was that the MWPD had a bead on a solid suspect in Bob Dow's murder. The bad news was that nobody knew where the young girl was. The TLETS/APB, which McAllester put out, had not yet yielded any hits. But then, it was still so early in the game.

"What'd you find out?" Boetz asked McAllester.

The seasoned investigator smiled. "Sit down."

There was a lot to explain.

Cops were still at the crime scene. Most of the evidence had been collected, but the scene hadn't been released yet—mainly because Bob Dow's mother's house was such a rat hole, inside and out. So it made for a longer-than-usual evidence-collecting process. That living room where the computer was located looked like a Texas twister had gone through it. There was no telling how much of what cops had sifted through was actual evidence or just plain garbage.

McAllester suggested to Boetz that he grab Detective Penny Judd and head over and interview Dorothy Smith, Bobbi Jo Smith's grandmother.

"Yeah," Boetz said.

"She'll have plenty to say."

The autopsy answers the final question: Why did life pass from a specific human body? Scott A. Wagner wrote in his graphic book *Color Atlas of the Autopsy.*

In the case of forty-nine-year-old Bob Dow, it was pretty damn obvious that he had been shot. Smart, competent, and experienced investigators, however, would never determine this early that those wounds were the cause of death—unless they had a medical examiner (ME) agreeing with them.

The autopsy is a complete evaluation of an individual's death and the circumstances surrounding that death, Wagner wrote.

This was the main reason behind Bob Dow's autopsy: to draw conclusions around the idea of what circumstance or circumstances had placed this man on that cold steel slab at the Southwestern Institute of Forensic Sciences (SWIFS) in Dallas.

It was 8:30 A.M., May 6, as Detectives Brian Boetz and Penny Judd headed off to interview Dorothy Smith, and the pathologist Dr. Christopher Young started dissecting Bob Dow.

Bob Dow had arrived nude, his body wrapped in

a light blue sheet. The first thing Young did after fingerprinting, photographing, and X-raying Dow's hands was place plastic bags over each and tie them off. The doctor did not want to contaminate any potential forensic "trace" evidence that Bob's hands might yield. Perhaps Bob Dow had swiped at his killer? Maybe he scratched his killer's face or arms? Anything—and everything—at this stage of the investigation was possible.

Dow weighed in at 234 pounds. He was six feet tall. His body was "cold" to the touch, Young noted. He wrote: *Rigor [had] fully developed . . . lividity posterior and fixed.*

Scott A. Wagner quoted Voltaire at the beginning of his "A to Z" autopsy textbook: *"To the living we owe respect, but to the dead we owe only the truth."* That truth was, in certain respects, somewhere inside or outside Bob Dow's corpse, and it would slowly emerge as Young went about the business of examining him.

The best place to begin was with the four gunshot wounds visible on Bob's upper body. One shot was to the right side of Bob's chin. Dr. Young found "no soot or stippling" on the skin around that particular hole. Young called this an "entrance" wound. Stippling is unburned gunpowder and other essential material from the bullet exiting the barrel and left behind when someone is shot at close range. Stippling usually looks like small black dots surrounding the bullet wound. This particular gunshot, Young wrote, after "perforating the skin" and the "subcutaneous tissues" of the "right side of the chin," went through the mandible before striking and avulsing through the "right lower molars." The bullet essentially shattered a few of Bob's teeth before "one fragment" penetrated "the right lateral surface of the tongue." When projectiles enter the body—suffice it to say at close range (say, within an arm's length)—they can travel tricky and unpredictable paths, splitting apart and heading off into all sorts of directions after passing through the skin and hitting the hard surface of bone or teeth. It's not uncommon for a pathologist to see a bullet enter the body at the jawline, let's say, split in half, head directly south, and penetrate the stomach or another major organ. The .22-caliber bullet fragment that ripped through Bob's two lower molars had actually propelled those broken teeth down into his esophagus about midway between his mouth and stomach. Young recovered one fragment from the "musculature of the tongue." The other section was found in Bob's right cheek. That one bullet, in other words, about a quarter of an inch wide, struck Bob Dow on the right side of his chin, split in two, and traveled in opposite directions: *Front to back, right to left, and slightly upwards.*

The wounds Dow sustained to his head were fatal. There was no argument from Dr. Young there. If that shot to the side of his chin wasn't enough, another round entered the right side of Bob's face below his earlobe. There was "no soot or stippling" Dr. Young could find near this wound, either. What was interesting about the projectile was how it had perforated the skin and subcutaneous tissue of the right side of Bob's face and then entered his skull, continuing into the "calvarium" through the "right petrous ridge and the brain. . . ." What would become important later was that the path, or "trajectory," of this bullet went "upward, front to back, and right to left." The shooter held the weapon—the evidence left behind would presume—at an angle with the handle of the weapon *below* Bob's jawline, the barrel facing upward, toward his head. The shooter was likely positioned, one might determine from this evidence, in front of Bob, almost as if sitting on top of him. What turned out to be good news for the MWPD was that Young had been able to recover this bullet, too.

If one looked at this bullet wound without speculating where the shooter was positioned, however, one could also argue that Bob Dow's killer could have snuck up on him and put a cap— maybe the first one—into the back of his head near his ear. And there was one killer, any good investigator knew, that this sort of procedure worked best for: the hired hit man. Organized crime. If one took a complete look at Bob's life as it presented itself this early, one would have to take into account that he was treading in several areas of treacherous social water. For example: Did the father of one of these girls he was videotaping find out what was going on and pay back a pervert with a little bit of vigilante street justice? Had the brother, boyfriend, or father found out that Bob was supplying his sister, girlfriend, or daughter with unlimited amounts of dope for sex and thus sought revenge by murdering Bob and making it look like someone else had done it? In a case like this, it's easy to put blinders on when the evidence seems to be stacking up against one particular suspect. However, cops with integrity don't do that. They sit back and wait for *all* of the evidence to emerge, and then they evaluate their case, which was why Dr. Young's autopsy became so relevant.

Young noticed that another .22-caliber projectile had entered the right side of Bob's head, "posterior to the ear." There was no soot or stippling there, either. This shot entered Bob's brain also. Young recovered the fragment. The trajectory was basically the same: It went front to back, right to left, upward.

When the doctor put them together, these three shots had likely been fired in succession. Some type of order. Although there was no way to tell which was first or last, the shooter had done this quickly.

Bang! Bang! Bang!

And then an anomaly popped up. The doctor found a projectile entrance wound on Bob's "left upper arm." It was centered nineteen and a half inches "below the top of [his] head." On this wound, there was "sparse stippling" extending two inches "above and below the defect."

The shot had fractured Bob's left humerus, but had done nothing else. It was a strange wound, all told, when taken into context alongside the three money shots, which were certainly intended to kill the man. It almost appeared as though this shot took place *after* the fact.

Or was this shot meant to stun the man to allow the three kill shots to do their business?

A toxicology test was conducted on Bob's blood. The Dallas County medical examiner found no alcohol in his blood, but there was .05 milligrams of cannabinoids (cannabis) per liter of blood, which meant Bob had used marijuana not long before he expired. In addition to the cannabis, doctors found .002 milligrams per liter of blood of metoprolol, a heart medication, along with .012 milligrams of diltiazem, another heart med. Those made sense, seeing that Bob's heart weighed in at 640 grams, slightly more than double the weight of a normal heart. (The pathologist came to find out that Bob Dow was in terrible health and in desperate need of a new heart.) On top of that, there was a larger than normal amount, 1.3 milligrams, of meprobamate, a tranquilizer used to treat anxiety, uncovered. The drug is marketed as Miltown, but meprobamate is a short-term–relief drug designed to take the edge off if an individual is high-strung.

Another finding by Dr. Young was the presence of "black circular material" that resembled "gunpowder." These "flakes," as Young described them, adhered to the skin on Bob's "left lower chest," his "right upper abdomen," as well as the "dorsal surfaces of the hands bilaterally."

What did finding gunpowder residue on Bob Dow's chest mean?

Gunpowder would not be present on Bob's chest and stomach if the shooter *stood* in front of him and fired. The shooter would have to have been straddling Bob Dow (sitting on, or leaning over, his chest) in order to leave gunpowder flakes where the doctor found them. The only other possibility was that Bob fired the weapon, holding the gun out in front of himself, maybe framing someone for the crime.

Still, could a man fire three shots into his own head and one into his left arm?

It did not seem possible.

Brian Boetz and Penny Judd pulled up to Dorothy Smith's house. Dorothy lived in a modest white ranch-style home with a marvelous, almost picture-perfect, birch tree in the front yard. Looking around the family-skewed, suburban neighborhood, a globelike Texas skyline stretched as far as the eye could see. This part of Texas is flat as a griddle. Down the block, the one piece of visible infrastructure was an old water tower projecting into the sky like a rocket ship taking off.

Boetz and Judd looked around as they approached the porch.

Boetz knocked.

Clearly upset by their presence, Dorothy was expecting them.

"Come in," she said. "Come in."

CHAPTER 10

ACCORDING TO BOBBI JO SMITH, she had known Bob Dow for six years, as far back as 1998. Bobbi was twelve years old when she was first introduced to Bob.

"I met him," she explained to me, "through his stepson . . . my son's father."

Bobbi said Bob Dow became "a father" to her. "And I treated him as such."

From a young age, Bob had taught Bobbi how to work construction and wire electrical outlets and circuits.

"He had his own maintenance service and I helped . . . and did a lot of work for him." Thinking back on it all, Bobbi said, she was grateful for the skills, trade, and experience Bob Dow had given her. And his tragic, untimely death, Bobbi added somberly, was devastating to her, regardless of the ("perv") twisted things Bob Dow had done throughout his life.

"Robert fed me drugs from the time I woke up until I passed out," Bobbi admitted. "Sometimes I prayed that I'd *never* wake up."

Friends of Bobbi's said she was quiet, mostly, and would do anything for anyone.

"Bobbi had a huge, huge heart," said one of her girlfriends. "There is nothing that Bobbi wouldn't do for a friend in need, whether she was high or not."

Bob had a fixation with young females. Bob's first wife, Charlene Kay McQueary, was "ten or twelve" when she and Bob met. Bob married Charlene as soon as she turned sixteen. Incidentally, the age of consent in Texas has always been seventeen. So having sex with anyone under the age of seventeen (who is *not* your spouse) is illegal in the state. Unless Bob Dow married Charlene when he did, he would have been committing sexual assault.

"I've known [Bob] all my life," Charlene later said in court. "We were married for a while when I was sixteen and we . . . remained friends forever. . . . We just decided we couldn't have an intimate . . . a personal relationship. But we have always remained friends."

Charlene claimed she could live with Bob "under the same roof," but she just couldn't "have a real good working relationship. . . ."

There was one part of Bob Dow's character that Charlene talked about rather ambivalently when later pressed: The notion that he was heavily into witchcraft and satanic worship. Inside Bob's trailer at one time were all types of bizarre books about witchcraft and satanic worshipping. Bob, Charlene explained to police, was very possessive of these books, as far back, she said, as 1997 and 1998, when she became involved in a personal project and needed some books to "cut up to do decoupage."

"There's a bunch of books over there," Bob had said. He lived in an apartment in Fort Worth then.

"Great," Charlene responded, heading for the shelf.

Bob followed. He pointed to his collection of books on witchcraft and satanic worship. "Any books but those. Do not touch those."

Bob did not believe in God, Charlene claimed. "He told me that."

A woman Bob married in 1982, Elizabeth Smith (no relation to Bobbi Jo), the mother of Bob's only child, said he could be a good man, but once he started hanging out with young girls at his mother's house and his trailer (where Bobbi Jo also stayed from time to time), Bob changed.

Elizabeth Smith divorced Bob six months after marrying him.

Why?

"Bobby cheated on me with my best friend," Elizabeth explained—"who also happened to be my younger brother's wife."

They had been together for nearly four years

before marrying. And even after the divorce, Elizabeth stayed in touch with Bob.

"We ran an apartment complex in Eastland, Texas," Elizabeth later explained in court. They took care of the maintenance and other duties. After the split, however, Bob moved to Weatherford, the Twin Oaks section. He started living inside a trailer and working for a railroad. From there, Bob moved into his mother's house in Mineral Wells after his brother had a heart attack and passed away. That was December 2003. Elizabeth stayed in contact with Bob because, she explained, "We had a child together."

"He did the best he could as a father," Elizabeth claimed, defending Bob.

Yet, those who knew him said Bob was not always the best man he could be to his son; but once in a while, he tried to make up for it by paying a little bit of attention to him.

"I think he done a wonderful job in spending time, you know, and he always provided what [his boy] needed," Elizabeth added. "Whatever [he] needed, it was there."

Elizabeth routinely saw Bob throughout the years after their divorce. If she didn't spend time with him, she spoke to Bob on the phone. Bob was alone after his brother passed. He had no other siblings and his father had died many years before. Lila Dow, Bob's mother, was paralyzed on one side of her body after suffering a terrible stroke. After Bob's brother died, Elizabeth even stepped in and

bathed and fed Lila because Bob just couldn't do
it. It was one of the reasons, Elizabeth said, that
Bob was forced to move in with his mother: to care
for her. While Bob spent more time at his mother's
house, Elizabeth, who had been stopping every
weekend at Lila's, caring for her, saw Bob on a
more regular basis. They got to know each other
all over again.

By January 2004, Bob was living at his mother's
house in Mineral Wells, just about full-time, taking
fairly good care of Lila, according to Elizabeth.

"In the beginning, Bobby took very good care of
his mother. He cleaned her. He bathed her, which
was hard for him. He never had to do anything like
that in his life. And, you know, there was—she never
wanted for anything. And he didn't mind paying
anybody to come and do what he couldn't do."

By then, Lila Dow could only feed herself if food
was placed in front of her. She couldn't bathe herself or go to the bathroom without help.

Bob's life went along this path for about a
month. Then February 2004 came, Elizabeth explained, watching all of this from the sidelines. At
this point, someone Bob had known when she was
a child reentered his life.

"Bobbi Jo came into the picture . . . ," Elizabeth
recalled. She had never met Bobbi Jo before that
February day when Bobbi showed up and began
staying with Bob at his mother's house.

"Hey, Liz, this is Bobbi Jo," Bob said, introducing Elizabeth to Bobbi. They were inside Lila's

house. "She's one of my workers. . . . I've known her for years. She's going to be staying here."

Elizabeth thought, *Well, this is okay. If she helps take care of "grandma" and cleans and what-have-you, it'll be fine.*

"Nice to meet you, Bobbi Jo."

"Same here," Bobbi said.

And yet, what was clear to Bobbi later was how much Elizabeth despised her from that day on. Bobbi felt this coldness from Elizabeth, as if Elizabeth felt Bobbi was intruding on a good thing Elizabeth had going with Bob.

"She hated me," Bobbi said. "I don't know why."

As a "preteen," Bobbi Jo Smith said, she dated Bob's stepson. It was her first romantic relationship with a boy (with any person, in fact), and she added, "All that I knew." Bobbi had a child when she was sixteen, fathered by this same man. They planned on getting married. But the relationship didn't last, obviously, and Bobbi split with her soon-to-be husband. She was distraught and broken, not knowing what to do. She didn't really feel as though she could go to her mother, a woman Bobbi said had abandoned her at a young age and didn't teach her many social skills to survive the world.

So Bobbi Jo went to see Bob Dow, a man she knew and trusted to help her.

"He opened his door to me," Bobbi recalled, "and treated me just like one of his own children."

At the beginning, that is.

Bobbi blames her fiancé for introducing her to, as she put it, "hard-core drugs." She loved the man, she said, but it was the drugs and "infidelity" that drove their relationship into the ground. Bobbi never mentioned that her sexuality had anything to do with the demise of the relationship. But one would have to assume that suppressing homosexual feelings by staging a white-picket-fence family life and having no one—especially a mother figure—to turn to and discuss those feelings, would have a momentous effect on any relationship.

"I couldn't take it anymore," she said of his cheating and drugging, "especially after my son was born." Bobbi wanted to make it work because of the child. She wanted a better life for her son, whom she referred to as "the *only* love I've ever known and truly felt. . . ." She would have stayed with this man, despite having feelings for females, in order to give her son a home with a mother and a father.

To her credit, Bobbi felt she needed to protect her boy. She knew the road she was headed down with her fiancé was not going to end pleasantly. She could see their lives deteriorating a little every day. She didn't want her son to become a casualty of that life, a spoke in the cycle.

After the end of this first relationship, which

had turned into engagement and motherhood, Bobbi Jo turned her back on men altogether. The dissolution of what might have become a marriage to a male, a father for her son, in other words, sent Bobbi running to females, she suggested. She tossed out any notion of living life as a heterosexual—and she felt free, almost normal, for the first time.

"I've never been with another man (willingly) outside my son's father," Bobbi said.

It was women from that point on for Bobbi—lots of them. They came and went. Through those relationships, Bobbi learned about life and love and caring for her child. Bobbi's family always watched over the boy if Bobbi was ripping and running, chasing the bottle and the pipe. Bobbi knew enough not to be around the child when she was partying. She felt she could become the mother she'd always dreamed of and "desired to be," but the pull of alcohol and drugs, for which she had no control over, clouded her judgment and kept her from doing it.

Once the split settled on her, and the totality of it began to weigh on such a young and vulnerable heart, Bobbi Jo fell even deeper into that crazy, evil abyss of drugs, alcohol, and promiscuity. Sure, she started using drugs and alcohol before this, but she took it all to an entirely new level once she and her fiancé went their separate ways, and living that lesbian lifestyle didn't fill the hole in her heart, which she had thought it might.

"I began to get caught up with the fast life—drugs and sex with lots of women. . . . I was numb."

That hole in her soul, Bobbi explained, wasn't even that she and her fiancé had split, or that she had repressed her homosexuality for many years. That pain began back when "[someone close to me] began to sexually and physically abuse me—and my mother's . . . emotional and mental abuse and also abandoning me. I tried to make my mom proud of me. I played sports and hoped and prayed that just one time she showed up to watch. She never did . . . and then the terribly violent sexual abuse by someone close."

All before this girl could drive a motor vehicle legally.

It was too much. The pain broke Bobbi. For a while, the drugs and the booze filled up that space.

In Bobbi Jo, Jennifer Jones saw a gentle female, willing to party until the drugs and booze ran dry, full of lust for the same type of life Jen was leading. Jen viewed Bobbi as a counterpart, feeding her pain with whatever poison she could get her hands on. Jen had seen this firsthand whenever Audrey brought Bobbi over to the apartment, or wherever they ran into each other out in the small Mineral Wells world of teen partying. And yet, much like Jen, Bobbi hadn't always been the party girl and wild lesbian, up for anything, whose reputation followed her around like a storm cloud. At fifteen, Bobbi Jo lived next door to her grandmother's house in Graford, with her aunt Kathy and uncle Richard, the Cruzes. This was just before Bobbi became pregnant and talked of marrying the guy who had knocked her up.

A staunch believer, Bobbi went to church regularly. "And her participation in church [services] was good," Richard Cruz later said.

Bobbi was active in the youth groups as well. She'd go on retreats and other trips and act like a big sister/mentor to the younger girls, while befriending the girls her own age. She liked to participate in family outings, Richard Cruz explained later in court. She was a good girl. She was fun to be around, laughing and joking. She was always willing to do something for someone else. All of this despite the tempest of emotional pain that she was dealing with inside herself.

"Like, yeah, you know, we would play ball and stuff like that," Cruz commented. "My kids were grown and [Bobbi] was the only kid around the house."

It was great having Bobbi Jo around, Richard Cruz added. She always behaved and acted respectably.

Cruz was also privy to the other side of Bobbi, he said. She seemed like a naïve young girl, forced to grow up too damn fast, and maybe just beginning to embrace family as a good thing, when the bottom fell out. Bobbi was frightened of the same things other girls were, Cruz said. Like when they once went to shoot weapons off at a local firing range.

"She was very scared" of the guns, Cruz recalled.

Bobbi didn't want to mess with guns at all. She understood the power of a handgun, and she was well aware of what it could do to a human being.

CHAPTER 11

DETECTIVES BRIAN BOETZ AND PENNY Judd sat down with Dorothy Smith to get a better handle on what she had to say about her granddaughter, Bobbi Jo, who had just turned nineteen the previous week. Apparently, from the information Boetz and Judd had, Bobbi Jo told Dorothy that she had killed Bob Dow. Solid information, yes; but the statement alone still did not explain what happened, nor did it detail a possible motive—and, perhaps most important at this point, where Bobbi Jo was.

"Tell us what happened," Boetz encouraged Dorothy.

Dorothy took a sip from a glass of water on the table in front of her. This was not a hard recollection. The situation had occurred the day before. Under direction from Dorothy, Penny Judd took down the interviewee's statement, word for word.

"It was about two-thirty when I got home,"

Dorothy explained. She seemed a bit nervous, as would be expected, but also quite eager to explain what happened. She couldn't understand. There was something missing from all of what had happened.

"Yesterday?" Boetz confirmed.

"Yeah," Dorothy said, shaking her head. "Bobbi Jo was here."

As she began a narrative of what had occurred, Dorothy explained that her granddaughter was not herself.

"Grandma, I need your pickup," Bobbi had asked Dorothy.

"Why?" Dorothy said. Bobbi Jo was a child Dorothy thought highly of. She adored Bobbi. Sure, Bobbi had had some problems and had grown up rather fast. But what kid these days didn't have issues to contend with? The whole point of Bobbi moving from the Cruzes next door into Dorothy's home was to start anew. Bobbi and her mother were at different places in life, to put it mildly. Bobbi had given up on her mother after repeatedly giving her chances to make things up. Dorothy had always been there.

"I want to get my clothes out of Bob's," Bobbi explained after Dorothy pressed the issue of Bobbi wanting to use the truck. She was trying to find out what was going on. Bobbi had been staying with Bob Dow. However, Bobbi always had kept a room at Dorothy's house and traded off, at times, between the two places. Dorothy felt Bobbi had a love-hate relationship with Bob. She was always getting into arguments with him, but she looked up to him as a mentor. Something that not too many within Bobbi's inner circle knew was that Bob Dow had been providing Bobbi with her lifestyle: work, drugs, booze, women.

"They were very close," an ex-girlfriend of Bobbi's later said, explaining the often fragile and volatile relationship Bobbi Jo had with Bob Dow. "They planned on going on trips and going to work. They grouped up ideas from each other, just what to do, you know, for that day or the weekend. Like a . . . a . . . father-figure relationship, I guess you could say."

Dorothy wanted to know why Bobbi needed the truck. "Bobbi, what's going on?" Bobbi had "another girl" with her on this day. Bobbi's new friend was acting strangely, Dorothy felt: wiry and looking around, white as a ghost. Something had happened. Or, rather, something was *about* to happen.

"Look, I need to get my clothes out of there right now before Bob finds [out I'm leaving]," Bobbi said. "Bob is trying to make us"—Bobbi was referring to her and her new friend—"have sex with him to pay for our fines."

(Bobbi later disputed ever saying this, alleging that her grandmother was confusing what she had said on that day with what the girl she was with—Jennifer Jones—had said.)

Bobbi and Jen had been picked up at the mall the previous week for shoplifting. At first, nobody would bail them out, and nobody would pick them up at the jail.

Bob finally came through, according to Jen. He and Bobbi's mother picked them up and drove them to where Bobbi's mother was staying at the time.

As Dorothy continued to explain what Bobbi had said, she claimed Bobbi told her the previous day, "I need to pay my fine, or they'll pick me up."

(You see, this comment falls in line with what Bobbi later told me: She had signed herself out of jail after the shoplifting charge, but she still needed to pay the fine, or she would be in deeper trouble.)

"How much, Bobbi?" Dorothy asked.

"Two thousand."

Dorothy couldn't believe it. Where was Bobbi Jo going to get that sort of money?

"Bobbi—"

"Look, Grandma." Bobbi stopped what she was doing and focused on Dorothy, looking her in the eyes. "Bob said he wouldn't pay our fines unless we had sex with him."

The implication of this exchange was that Bob had lied to Bobbi and Jen. Bobbi was saying Bob had picked them up and agreed to pay the fines (as in a loan), but now they had to go to bed with him to pay off that debt. Bob had been after Jen ever since Bobbi hooked up with her, and Jen had started hanging around Lila Dow's house. That first time Bob had a look at Jennifer, he was infatuated with her. He was fixated on having sex with her (according to Jen).

It was Bobbi Jo's job, in one respect, to bring home young girls for Bob to fuel up with dope and booze and then bed down and film. (This was an accusation Bobbi voluntarily admitted to, adding that she never made any of the girls do this. How could she? She did, however, make the offer.) It was disgusting and illegal and immoral, but Bobbi knew the game and had gone along with it.

"Wow," Bob said the first time he met Jen (according to the version of this story that Jen later told *Texas Monthly,* although Bobbi did not recall this ever happening). "She's pretty. She could be a movie star!"

Bobbi, Jen later insisted, knew what Bob meant by that. Soon after, as the three of them were partying, Bob had a moment with Bobbi Jo to himself and said, "Ask her if she'll sleep with me." According to Jennifer, Bobbi was furious. Jennifer was hers.

Yet, Bobbi knew her place with Bob, so she asked Jennifer.

"No way," Jen supposedly snapped. "He's way too gross."

(However, when I asked Bobbi later, she said this never happened. "If Bob wanted to sleep with Jen, I could not have cared. He did sleep with her, as far as I knew. It was chaos in that house with the drugs, booze, and sex.")

Regardless, that was how the relationship among Bobbi, Bob, and Jen went along, Jennifer claimed. But as Bob pushed, Jen added (in one version) that Bobbi's answer was firm: "Have any of the other girls I bring home for you, just not her. She's mine."

Bobbi later told me this was nonsense. That if Bob had wanted Jen, he could have had her. Bobbi would not have balked one way or the other, because there were always plenty of girls around the house for Bobbi to party and have sex with.

And Jennifer knew this.

What's more, Bobbi insisted, at that point, Jen would have done anything for money so she could buy dope. She was a coke whore in the bare essence of the term, Bobbi insisted.

What Bobbi didn't see—likely because her judgment was so clouded by the sex, booze, and drug culture inside that house—was that Jen had become increasingly obsessed with her new girl/girl relationship. She viewed the romance entirely differently than Bobbi did. Bobbi went to work; Jen followed. Bobbi went to the store; Jen demanded to tag along. Wherever Bobbi went, whatever Bobbi did, Jen seemed to be right by her side. Bobbi would go to the bathroom, and there was Jen, waiting outside the door, according to several sources.

For Bobbi Jo, at that time in her life, she had stumbled into a win-win situation.

"I liked Jennifer. She was cool. Fun to be with."

Heck, Bobbi Jo had turned a heterosexual female. She enjoyed every moment of that new lifestyle Jen had thrown herself into.

"She was going to get her stuff," Dorothy Smith explained to Detectives Brian Boetz and Penny Judd on May 5, 2004, bringing the MWPD back to her narrative of what had taken place the day before. They were in Dorothy's kitchen. She was clearly broken up about the entire mess. "She [Bobbi] had a place to go."

(This part of Dorothy's statement adds up with what Bobbi Jo later told me. Bobbi said Bob Dow had pissed her off and she was going over to the house on that day to get her belongings and some money Bob owed her. She was done with him. Never going back.)

"Did you give them the truck?" Boetz asked.

Bobbi and Jennifer, Dorothy explained, "left in my truck."

"What happened next?" Boetz pressed.

"They came back in about an hour, hour and a half."

Bobbi was driving Dorothy's pickup and Jennifer was in Bob Dow's truck. It was strange, the two of them in different vehicles. However, Dorothy didn't think much of it at the time—just that they were back at the house dropping off her vehicle.

"Was there anyone else with them?"

Dorothy said a few other girls.

Bobbi rushed into the house. Dorothy was certain of this fact.

"What's going on?" Dorothy asked her granddaughter.

Bobbi didn't answer.

"Bobbi?" Dorothy said sharply.

"I have to leave," Bobbi said. "Grandma . . . I . . . Grandma . . . I killed Bob. I shot him in the head."

"No, you didn't," Dorothy said. She knew when Bobbi was making something up—and this surely seemed like one of those moments. Bobbi Jo had tears in her eyes and became more nervous as she talked about what she claimed had happened at Bob Dow's.

"Yes," Bobbi said as she grabbed a bag, flung it over her shoulder, and then started for the door. "I did, Grandma. He is *not* going to molest me again."

"Wait . . . wait, Bobbi . . . please." (Several of the other girls there that day, beyond Jen, claimed Dorothy pulled at Bobbi's shirt, beckoning her to stay and explain. Bobbi did not want to look her grandmother in the eye. "Because," Bobbi told me, "I was lying.")

"I've got to go, Grandma," Bobbi said.

"Please stay, Bobbi. We can work this out."

"No. I need to get out of here now, Grandma. I'm sorry."

Jen stood by as Bobbi and Dorothy talked. The others, who had been waiting outside in the two vehicles, were now standing near the three of them in front of Dorothy's house.

"Bobbi, please. Don't go. You didn't kill anybody," Dorothy said.

"Yes, I did," Bobbi insisted. Standing next to her, Jen nodded yes to Dorothy, agreeing with Bobbi, trying to get Dorothy to believe that Bobbi had done it: shot Bob Dow.

"But, Bobbi, you don't even have a driver's license," Dorothy said. Just then, Bobbi was getting into the driver's side of the other vehicle.

The other girls piled into the truck: Five females, including Bobbi and Jennifer, were now preparing to take off on what appeared to be some sort of a run.

"Did you kill Bob, Bobbi?" Dorothy asked pointedly.

"Yes, Grandma. I did."

"Did she?" Dorothy asked the other girls.

"They all shook their heads yes," Dorothy explained to Boetz and Judd.

And then they were gone.

"That was the last I seen of her," Dorothy told the detectives. "I called Richard [Cruz] over here when he got home, and he called the police."

"Have you heard from her?" Boetz asked.

"No."

Boetz told Dorothy that should Bobbi Jo try to contact her, Dorothy needed to call the MWPD immediately. Now was not the time to try and protect a loved one from the law. The faster they got Bobbi Jo in custody, the better it would work out for her in the end.

Dorothy understood.

Boetz and Judd drove back to the MWPD. Boetz sat down at his desk and began filing a probable cause affidavit, a process that needed to be done in order to get an arrest warrant issued for the apprehension and arrest of Bobbi Jo Smith. Filing the affidavit didn't mean they could arrest Bobbi Jo on murder charges; Boetz still needed to prove to a judge the MWPD had enough evidence to claim Bobbi Jo had committed the offense.

In the scope of it all, however, Boetz didn't have much more than hearsay—a source claiming that someone had shot a man the MWPD had found dead.

Was that *proof* of murder?

After he finished typing, Boetz tracked down Judge Hart, who had been at the crime scene the previous night.

Hart looked the affidavit over while Boetz waited, asked a few questions, and then agreed there was enough to issue an arrest warrant.

Somewhere out in the world, traveling with four other women, Bobbi Jo Smith was wanted for first-degree murder—a charge, in Texas, that could place this teenager (if convicted under the right circumstances) on a gurney, with a hot needle filled with a state-issued death potion plunging into her skinny arm.

CHAPTER 12

IT DID NOT TAKE LONG for Elizabeth Smith to begin hating on Bobbi Jo once the two met inside Lila's house after Bob introduced them. And yet, according to what Elizabeth Smith later testified to, based on what she witnessed during the time she spent at the house in February and March 2004, all she knew about Bobbi was that "Bob had worked with her, on and off, for years. . . ." As Elizabeth later described her feelings, what was clear was that she did not care much for Bobbi Jo.

"I think she was jealous of me, for some weird reason," Bobbi told me later. "I have no idea why that would be."

Elizabeth had no idea that Bob had known Bobbi since Bobbi was a child; nor, according to Bobbi, that Bob had been forcing her to have sex with him all those years. There was certainly a lot more to the relationship between Bob and Bobbi than Elizabeth knew.

"She's one of the hardest workers I have ever met and have ever employed," Bob told Elizabeth one day after Bobbi Jo moved some of her stuff into the party house.

Bob was repairing apartment complexes at the time. He hired Bobbi mainly as a painter, but he also taught her to do all sorts of miscellaneous maintenance jobs. She also cleaned swimming pools with Bob on occasion.

"He could just do anything," Elizabeth remembered, shining up Bob's memory best she could. "He was just *that* talented."

Bob had been in the U.S. Navy. At one time, he implored values favorable to the navy's golden standard of living, especially where cleanliness was concerned. But all that changed, Elizabeth assumed, after Bobbi Jo moved into the living room and began sleeping on a mattress.

"Change?" she said. "A lot of things began to change, yes. . . ."

Bob wasn't keeping the house clean. Elizabeth blamed Bobbi. "He wasn't staying at home taking care of his mother. I was spending more and more time there," Elizabeth added.

And this, too, was easy for Elizabeth to blame on Bobbi.

It wasn't just Bob being gone all of the time, out and about, working with Bobbi Jo, running around,

Elizabeth said. There was "a lot of drug use" going on around the house. "A *lot* of drug use."

What Elizabeth didn't see and never quite understood was that Bob Dow had turned into a drug addict. He had been heavily involved with all sorts of drugs long before Bobbi Jo stepped back into his life and asked him for help. It wasn't Bobbi Jo who turned Bob into a doper and influenced his life in negative ways. In fact, one could argue it was Bob Dow who did this exact thing to Bobbi Jo.

When Audrey Sawyer first met Bobbi Jo, Audrey had just been released from prison, completing time on a two-year bid. The crime that put Audrey behind bars had been committed in Strawn while Jennifer and Audrey's other sister were living there. Jennifer and a friend had broken into a store directly across the street from Jen's friends' house, where a group of teens had been partying one afternoon. After Jen and her friend committed the crime, they showed up where Audrey was hanging out with their other sister.

"And we all got drunk," Audrey explained with a laugh.

There were other friends there, too.

"Well, they, Jen and her friend," Audrey added, "they told us that they had broken into the store. They said it was easy."

So Jen and her friend went back into the store. Audrey and the other girls followed. One thing led to another and, Audrey explained, "we all ended up getting into trouble for it."

Most of the girls were underage and placed on probation, including Jennifer. Audrey and Jen's friend, both eighteen, were arrested. Audrey was on probation then for a separate charge and wound up with a two-year bid.

When she got out of prison, Audrey moved into the Spanish Trace Apartments, where Jerry Jones and Jennifer lived. Between the time they all got pinched for robbing the store and Audrey went off to prison, Jen had evolved as a would-be, aspiring criminal, graduating from small theft to more risky things. She got busted two months after the store theft, for example, for writing bad checks—for the most part, an adult crime. Her drug use had escalated by then. She needed money to fund those good times.

After that, Jen stole a car. As time went on and she got older, it was clear her crimes were becoming more serious. She had set the risk-taking bar higher.

Whenever Jen felt backed into a corner—no one else to turn to, her big sister not there—she wrote. Near this time when she was breaking the law and getting caught, Jen wrote about going to visit her mother, Kathy Jones, who was herself working on a prison bid. And yet, Jen seemed to joke about a drug bender she had been on herself, writing, *I have been awake for 36 hours. I feel ditzy!* And so she decided, since she was already awake, she might as well write Audrey a letter: *Then paint my toenails red.*

Feeling guilty the following day, Jen again turned to her journal, adding, *I am such a bad person [who does] the stupidest things. Well, I am going to try and get some sleep. . . . Please pray for me tonight.*

Drugs were controlling Jen's thoughts and actions. Telling her when to sleep, eat, shit, get up, work, do the right thing—and she was only sixteen years old. Jennifer Jones, with a mother and big sister in prison, was following right along in the wake of her pedigree, but maybe, in some ways, hoping to surpass her sibling and mother and grasp that Clyde Barrow dream of becoming criminally infamous.

It's worth noting, this was long before she ever heard the name Bobbi Jo Smith.

It was not long after Audrey served her time and was released that she met Bobbi Jo. Mostly, the time they spent together was at Bob's mother's house, a five-to-ten-minute drive south of the Second Street Spanish Trace apartment complex. Audrey would go over to what all of them—including Bob Dow—referred to as the "party house" and hang out with Bobbi Jo. Audrey and the others felt safe at the house: a place to party and do what they wanted without worrying about being busted. There would be girls, young and old alike, hanging out, Audrey said, all the time.

"Drinking, popping pills, smoking weed . . . what-ever." It was one big, perpetual bash. As far as Audrey could tell, Bob Dow was the ringleader, keeping tabs on and providing what was a nonstop conveyor belt of drugs, sex, and booze. Bob had what seemed to be an endless stash of pills, weed, booze, and other hard-core drugs—meth and coke included, two popular drugs of the time that attracted lots of girls. Unbeknownst to her at the time, what Elizabeth Smith later discovered was that Lila Dow's house had been gifted to Bob the previous fall by his younger brother after he died. According to several sources, from the time he took over for his brother, Bob received (and cashed) his mother's Social Security checks as pay-ments for taking care of her. Many of the girls who frequented the house claimed that Bob's idea of tending to his mother's needs, however, consisted of tossing her a Value or Happy Meal from McDon-ald's every once in a while, or warming up some canned soup. The old lady was "incapacitated" in many ways, mostly due to the stroke she had suf-fered. She stayed in her room, staring blankly at a television screen, seemingly waiting to die. She did not have a clue about what was going on just out-side the walls of her bedroom. When Bob had his little parties with the girls, he'd lock his mother inside her room by placing a padlock on the out-side of her door.

Certainly not that loveable "good father" and "good son" Elizabeth Smith later described. Which would lead one to believe that Bob Dow put on a show for his ex-wife whenever she was around.

"Bob Dow was pretty quiet when I went over there, most of the time," Audrey remembered. "But he could be very perverted, too. Weird guy. He's hard to explain. He was kind of dorky, you could say."

Bob wore big tortoiseshell-style glasses over his hazel eyes. He had a receding hairline, but he was not bald. He had some gray hair, generally greasy and unkempt, and what seemed to be continuous stubble of beard growth. He wasn't fat, but he carried a large beer gut. Bob Dow did not take care of himself. He was viewed by most of the girls hanging around the house as "scuzzy" and "dirty."

"He'd stare at people (the girls, mainly). He'd . . . just . . . He was *very* strange," Audrey said.

The one thing most agreed on was that Bob used the hell out of Bobbi Jo, who became, in a sense, Bob's personal prostitute, employee, drinking and drugging buddy, and madam—all wrapped up in one.

"Sometimes," Jen later testified, "Bobbi would have . . . she would have to sexually give herself to him in order to get something in return, like drugs or money. She would have to sometimes give up her girlfriend and sleep with Bob to get what she wanted. . . ."

(Here was an interesting turn of phrase by Jen: "her girlfriend." Why not "me"? If what Jen later claimed was true, that she and Bobbi were totally in love, why say "her girlfriend" in place of herself? This statement, which Jen made in court, fell more in line with Bobbi's analysis of the relationship—that she and Jennifer were party friends and sometimes sexual partners, nothing more. It made sense that Jen would describe this aspect of Bobbi's life by stating how Bobbi would have to "give up her girlfriend." Jen never saw herself as Bobbi's exclusive girl, because she wasn't.)

According to Jen, Bobbi came up with a name for what Bob forced her into doing: "paying the rent." Jen was never jealous of the relationship between Bobbi Jo and Bob, she claimed. But she felt it "wasn't right," adding, "It made me . . . disgusted more than anything that a man would go to that level, you know, to say, 'You need to sleep with me in order to be able to live in my house, to be able to get what you want, instead of working for it.'"

Jen said she witnessed times when Bob would "force himself" on Bobbi Jo, even though Bobbi made it clear she didn't want to have sex with him. Afterward, Jen would ask Bobbi how she felt.

"I don't want to talk about it," Bobbi would say. ("Dismissing it," Jen exclaimed.)

Before Jen moved herself into the party house—an important fact in this case—and started sleeping with Bobbi Jo, Bob forced Bobbi to have sex with him, Jen claimed.

"I would say at least maybe three times a week," Jen explained in court.

* * *

For Audrey Sawyer, she found hanging out, having sex, and partying with Bobbi Jo to be a blast. Audrey never spent enough time over at the party house to witness what her half sister later claimed—nor had she recalled Bobbi ever talking about Bob forcing himself on her.

Bobbi told me she accepted Bob's deal as part of getting the things she wanted out of the guy. Bobbi was young when the sexual abuse started (in her early teens). She didn't know any better. The guy was sexually abusing her and making her feel as though it was no big deal. If a person wants something, she pays for it. Sometimes with cash, but other times with her body. That was how Bobbi understood her deal with Bob Dow.

"Bobbi was cool," Audrey said of her former girlfriend. "She was hyper, fun to be around. She'd make you laugh."

Everyone said this about Bobbi.

There was never a time during their relationship when Bobbi ever talked of wanting Bob Dow dead or hating him, Audrey explained. Bobbi absolutely loved the guy, from where Audrey saw it.

Bobbi Jo was the life of the party. But still, there was an immense pain deep down, always. Bobbi sometimes had this sad, heavy look to her. When she'd get really high, her eyes bulged and turned to slits, as if she had a hard time keeping them open. She would get into a droopy sort of mood and become sloppy and lethargic. Still, it was the sex with girls that Bobbi craved more than anything—it drove her emotionally and helped to cover up and stuff all that emotional pain she suffered. Bobbi connected with the same sex on this level and never felt more alive than when she was involved intimately with another female. The problem arose when her lifestyle became a promiscuous mesh of sexual encounters with so many different girls that she'd had no emotional connection with. She'd bed down with just about any female who was around at the time.

There are photographs of Bobbi having oral sex with women; others of Bobbi passed out on a mattress on the floor in the party house, with a female having her way with Bobbi's chest and vagina. There is maybe a third female in the background, handcuffed, waiting her turn. There are also photos of Bobbi kissing two girls at the same time, smoking weed and smoking coke and meth, along with photos of Bobbi putting a gun to her head in a mock version of pulling the trigger.

"When I first seen her, I did think she was a little boy—I didn't know she was a girl," Audrey recalled.

Bobbi liked to wear a leather jacket, jeans, a chain wallet. She could have easily passed, at times, for a male, especially from the backside. And this was, Bobbi later explained to me, one of the reasons why some people hated her: She was a lesbian.

Once she turned around, however, it was easy to recognize the feminine side Bobbi could not hide from. She is pretty, effeminate, and sensual. When it came to lovemaking, Bobbi might have been the aggressor, but past lovers told me that Bobbi was gentle and quiet and never demanded anything weird. She took her time if a girl was nervous. Taking into account the number of females she slept with, it was about the sex for Bobbi, not scaring anyone. Like the booze and dope, Bobbi developed an addiction to sex.

Whenever she needed to get high, there was Bob Dow with a handful of drugs, gallons of booze, standing in front of whichever lover Bobbi had that day, with a camera, the green light flashing, encouraging the two (or three or four) of them to get on with the sex so he could get all of it on film. Bobbi didn't balk because she was getting what she wanted all around, feeding her habits quite ravenously.

Bobbi was not Audrey's first lesbian experience: "It was like my fourth," Audrey said.

According to Audrey, one of the drugs Bobbi Jo introduced her to was whip-its, a cheap and quick high that users get from inhaling small canisters filled with nitrous oxide.

"What makes them really popular is they're easily accessible," William Oswald, founder of the Summit Malibu drug treatment center, told ABC News during an interview some years back. Oswald is an expert on whip-it use.

Long after Audrey and Bobbi Jo were into whip-its, the drug made a comeback when actress Demi Moore was rushed to the ER after reportedly inhaling several canisters.

"You can get them at a head shop, you can get it out of a whipped-cream bottle," Oswald added.

This type of over-the-counter drug seems almost harmless to the naïve mind of a teen. (It's also readily available online, which has made this drug extremely common.) It's marketed in the same casual way, as if it's some sort of recreational drug that won't hurt you. But the reality is that whip-its can cause severe brain damage, and even death. Reports claim that over 12 million people in the United States have tried whip-its—a remarkable number, by any standards—which does speak to how "innocent" users view the drug.

Audrey said, "They're these little canisters that you pop open and suck up—it's kinda like helium, but it's not helium. Bobbi and me would get them from the local smoke shop."

The two of them would grab several canisters and head down by the lake and "do one or two of them." They'd get light-headed and dizzy, laugh and joke around, smoke cigarettes, and then have sex.

This was the life they led.

"They would do them all the time," Audrey said of all the girls hanging out at Bob Dow's house.

There was a revolving door of girls constantly in and out of the party house. There were three-somes going on at any given time: girls on girls on girls. Sometimes Bob would partake; sometimes he'd just film. Bob had a problem getting an erection, so there were lots of times when he'd simply watch and masturbate himself, hoping to get hard so he could participate.

"They would take crazy pictures," one girl who frequented the house later told me.

Bobbi and Audrey had what Audrey described as a "party thing." Their relationship was centered on booze, drugs, and sex. Audrey never saw a long-term thing with Bobbi.

"Yes, I loved Audrey," Bobbi explained to me. "I cared about her more than I cared about Jennifer. After I cheated on Audrey with Jennifer, Jennifer would not leave. I was used to just messing around with women and not caring and not thinking twice about anything. Audrey and I were together for a while." But, as Bobbi learned, Audrey started doing something Bobbi felt explained to her what type of person Audrey truly was. "I didn't like her sleeping with Bob [Dow], but she made her own choices freely. I believe that's what kept me from 'falling in love' with her. But, yes, Audrey was loved deeply by me."

None of the girls who ever hooked up with Bobbi considered Bobbi all theirs—that is, until Jen decided she was Bobbi's girlfriend. As a mate of Bobbi's, a lover knew Bobbi was a party girl, and accepted that going into the relationship. A good time was a good time. Audrey was into partying back then, and Bobbi came along at the right moment. Most of the girls who ended up with Bobbi later said it was easy to love her. She made them feel good almost instantly. Even Jen, with Bobbi being her first lesbian experience, couldn't explain how or why, but she became instantly infatuated with Bobbi.

"The relationship that we had, I felt I was real close to her, and felt I needed her more than anything," Jennifer later said. "That if I . . . initially, if I didn't have her, I couldn't go on."

("If I didn't have her, I couldn't go on" becomes an important part of this narrative—remember it.)

Bear in mind, this statement came from a female who had denounced lesbian relationships (insulting Bobbi Jo in the process) a week before hooking up with Bobbi by calling Bobbi Jo Audrey's "dike [sic] girlfriend."

"It was . . . I cared for her," Jen continued. "And that right there is what I felt I needed—just someone that gave me that attention and that cared for me and loved me."

Bobbi's lovers—especially Jen—would later talk about a feeling of being able to take on the world when they were with Bobbi, that nothing could stop them. Being with Bobbi was like believing that between the two of them, the new girl became infallible. Nothing could penetrate how important and how indestructible Bobbi made a girl feel. Everything and everyone else melted away.

That relationship was going fairly well, Audrey explained, after she got out of prison and hooked up with Bobbi Jo. But then Bobbi went and ruined it by bringing something up one night that threw Audrey off. There were certain things, Audrey said later, she just wasn't going to do. And when Bobbi approached Audrey with a plan she had, Audrey took a step back from the relationship and reevaluated what she wanted from it.

"I want to have a threesome," Bobbi suggested one night.

"You what?"

"You heard me. A threesome with another girl."

"Not me, Bobbi," Audrey responded. It was one of those out-of-sight, out-of-mind things. Naïve as this sounds, Audrey may have assumed it was going on at the party house with other girls whom Bob was filming, but she had never heard of Bobbi being involved and claimed to have never seen it herself. And Audrey wasn't into kinky, weird stuff. She was a lesbian and proud of it. She wanted monogamy. She wanted love. She wanted a partner. Being a lesbian didn't mean you had to partake in all sorts of frivolous, unhealthy behavior. All that stuff with Bob, that was for money and drugs.

They were at the party house, of course, waiting for some friends to come over.

"Come on," Bobbi pressed. "It'll be fun."

"I'm out of here, Bobbi," Audrey said, gathering her things, walking toward the door. "You go have some fun with that other girl. Not me."

This was how Audrey explained the breakup of their relationship.

It was around this same time, however, middle of March 2004, when Jen later said she had that little exchange with Bobbi as she sat on the front stoop, smoking a cigarette, and Bobbi pulled up with Audrey and a few other friends. Audrey and Bobbi were having problems already. They hadn't necessarily broken up, but Audrey knew her time with Bobbi was limited.

Audrey felt that if she got involved in a threesome, Bob would film it—and Lord knows where it would end up. As it was, Audrey had heard Bob was putting all of the videos on a website. Audrey had found out Bob had even set up hidden cameras all over the house so he could get the girls on video when they didn't know it.

"I'm going out to the grocery store," Bobbi told Audrey the following day (after Bobbi and Jen supposedly had that conversation at the apartment). They were at the party house. Audrey said that the threesome request came around this same time.

"Whatever," Audrey said.

And that was the end of the relationship, according to Bobbi and Audrey. Bobbi said later it was part of her normal routine. She was involved with scores of women. Audrey was just *one* more. And then Jen showed up (at the party house) just around that time.

"And wouldn't leave," Bobbi said, "so we started hanging out."

In one of three vastly different versions of hooking up with Bobbi Jo that Jennifer Jones would later tell, she claimed Bobbi called her after Bobbi had an argument with Audrey about the threesome.

(Bobbi does not recall the following scenario ever taking place, and she equates it to Jen's drug-induced fantasy version of their brief life together.)

"Can you meet me at the library?" Bobbi asked, according to what Jen claimed in an interview she gave to *Texas Monthly*. (Granted, this was published merely weeks *before* Bobbi would face trial for murdering Bob Dow.)

Jen was taken aback by the phone call. "Why?" she supposedly asked Bobbi.

"I want to talk to you."

Jen had been over to the party house by then a few times, she claimed. She knew what went on. The drugs. The sex. The moviemaking. The first time Audrey brought Jen over to the house, Bob took one look at Jen and, Audrey could tell, was instantly infatuated. "She's *purty*, Audrey," Bob had said, allegedly. "Wow."

"Well, Bobbi and Audrey," Jen later said in court, thinking back on that moment when she first hooked up with Bobbi (totally contradicting that later version of the same story she gave to *Texas Monthly*), "had asked me to go to a party, a get-together, whatever. And I went over there and I stayed the night."

Jen slept on a floor mattress; yet, "sleep" was not the best way to describe that first night. "Passed out" was better. Nonetheless, Jen liked the idea that she could do whatever she wanted at the party house and not have to answer to anyone. Jerry Jones was not an iron-fisted parent by any means; but at the time, Jen didn't want to report to him about certain things. She was underage. Her mother, Kathy Jones, didn't mind Jen's drinking (and, hell, Kathy admitted to me that she'd even buy the beer), but Jerry forbade it. Over at Bob Dow's party house with Bobbi and Audrey, however, Jen could do whatever she wanted and not be called on it. She was eighteen and, arguably, an adult. But Jerry demanded certain behaviors from Jen if she wanted to remain living in the apartment.

"To . . . just . . . to just party and hang out with friends," Jen said in court, referring to what she liked best about Bob Dow's party house. "To do things that my dad wouldn't let me do, like drugs and drinking."

And it was during that time when Jen was hanging out over at the party house—every other person involved in this case agreed, even Jen, in one of her versions—when Jen and Bobbi started eyeing each other and wound up in bed.

Going back to that story Jen would later tell *Texas Monthly* reporter Katy Vine, Jen claimed that when she met Bobbi at the library on that day when Bobbi called out of the blue, they stood near a large tree, at first just talking about their lives. The way Jen described the scene on this afternoon, it almost sounded like a fairy tale, as if the way Jen remembered the day had come from a storybook she had recently read—or perhaps a Miranda Lambert song she'd heard before the interview!

She claimed that she and Bobbi were standing there, just talking (you could almost picture Jen holding a dandelion, plucking its leaves one moment, staring up into Bobbi's eyes the next), and Bobbi took Jen by the head and planted a long, slow French kiss on her.

And all of a sudden, the *Texas Monthly* article reported of that moment, *Jennifer didn't care that Bobbi Jo was a lesbian or even kissing her meant she was one too.*

If this version of their hookup is true, at that exact instant, underneath a tree out on the lawn near the town library, after Bobbi kissed Jen for the first time (the first time, Jennifer said, she had *ever* been intimate with a female), Jen decided she had found true love.

"Come with me," Bobbi apparently said, taking Jennifer by the hand.

As Jen told it, the scene took on that Grimm-like imagery, as if they were trapped inside a dream Jen once had.

And so, once upon a time, Jen went over to Bob's house with Bobbi on that day, she explained to *Texas Monthly*, and returned to her Spanish Trace apartment, only to pick up all of her belongings, so she could effectively move in with Bobbi. Jen was taken in completely by Bobbi, she said. She was Bobbi's girl now.

Later, under oath, Jen would refer to her hooking up with Bobbi Jo under yet vastly different circumstances, saying: "I went over to Bob Dow's house and stayed the night." She was referring to early March, after being invited to the party house by Bobbi and Audrey. "And from there, it's kind of like me and Bobbi Jo kind of hit it off. You know, we were talking. We were just, you know, getting to know each other, and . . . one thing leads to another and, you know, just together."

Audrey was out and Jennifer was in.

Simple as that.

In a statement Audrey later gave to police, she said, "I introduced Bobbi Jo to Jennifer and . . . then I found them in bed together one night." The implication was that Audrey had left Jen at the party house, went out, came back, and caught Bobbi and Jen having sex.

"I don't know where that story came from,"

Audrey told me later. "I never told that to the police. There was a lot of stuff that was later reported that simply wasn't true. When Bobbi Jo and me was together, we was never separated."

It seems impractical to believe that. What seems about right, according to most of those involved, is that Bobbi, in keeping with her promiscuous ways, replaced Audrey with her sister. Audrey got pissed and broke up with her. Sure, it sounds so *The Jerry Springer Show;* but in the lives of these women, it is definitely plausible.

Another piece of erroneous information Audrey wanted to clear up, she said, was a report that she had sex with Bob Dow two times for money.

"They—Bob and Bobbi—tried to talk me into it several times, but I never went through with it," Audrey said. "It never happened. What happened was, Bob Dow had paid me and this other girl to mess around [together, without him]. Me and Bobbi Jo were together at the time."

Bobbi Jo "didn't mind." She encouraged it, in fact, according to Audrey.

Yet Audrey later told me (during a separate conversation) that when Bobbi presented her with the idea of a threesome, she relented and left, never to return.

From Jen's point of view, what can never be in dispute, no matter which story is believed, was the way that Bobbi Jo made Jen feel. Jen adored Bobbi from the first moment they spent the night partying and having sex. Jen was hooked. Bobbi made her feel more special than anyone else ever had. Bobbi paid attention to Jen in a way that made Jen believe she was the only woman in Bobbi Jo's life.

"The attention I was getting, it was like I was being involved with everything that was happening," Jen confirmed in court. "I wasn't left out."

This is important. Jen believed that in Bobbi's eyes, she *mattered*. What Jen had to say and what she did was central. She wasn't the little sister anymore, the daughter to a drug-saddled mother who was never around. The troubled child no one could handle.

"Just not exactly cling to, but, you know, it's kind of cuddly . . . flirty," Jen said, explaining those first days with Bobbi Jo. "She just . . . *really* cared about me."

"Bobbi Jo gave my sister a lot of attention that Jennifer never got from anybody else," Audrey explained.

And Jen lapped it up.

Bobbi Jo and Jen became inseparable. Never out of each other's sight. Not for what Bobbi Jo wanted. But if Bobbi Jo went to work for Bob, painting or cleaning, Jen tagged along and waited in the car or helped out. If Bobbi had to run to the bank or over to her grandmother's to help out, Jen was there, by her side.

There were times when Audrey stopped by the house unexpectedly to try and convince Jennifer it was a bad idea to be hanging out with Bobbi, possibly more out of a jealous agenda than her worrying about Jen's well-being.

Jen would lock herself in the bathroom and refuse to come out. She was addicted to Bobbi by then. Nobody could tell her differently.

"Leave me alone. I love Bobbi Jo."

Jen later said she was in a state of euphoria with Bobbi and truly felt that she had found her soul mate, the person she wanted to spend the rest of her life with.

Kathy Jones said she was equally concerned when she heard that Jen had entered into a lesbian relationship with Bobbi Jo and was now staying with Bobbi at Bob Dow's. Jen was not ready for that type of world, Kathy knew—the one that Bob Dow created, that is. So Kathy headed over to Bob's to see what she could do about convincing Jen that this was not the proper life for her. There were people who could handle the lifestyle, Kathy knew. Her daughter was not one of them. Jen wasn't built for it, emotionally or psychologically. She wasn't tough enough.

This made Jen fuming mad. She was always the little sister.

"[Kathy] went over there a few times to try and get Jen out of there," Audrey explained. "But you know what, [Kathy] ended up partying over there with them! Apparently, Jen wouldn't leave, so [Kathy] just stayed there and partied with them all."

"She put Bob's [penis] in her mouth on camera

plenty of times," Bobbi later told me, speaking of Kathy. Photographs and interviews with people at the house later proved this.

The same thing happened to Audrey. She'd go over to the party house with the intention of trying to convince Jen to come back to the apartment, that Bob Dow was a bad influence on her, only to find herself staying and caught back up in the partying.

There are photographs of Kathy with Bob and other women, not only drinking and getting high, but indulging in the sexual behaviors as well. Kathy was going back over there when Jen and Bobbi weren't around, once she realized Bob was funding all of the parties. Kathy admitted in court later that she'd had sex with Bob on a number of occasions.

Nobody could do or say anything to convince Jen that Bobbi Jo wasn't right for her. To Jen, the relationship was like nothing she had ever experienced. It wasn't just the female-on-female sex with Bobbi that Jen found out she liked. It was everything. The way Bobbi made her believe she could have that white-picket-fence life she'd always dreamed of as a child and stared at inside the pages of *Better Homes and Gardens*. Jen felt it. She thought the answer to her woes was with Bobbi Jo.

"It was the attention," Jen said in court, looking back. "The love that I felt from her. I felt the caring and the nurturing that she . . . she was giving me— that *I* was being a part of the relationship, that I could just, like I said, not have to prove, you know, anything to her." Jen stopped here, turned on the tears, choking up. Then: "Bobbi Jo took me as I was."

Which was all Jen ever wanted.

Something else, however, was playing out here within the relationship Bobbi Jo had with Bob Dow. Something that was much more dangerous and dark.

"Bobby [Dow] used—he took Xanax and some painkiller," Elizabeth Smith said. "But Bobbi Jo was bringing in heroin, which Robert objected to. He threw her out, as a matter of fact, because he caught her shooting it up. . . . I seen it with my own eyes."

According to Bobbi, Bob would lace cigars and cigarettes with heroin, and he smoked it right along with her. Furthermore, Bob Dow was copping the dope—not Bobbi. She didn't have the connections; Bob did.

Elizabeth seemed to see things differently, or as she wanted to see them. She claimed to have been over at the house one weekend, sometime in February. This was before Bobbi hooked up with Jen. Elizabeth walked in, through the back door. She was stopping in to check on Bob and Lila, maybe help out. That was when, she later claimed, she saw Bobbi sitting at the kitchen table, prepping some dope to be booted in her arm.

So Elizabeth ran and got Bob.

According to his former wife, Bob shouted at Bobbi, "Get the hell out!" He ran into the kitchen from another room.

The house was the size of a shoe box, however; so the obvious question would have to be: How could Bob have not known Bobbi was using heroin in the next room? It didn't seem likely.

"I was *smoking* dope," Bobbi told me when I asked her about this. "Not *shooting* it. Elizabeth knows that. [Her] trailer house and her life speak for itself—look into it." Moreover, Bobbi claimed, she was not the one shooting dope in that house— but someone else was. "I'm not going to . . . stress myself out over a lie," she added when I pressed.

Elizabeth witnessed a parade of girls coming in and out of the house. When Bob and Bobbi would have their little sex parties, Elizabeth said, she'd walk out of the house and "go outside" to wait, adding, "I wanted no part of it."

She spoke to Bob about her concerns one day. "I'm worried about Lila," she told him. "What if I take her to my home and care for her there?"

Bob didn't like the idea. In fact, he became incensed. It had to be the check. Who would get Lila's Social Security money then?

"You could live life as you see fit, Bob," Elizabeth said.

"You get out," Bob raged.

CHAPTER 13

DETECTIVE BRIAN BOETZ was back at the crime scene on May 5, 2004, looking things over, searching for that lead that might put him like a bloodhound on Bobbi Jo's trail. One would think that Boetz needed more than a short—however powerful—statement from Bobbi's grandmother in order to make the charge against Bobbi stick. Sure, once he got Bobbi inside the box, door closed, hands cuffed, her future not looking so promising, an experienced interrogator could probably crack the young girl. But right now, no one knew where Bobbi had run off to with her girlfriends.

At some point late that same evening, Boetz made contact with Jerry Jones. The two men had a short conversation. By this time, Boetz figured Jen was Bobbi's girlfriend. After talking to Dorothy a bit more and getting Richard Cruz's entire story, it wasn't hard to work out. Obviously, talking to the girl's father could yield important information.

Boetz explained to Jerry how the MWPD had obtained a warrant for Bobbi's arrest. He mentioned that Bobbi likely took off with Jen and several others.

"I saw Jennifer and the others earlier that day," Jerry explained.

"Who are we talking about?" Boetz wondered.

Jerry ran down the names and explained who each female was: Bobbi, Audrey, Kathy Jones, and a girl named Krystal Bailey. Krystal was Audrey's new girlfriend, Jerry said. Kathy was Jen's mother.

"Her *mother*?" Boetz asked.

"Yup."

Boetz couldn't believe it. Jen and Bobbi were traveling with Jen's mother and Bobbi's ex-girlfriend.

"Where were they headed, Jerry?" Boetz asked.

"Out of town. They were all in Bob Dow's truck."

Boetz asked if there was anything else.

"Yeah," Jerry said, "Jennifer hugged me . . . and thanked me for everything." That was a fairly telling statement, perhaps letting Jerry know that Jennifer was planning on checking out somehow.

At this juncture, the fact remained that Bobbi, now wanted for murder, was on the run in Bob Dow's pickup. She and the others could be just about anywhere; they'd had a half day's jump on the MWPD. At *least* twelve hours. A person on the run could cover lots of roadway in half a day.

"We knew who we wanted to speak to," Boetz

explained to me. "Now it was just a question of 'Where is she at?' It was the only way for us to work the case."

As Boetz saw it, even after speaking to Jerry Jones, "We didn't have a clue as to where they were. At worst, we thought they were somewhere around Mineral Wells."

Boetz had underestimated these women. He and his colleagues were way off in their assessment—because Bobbi Jo and the others were halfway to California by then. They were traveling in a truck full of booze, weed, a few guns, and very little money.

PART TWO

THE SECRET AGONY OF THEIR SOULS

CHAPTER 14

I N KRYSTAL BAILEY, Audrey Sawyer hadn't necessarily found the ideal lover, committed in the way Audrey might have dreamed a woman would one day be. However, Jen's blond-haired, light-skinned, attractive half sister, with the aqua blue eyes, did find a companion in Krystal whom she could count on more than her last lover, Bobbi. Yet, even in that kernel of intimacy that Audrey found, by May 2004, just weeks after she and Bobbi Jo split, Audrey was already singing the blues; and the title of the tune was Krystal Bailey.

Krystal worked at a local factory, a business that seemed to have employed just about everybody in town at one time or another. Like Audrey, she was young, pretty, and willing to give her lover companionship on top of intimacy. Krystal lived in a small, redbrick, one-story ranch in a quaint Texas suburban neighborhood. It was definitely the polar opposite to where Audrey had lived the past

ten years or more. Krystal grew up in a place where
kids played tag after school, and home owners cut
their lawns on Saturdays and washed their cars on
Sundays. It was a "normal" life, outside the confines of that unpleasant drug and sex culture that
Audrey and Jen and Bobbi had been groomed in
and thrived on. And the funny thing is, Krystal
lived just a soccer ball's kick away from the back of
the Spanish Trace Apartments.

On that Wednesday, May 5, 2004, somewhere
near 2:00 P.M., not long after Bobbi and Jen left
Bob Dow's house—Bob Dow lying on his bed, a
laundry bag over his face, blood and pieces of his
face running down his chin—they showed up at
the Spanish Trace complex. Krystal was in the
bathroom with Audrey. They were quarreling.
Krystal wanted to continue the relationship;
Audrey was finished.

"Get out," Audrey said. "We're done, Krystal."

"What?" Krystal was crying. Audrey sounded
frustrated. The relationship had run its course.
Why isn't this chick getting it?

Krystal had been stopping by the apartment over
the past few days to pick up some of the belongings
she had left at Audrey's throughout the relationship. We've all been there. Lovers like to leave
something at their other half's place, using it as
an excuse to drive over and talk. These personal
items become an insurance policy. This was where
Audrey and Krystal's relationship currently stood.

Audrey didn't want her anymore. Krystal was fighting the end, trying whatever way possible to stay connected. She didn't want to leave that day and bring her possessions back home.

As one version of this part of the day went (and Kathy changed her story a few times, too), Kathy Jones was in the living room. She was watching a movie, listening to the argument going on in the bathroom, shaking her head, when Jen and Bobbi came bursting into the apartment enthusiastically. Both girls seemed excited and freaked out about something that had just happened.

Audrey heard the racket from the bathroom, where she was fighting with Krystal.

Jen was crying, Kathy noticed after jumping off the couch from the shock of the girls' arrival.

"I just killed Bob." Kathy later recalled Jen had said first.

Bobbi was jumping up and down, hyped up and manic. She said (according to Kathy): "We shot Bob."

We?

This announcement got everyone's attention. Audrey and Krystal were now in the kitchen, standing next to Kathy, staring at Jen and Bobbi, wondering what all the commotion was about.

"What's going on?" Audrey asked.

"Slow down," one of them suggested.

"Okay, what the hell is going on?" Audrey

said again, taking control. This was no way to joke around.

They told her.

Audrey laughed. "Y'all are full of shit."

"Yeah, right," Kathy said, reacting to what Jen said about killing Bob. Kathy smiled, shrugged, and threw her hands at them. Then she walked back into the living room to continue watching her movie. There was no way Kathy Jones was going to believe that Bobbi or Jen had shot Bob Dow. It wasn't possible. It was just some story Bobbi and Jen were telling, Kathy and Audrey both assumed, to inject a bit of excitement into the day. They were probably coked out, hyped up on meth, totally drunk out of their minds, or all three. Simply talking gibberish. This was something Audrey recalled Bobbi and Jen doing when they were high or drunk (something, incidentally, Bobbi Jo later agreed with when I asked).

"You're full of shit," Krystal said. "That's bull-shit."

But Audrey noticed Jen had a look on her face that spoke to the point of this perhaps not being a joke. Audrey had never seen Jen look so stunned, so shaken up. Jen was naturally pale, anyway; but she now had a ghostly, pasty sheen to her, which Audrey had trouble writing off.

Still, taking into account what her gut said, Audrey was going along with Kathy and Krystal, adding, "You're lying."

Jen tried to speak, but she couldn't. She was crying. Her hands shook.

Kathy got back up off the couch. "Okay," she said, walking toward them, "just *shut* up . . . and listen to me. If you shot Bob, take us over there right now to see the body."

"Yeah," Audrey added.

"Damn straight," Krystal said. "Let's go see the body."

Audrey looked outside. There was Bob's truck. Just then, Bobbi took out $100 in cash, according to Kathy and Audrey. Then (Kathy and Audrey later claimed) Bobbi showed them the gun. ("We just thought maybe they had rolled Bob," Audrey remembered, "that he passed out and they took his money and his truck.")

Jen finally spoke up, according to one of Kathy's later recollections. Jen said quite pointedly, very seriously: "I killed him—"

"*We* killed him," Bobbi interrupted, seemingly covering for her friend.

("I was protecting Jen," Bobbi later said.)

Audrey and Krystal looked at each other. Kathy went quiet.

"We gotta do something," Bobbi said. "Mom, we gotta get out of here." (Kathy Jones had instructed all of her children's friends to use this appellation for her.)

Kathy laughed.

"What's so funny?" Bobbi asked.

"Y'all are just joking." Kathy thought about it. "Listen to me . . . I want to go see Bob right now."

"You cannot see Bob," Bobbi said.

"I killed him . . . ," Jen kept saying. She continued to shake uncontrollably. She repeated that sentence over and over, as if stunned by her own words.

"They started telling details [about the murder] and I figured out that they were telling the truth," Kathy later told police. Kathy felt the specifics Jennifer shared were enough for her to change her mind. Plus, Kathy later explained, she walked up to Jen at one point, and "I . . . just felt her whole body shaking."

Kathy stared at her daughter, holding her face by the cheeks. "Jennifer, what happened?" she whispered. "You know . . . tell me . . . what happened?"

"Look, listen to me," Bobbi said, "Bob was raping Jen and she shot him."

"Jennifer, if that is true, it was self-defense," Kathy explained. "We need to call the cops and tell them what happened."

Later, Krystal vividly recalled the moment when she believed them, telling police: "Jennifer was crying. She was in hysterics. And Bobbi Jo was just kind of, like, jumping, like—I don't know—like she was bragging about it."

Krystal and Audrey still had a hard time believing that Bobbi and Jen shot and killed Bob Dow. Bob had held such power over Bobbi. He was so much more controlling and bigger and stronger and mature. He definitely had Bobbi wrapped around his finger and whupped, Audrey knew. She had witnessed the behavior herself. Whatever the reason, Bobbi had been consistently loyal to the guy. It didn't make sense to Audrey that Bobbi would be involved in killing him. Bobbi would not benefit at all by Bob's demise; quite the opposite, she had everything to lose by his death.

Over the past few weeks, as they hung out together and did lots of dope, Krystal had gotten to know Bobbi fairly well. They spent time talking and dreaming about getting out of Mineral Wells. Krystal, particularly, did a lot of listening.

In this regard, as Krystal stood, staring at the two of them, she was torn. "I thought it was a joke, actually."

Bobbi said, "Pack your shit. Come with us." She meant all three of them.

Audrey, Krystal, and Kathy looked at one another; then they shrugged their shoulders in a "what the hell" moment.

"Why not?" Kathy said. Then she stopped herself: "But wait. If this is true, if you killed Bob, why not go to the police department? Let's turn yourselves in. If he raped Jennifer, you need to tell them that."

No one said anything.

Then Bobbi spoke up. "No. We're *not* calling the police. Let's go."

"Jennifer, you should stay," Kathy said.

Jennifer shook her head.

("I could not talk Jennifer into staying," Kathy later told police. "I felt like it was better if I went with her to try to talk her into giving herself up rather than her be with Bobbi Jo alone.")

Jennifer was apparently in a state of shock. She was shaking and crying and could barely utter but a few coherent words.

As Jen stood in the living room, unable to speak, Bobbi said, "No. No. No. We cannot do that. We cannot do it." She meant go to the police. "We've *got* to get out of here—right now. We're going to Mexico."

"You ain't going to Mexico," Kathy said. "And you ain't takin' my daughter with you." Kathy walked over and put her arms around Jen.

"Ma, I am going with Bobbi Jo—no matter what you say," Jen explained.

"Well, shit, if y'all are going, I'm going, too," Kathy said.

Kathy said she noticed something about the relationship her daughter had with Bobbi Jo. "Bobbi Jo was making the decisions. . . . The only decisions Jennifer was making—whatever Bobbi Jo was going to do, [Jen] was going to do it, too."

And this comment fits perfectly into the nature of their relationship: Jen had been looking for someone to tell her how to live. Bobbi came along, and Jen found that mother figure to nurture her.

As Kathy stood, contemplating what to advise the two of them to do next, Kathy decided that

Jen would be better off with her mother along for the ride.

"I was—the thing for me, just the thought was, just doing whatever they wanted to do to start with. I didn't really know the whole situation." Kathy was on probation; she wasn't allowed to leave the state. She'd be tossed back into prison. "I just knew, though, that what they were saying had happened, and I had to believe it, you know, because of the seriousness of the way Jennifer was acting. And Bobbi Jo, too, just wanting to get out of there. I really had no intentions of crossing the border."

Every minute counted. The girls must have considered that someone had heard the gunshots and called the cops. Bobbi was getting extremely antsy, everyone later said, as the immensity of the situation and what Jen had done settled on her.

"I wanted to protect Jennifer," Bobbi later told me. "She was my friend, one of my lovers."

Krystal stood next to the girls, waiting for what Audrey was going to do. If Audrey went, Krystal decided, she was going, too. ("I was chasing Audrey," Krystal later said, explaining how she was still deeply in love with Audrey and unable to let go of her.)

"Let's get out of here," Bobbi said again.

They split up and hopped into the two trucks: Bob's and Dorothy's.

"I need to get some clothes or something," Krystal said.

"We need to stop at Krystal's," Audrey said.

Bobbi led the way in Bob's truck, with Kathy riding shotgun. Krystal drove her car. Jen and Audrey followed in Dorothy's truck.

Bobbi Jo described for me in detail this scene at the Spanish Trace Apartments during those moments directly following Bob Dow's murder. Her version was quite a bit different from what you've just read, which I composed from the court record and various interviews with Audrey and Kathy, along with police reports and interviews police conducted with all of the players involved. (That is, all of the participants except for Bobbi, I might add. Bobbi did not talk about this moment at any length and, surprisingly, was never really asked to do so by the police later on.)

"On the day that Jennifer murdered Bob," Bobbi began, trying to clarify the record, "I was not drunk. Indeed, very sober I was, and so was she [Jen]. Neither drugs nor alcohol were a factor on that given day."

Tracking the movements of the girls, looking at it from Bobbi's point of view, it's easy to see how that last statement could be true.

Bobbi said, "Jennifer told me she killed Bob and how." Bobbi claimed to be outside the party house in the yard. Jen ran out the door and said, "Take me to my mother's. . . ."

"And, of course, I complied."

"Mother's" was an odd word choice, but very

telling. Jen knew the apartment belonged to Jerry Jones.

In any event, Bobbi took Jen over to the apartment.

When they arrived, Bobbi said, "they [Kathy and Audrey] were already packed and ready to leave, as if they already *knew* what was happening and what had happened." Bobbi was referring to the ordeal back at Bob's. Bobbi was saying that Audrey, Krystal, and Kathy already knew Jen had killed Bob and were waiting for her to arrive at the apartment. Bobbi was certain of this.

"I never really spoke to anyone at the apartment," Bobbi later insisted. "That's all Kathy and Jennifer's bullshit that they had come up with. . . . Even while we were on the run, I never spoke much. Kathy was the one ordering us around. I got into it with her once. . . ."

I asked the MWPD if they subpoenaed phone records from Bob's cell phone, Lila's house, Jerry Jones's apartment, or any of the cell phones that the girls had, so I could see if someone had maybe called over to the Spanish Trace or one of the girls' cell phones *after* Bob was murdered.

Detective Brian Boetz told me, "No, there were no phone calls made moments after the murder. . . ." Boetz never clarified how he had drawn this conclusion, but I can say that there were no phone records I ever saw as part of the court file.

As she walked into the apartment at Spanish Trace, Bobbi revealed to me, "it seemed everyone knew what was happening and what was going on—but me."

As they stood and talked, Kathy Jones, whom Bobbi referred to as "drug-crazed" on that day and most others, pulled Bobbi aside and said, "You need to take the blame for Jennifer."

"Huh?" Bobbi responded.

"You need to take the blame . . . Bobbi. You're gay. You'll *love* prison."

Bobbi looked at her: *Are you as crazy as you sound?*

("She tried to make prison [sound] *comfortable*," Bobbi recalled.)

"You're crazy," Bobbi said.

According to Bobbi's version, Kathy next said, "Look, I need you to take me back to Bob's so I can recover all of that computer equipment."

"You'd have to kill me first," Bobbi responded.

Bobbi admitted that she was well aware of Bob's sordid, vile history of "making movies and taking photos with *all* the women he had sex with." Bobbi admitted, "At times, I would be the one behind the camera." She believed that Kathy wanted to go over to Bob's so she could grab all the videos before police got there. She didn't want the videos made public—because she and her two daughters were featured in some of them, sometimes to-gether.

According to Bobbi's recollection, she believed Kathy, Audrey, and Jen thought it was some sort of joke that Jen had murdered Bob. They felt that it didn't matter. They thought of the murder as being "light," as Bobbi called it, as if Jennifer had done the world a favor, ridding the planet of an evil, dirty man whom nobody cared much about.

"I was in shock, to say the least," Bobbi told me. "Shocked. Confused. Scared. And young."

As they took off from Spanish Trace, Bobbi said, the girls were still making light of "Bob's death." They were telling jokes and laughing.

"I was disgusted and devastated."

CHAPTER 15

ALL THE MWPD felt it could do at this point was wait. Bobbi, Jen, and the others had taken off, and the MWPD had no idea where they'd gone. That was the short end of it. A "statewide broadcast" sent out by the department indicated how a "possible homicide [had] occurred in our city," and the MWPD was looking for a "red-and-white crew cab Chevy truck" (Bob Dow's) being "occupied by 5 W/F's possibly en route to Mexico." The report called the girls "armed and extremely dangerous." A follow-up report, sent two hours after the first—again statewide—reported that Bob's truck could be "possibly dark blue or green over tan." This follow-up report named Audrey, Bobbi, Jen, and Kathy, leaving out Krystal.

I asked Detective Brian Boetz about alerting major media outlets, especially seeing that the tele-type qualified the girls as "armed and dangerous."

This seemed like big, potentially important news to me.

"We did not notify the local news," Boetz told me. "My chief would have been the person that would have notified the public."

The APB had yielded nothing in the sense of a lead. No other police departments had spotted the vehicle. As Boetz and the MWPD checked back with Jerry Jones and Dorothy Smith, neither had seen nor heard from the girls.

The MWPD had done nothing that I could find to track down friends and family and try to develop a sense of who Bobbi (their major suspect in a brutal murder) was, where she might have taken off to, or whom she might be hiding out with. Bobbi had a son, after all. She had an ex-fiancé. She had brothers, a mother, ex-lovers. She had other family *besides* Dorothy and the Cruzes.

"We thought she was still in town," one law enforcement source told me.

The MWPD zeroed in on Bobbi Jo Smith as a "possible" murder suspect and stopped there. They had the grandmother of a person of interest fingering her, a statement from that witness, a hearsay statement from the suspect's aunt and uncle backing it up, and an arrest warrant for murder. On paper, it didn't seem like much, but the MWPD was satisfied, and now they were waiting for someone to call in and say he or she knew where Bobbi had run off to.

And so, as Bobbi, Audrey, Krystal, Jen, and

Kathy headed out of town, the MWPD sat back and waited.

"As for the cops and Bobbi Jo," said a source close to the investigation, "just about every person in Bobbi Jo's inner circle [which I, the author, feel is quite a stretch to say here] was either dead or in that truck with her. She lived and worked with Bob (dead). Was dating Jennifer (in truck). Used to date Audrey (in truck). The only people that knew her well, who the cops could talk to, were her mother (who had no fixed address, I believe), her grandmother, and Jerry Jones (who did not know Bobbi at all), all of whom Detective Boetz spoke to. . . . So, at that point, he knew that Bobbi Jo, Jen, [Kathy], Audrey, and Krystal had hit the road for parts unknown."

Still, there was no rush to find them.

"Neither Jen nor Bobbi Jo," this same source added, "had the kinds of things cops usually use to track people—cell phone, credit cards, or bank accounts. All [law enforcement] knew was that they were in Bob's truck. The best detectives in the country would have been hard-pressed to find them without a lucky break or inside information. . . ."

The fact remained: A quick check would have produced the information that Audrey Sawyer had a cell phone on her (which she was constantly using), as well as Kathy Jones.

* * *

After Krystal dropped off her car around the corner from Spanish Trace and grabbed a few belongings from her house, she hopped into the truck with Audrey. (Jen was now driving; apparently, she wasn't too distraught any longer and could operate a motor vehicle.) The girls made their way to Bobbi's grandmother Dorothy Smith's house, in Graford. They wanted to drop off Dorothy's truck. They had a stash of booze, some weed, which Jen jacked from Bob after killing him, but not a lot of money. Bob Dow never carried much cash, so they were only able to get gas money, per se. That would be just enough to make it through Texas, if they were lucky.

According to Kathy's later testimony, the murder weapon was sitting inside a blanket in back of Bobbi as she drove.

Kathy looked on as Bobbi told Jen (who, contradicting what the others said, Kathy claimed was riding with her and Bobbi at that time) to grab the weapon.

"What?" Jen supposedly asked. They were going about sixty miles per hour.

"It's inside the blanket."

Jen reached in back, found what Kathy later described as a "bloody comforter," and handed it off to Bobbi.

"Hold the wheel," Bobbi said (according to Kathy).

Jen did as she was told. Bobbi took a yellow T-shirt and wiped the gun down, Kathy recalled.

The girls were thinking they had to get some additional cash for the trip. One hundred dollars wasn't going to get them very far. The more money they had, the farther into Mexico and away from Mineral Wells they could get.

Bobbi said, "Steer the truck. . . ."

In Kathy's version, Jen steered as they drove across the city limit of Mineral Wells on the FM (Farm to Market) 1821 N, with Audrey and Krystal following behind, watching as Bobbi "leaned out of the window and threw the gun toward the left side of the roadway. . . ."

But in Jen's courtroom version of this same event, she said: "We were driving down the road—I don't know which one. Bobbi Jo took the gun out from the blanket in the backseat. And she opened it up, and she was beating it against the door, whatever, trying to get the bullets out. And then she threw it in a ditch. We kept on driving, and then Bobbi Jo said that I need to drive her grandmother's truck back to the house, since I was the one that took it."

So they pulled over, let Jen out, and switched there, on the road (according to Jennifer's recollection).

Audrey and Krystal looked at each other as they saw the weapon fly out the window. Neither could clarify who was driving the truck at this time or who actually tossed the weapon out the window. ("I think it was Bobbi," Audrey told me.)

For some reason, as they drove by the area in the tall weeds where the weapon landed, Audrey and Krystal took note of where they were.

Things were a bit calmer when they arrived at Dorothy Smith's house. Bobbi and Jen were manic, but Kathy—arguably the adult in the bunch— knew the farther away from the crime scene they were, the better their chances became of getting out of Dodge without wearing metal bracelets.

Kathy waited with Audrey and Krystal outside for several minutes as Bobbi and Jen went in. Jen said they stopped at Dorothy's to get "our things."

Dorothy soon came out of the house, tugging at Bobbi's shirt, pleading there in front of everyone for Bobbi to stay.

Kathy later claimed she heard Bobbi tell her grandmother, "I killed Bob. . . ." ("I was really confused," Kathy added as she recalled this moment for police. "Because Jen had told me that *she* shot Bob.")

Jen told the court (during her sentencing hearing, months before she was interviewed by *Texas Monthly* and Bobbi's case went to trial), "And then we reached her grandmother's house. And that's where Bobbi Jo told her grandmother, 'I killed Bob. I killed Bob.'" When asked if she had said anything while at Bobbi's grandmother's house, Jennifer claimed, "No, I didn't."

Krystal heard them talking and walked closer. She heard Bobbi Jo say, "I killed Bob. I shot him. I killed him."

But Dorothy didn't "believe her and asked Jennifer" if it was true.

"Bobbi Jo killed him," Jen said (this by Krystal's recollection).

What was clear was that Bobbi wanted to leave right away.

Bobbi and Jen walked toward Bob's truck as Dorothy followed close behind, peppering the girls with questions. Dorothy became increasingly upset the more time she spent with the girls, Krystal said.

"We have to go, Grandma," Bobbi told Dorothy. "I wanted to return your truck."

The first time Kathy Jones met Bob Dow was on the night of April 28, 2004, Bobbi Jo's nineteenth birthday. When they talked about it later, this particular night seemed to be a turning point for all the girls involved in the madness that was taking place at Bob's party house for the past few months—not to mention the dark end to it all of it, which was to come a week later with Bob's murder. Each woman—Krystal, Audrey, Kathy, Jen, and Bobbi Jo—spoke of this night as a defining moment. And each had her own story to tell.

"Bobbi Jo's birthday—I don't know what day that is, but that's the day I met [Bob]," Kathy explained in court. "It's whenever I went over [to Bob's] that night and I had left my [second] husband in Albany [Texas], (an hour-and-a-half drive west of Mineral Wells). That night I went over there and they was having her birthday party."

Kathy drove to Bob's, not realizing there was a celebration going on. Bobbi was growing up. No longer that "kid" of eighteen, struggling—or being forced—into (true) adulthood. Nineteen felt so much more mature than eighteen, suffice it to say, within the world Bobbi lived. Bobbi was feeling good. There was a new girl, a little younger than her, hanging around Bob's house. She was a hot female, obsessed with her every move. Bobbi was making money from Bob, providing him with a train of girls to film at all hours of the night and day, on top of her hourly rate while working maintenance jobs. She was learning several different trades from Bob. Despite her upbringing, as Bobbi claims, of an absent mother and father, she still had a strong family core—her grandmother, aunt and uncle, a brother she was very close to—to fall back on when she desired normalcy. Bobbi understood now that she didn't need her mother, though she had a hard time keeping track of where the woman was at any given time, anyway. Bobbi felt as though she had a place of her own to live, drink, do all the drugs she wanted—all of this without anyone looking over her shoulder. To boot, she could sleep with as many women as she wanted, without anyone bothering her. Effectively, she

could finally live the lifestyle she had so desperately
wanted since realizing she was gay.

Bobbi said Bob was like a father to her.

"Bob and I never had sex with each other."
Bobbi denied reports that Bob was some sort of
sexual slave master, turning her into his personal
sex goddess, whether she was into it or not. "But
we did share all of the same women."

In addition, Bobbi insisted, it was not Bob Dow
who had turned her into a doper, dependent on
various drugs and alcohol. Sure, Bob fed her addictions. But it was "my son's father that introduced
me to drugs," Bobbi explained to me. "And I
could not break myself away from pills and alcohol. I was drunk often and loved to smoke weed."

Bobbi was away from that man (her son's dad)
now and on her own. It had taken some time to
become independent; but by nineteen, Bobbi had
done it. The only pang of guilt nagging at Bobbi
Jo as she contemplated her life at nineteen, and
where she was headed, was the one thing that
meant more to Bobbi than anything else: her son.

Still, life, as far as Bobbi could tell, was going
along okay. She had plans to obtain sole custody of
her son eventually, get her own place, and get off
the hooch. Moreover, she saw her son when she
wanted. One could argue that Bobbi had the best
of all worlds during that time before Bob was murdered.

This relationship with Jen—however intimate
and emotionally connected Jen may have felt it

had become—was a train carrying a lot of baggage, rushing on a violent collision course. Going back to March, when they first met, from day one, the relationship was built on a platform of betrayal. Since then, at best, it had grown into what was both an abnormally codependent, dysfunctional, and masochistic union; at worst, it was a manufactured love affair based on nothing more than sex, lies, lust, and drug use.

According to what Jen later told *Texas Monthly* (maybe the one thing Bobbi Jo agrees with her today), Bobbi's and her entire "existence" together as a couple was centered on abusing drugs and alcohol. *They'd get drunk and high for 48 hours straight,* Katy Vine wrote in her article "Girls Gone Wild," published in the *Texas Monthly*'s September 2005 issue. *One week of partying led to two weeks, then three weeks,* Vine reported, adding how Jen had told her that she and Bobbi favored Xanax and meth, weed and shots of vodka. They slept very little and "hardly ever ate." After a two- or three-day binge, for example, as they were coming down from all of the dope, *constantly telling each other how in love they were* (according to Jennifer), Bobbi and Jen found themselves strung out to the point of unremitting paranoia. The withdrawal was intoxicating in and of itself, sucking their emotions dry; they'd feel so depleted and depressed, they'd have to start the bender all over again to feel *normal.*

"Bobbi Jo was a self-destructive addict," clinical social worker and addiction specialist John Kelly said after studying this case for me. "To quiet her demons, she used drugs to live and lived to use drugs. Unfortunately for Bobbi Jo, her main enabler was Bob, her dealer. Bob was a lust-filled, sexual deviate who enjoyed the power, control, and sex he exhibited over Bobbi Jo [and others]. It seems Bob's enabling manipulation over Bobbi Jo was for pure sexual gratification."

There can be no doubt that Jen and Bobbi both seemed to take pleasure—unwittingly—in the pain, without realizing it was the source fueling their desire. This was the food that kept the relationship from not only starving completely, but running at one hundred miles per hour. Maybe they were too young, too far gone when they met, too wrapped up in the drugs to realize what was happening. Whatever the case, from where Jen viewed the relationship, it went from zero to one hundred, seemingly overnight, and turned into a nonstop ride in the fast lane, where she did not feel she could (or even wanted to) jump off.

Kathy Jones was at her ex-husband Jerry Jones's Spanish Trace apartment with Audrey and Krystal on April 28, 2004. She had just been released from prison. Kathy had taken off from her home in Albany.

"Jerry, I need to use your truck," Kathy mentioned.

Jerry knew better, but he had a soft spot for

Kathy. From what Kathy has said, she left Jerry back on Father's Day, 1989. Jen was three and a half years old. Jerry had tried every which way he could (as Audrey later confirmed) to get Kathy to come back, going so far as to give her money, attempting to rescue her out of the trenches of crack cocaine, which she had jumped headfirst into. So Kathy knew where to go when she needed something; Jerry had trained her that way.

"Jerry tried to get me to come back to him a number of times, but I kept refusing," Kathy said later. "And about the only time I would get to see Jennifer and [Audrey] was whenever I would go stay at the house with Jerry. . . . I had a boyfriend at the time (just after she left Jerry), and then I started refusing to go back or stay."

It was that alienation from her kids that drove Kathy, she claimed, to hit the streets for a little smoke to relieve the stressors of not being able to see the kids. That little buzz turned into a pipe and crack cocaine, she later told the court (and me), spending years chasing the red dragon. The crack led to a drinking problem. Those new habits were not easy to afford; thus, a new career in crime was born out of necessity. Kathy's specialty now was burglarizing businesses and homes. Soon Kathy started her disappearing act—the bottom of that magician's black hat was a prison cell with her name on it and a revolving door.

Kathy, Audrey, and Krystal stopped by another friend's house to pick her up on April 28, 2004;

then all of them headed over to Bob's party house after borrowing Jerry's truck. They had no idea what Jen or Bobbi had been up to all day. But no sooner had they walked into the party house that evening of Bobbi's birthday bash than Kathy realized this night was going to be like no other.

CHAPTER 16

FOR BOBBI AND JEN, the birthday celebration on April 28, 2004, started long before Audrey, Krystal, and Kathy showed up at the party house looking for them that night. If you believe the *fourth* version of this day, which Jen shared with *Texas Monthly,* Jen and Bobbi were at Bobbi's grandmother's house in Graford with another friend, Abigail (pseudonym), just after noon on that same day. (Bobbi said there was never anyone else with them at the house—that she would "never disrespect" her grandparents and allow someone other than Jen, whom her grandparents knew, to be in the house when they weren't home.)

Beginning Bobbi's birthday celebration with a tradition—that actually was a habit—all three girls fired up the pipe and smoked some meth, Jen explained. After that, they swallowed some pills (likely Xanax, as both would later talk about a penchant for Xanax bars, also known as "school buses" and "white ladders"). Not quite the typical birthday lunch of maybe ribs and French fries, topped off with a buttercream-frosted cake, and a group of restaurant servers singing "Happy Birthday." But the kind of party, nonetheless, that Bobbi and Jen had grown accustomed to having just about every other day—if not every day, by then.

There came a point where the paranoia brought on by the meth they smoked got out of control. Jen told *Texas Monthly* (a somewhat different version than she would later tell police about this same afternoon) that she was sitting down watching television, giggling and having a laugh while watching some zany cartoon. Bobbi was in the shower getting herself cleaned up for the real party they had planned later on at Bob's.

Abby was in the living room with Jen. Neither spoke. Jen said that at one point, however, she heard something. It was Abby speaking to her, and yet Abby's lips never moved. (Jen later claimed that she, Bobbi, and a few of their friends could read minds.) Jen was, she maintained, reading Abby's mind at that moment.

Later, in court, Jen talked about how this mind reading actually worked, testifying to these words under oath: "Well, it's not really mind games in a sense. It's more like Wiccan witchcraft, and stuff like that. There was a lot of—there was—I felt, you know, like, there was a lot of that going on [with Bobbi and me]. You're under the influence of drugs and you just—you're in that *other*world. And it's just so easy to fall in there, and it's so easy to be in one room with someone else not saying a word and you can read their minds. You can just go into a trance state of mind."

That day, as Abby sat next to her, Jen was in that "otherworld . . . trance state of mind."

I want you to leave Bobbi Jo alone and never come back was what Jen believed she heard Abby tele-pathically communicate to her through their minds.

After she heard it, Jen looked at Abby. She had an urge to jump off the couch and beat up Abby. How dare Abby tell her to leave Bobbi? She was madly in love with Bobbi. Nothing—and no one—was going to keep them apart.

Jen listened closely again to make sure she had heard Abby correctly. And for a second time, Jen didn't like what Abby was telepathically communi-cating.

While in court, Jen went on to explain in more detail about a version of Wiccan witchcraft she and—she insisted—Bobbi understood and, at times, practiced. "It's like spells. You . . . basically, you take part of . . . bodily part of someone's body, like a . . . like a piece of hair, or you take, like, a fingernail, something that's part of someone's body, and you have that, and you can put a spell over it. You can . . . you can just have a possession of that part. It's basically . . . you can control that person whenever, like in your mind."

Jen said she absolutely believed it was possible

and that it was taking place on this day at Bobbi's grandparents' house.

The strangest part of it all, Jen later insisted, was that as she sat there on the couch, listening to Abby tell her to leave Bobbi, Bobbi came running out of the bathroom while Abby was talking vis-à-vis their minds. Apparently, Bobbi had heard Abby, too.

"What the *hell* are you talking about?" Jen later said Bobbi screamed, dripping wet, staring at Abby.

Jen couldn't believe it. *Bobbi heard it, too?*

"I didn't say anything," Abby pled, standing up.

"I heard it all," Bobbi supposedly said.

Abby would hang out with the girls at Dorothy's sometimes, Jen said (and, to be clear, Jen gave *Texas Monthly* a pseudonym for Abby, so her true identity was never established. I also contacted *Texas Monthly* and asked to be put in touch with Abby, so I could confirm this story, but I never heard from her.) They liked to party together. Abby also wrote. She kept a book of poems at Dorothy's house inside Bobbi's room, Jen claimed. They'd get high and Abby would write things.

("Notebook . . . poems . . . ?" Bobbi later asked rhetorically, when I pressed her on this story. She had no idea what Jen was talking about.)

"Where's that notebook?" Bobbi demanded angrily—that is, in Jen's version of the story. Bobbi had seen Abby writing in it earlier, after they smoked some meth.

Jen took one look at Bobbi and knew she wasn't going to stop until she got her hands on the book.

Bobbi was certain Abby was writing bad things about them. Not that they were sluts, whores, liars, or anything like that. Bobbi didn't care too much what people said about her. What worried Bobbi was that Abby was writing (and casting) "magic spells," as Jen referred to them, over the two of them, using the book.

Bobbi looked all over the house and came up with the notebook.

"Let's take a look," she said, walking back into the living room, where Abby and Jen were sitting. Bobbi held the notebook.

Abby looked terrified. What the hell were they talking about? They were too high. A bad trip or something, she must have rationalized. They'd smoked too much meth. Wired beyond belief, their minds were playing tricks.

Bobbi opened the notebook, but then she realized that all of the pages had been torn out.

"Where is it all?"

Abby looked confused.

Bobbi rummaged through the house: drawers, shelves, under couches and chairs and cushions, closets.

Everywhere.

She hit pay dirt in the kitchen, Jen claimed, inside one of the drawers and underneath the couch cushions in the living room. Abby had torn the notebook pages into tiny little pieces and stuffed them in the drawer and under the cushions.

"What the hell!" Bobbi said. She was now more certain than ever that Abby had "put a hex on them," Jen said in *Texas Monthly*.

"You're not coming between me and my girl-friend!" Bobbi screamed in a rage, according to Jen. "Get out. . . ."

Abby took off.

"I need to see [my son]," Bobbi told Jen after Abby left. "I'm going to get him."

("Never happened," Bobbi told me. "I would *never* go and get my son after getting high. *Never*. It's another set of lies Jennifer told.")

During the afternoon of Bobbi's birthday, after the hypothetical mind games with Abby, Bobbi went over to her baby daddy's house and picked up her two-year-old son. (Again, this is from Jen's *Texas Monthly* version of the events; Bobbi claimed this never happened.)

One thing that cannot be disputed is that for Bobbi this child was the essence of life. The pain of not being able to spend every moment with him was one of the reasons why the drugs felt so good: The numbing effect did its job. The drugs allowed Bobbi to disengage emotionally from those feel-ings of loss and detachment.

Interestingly, here were two generations of the

same cycle playing out in the lives of Jen and Bobbi. Kathy Jones and Bobbi Smith were two mothers who used the deadening influence of chronic drug use to stifle the pain of not being the parents that they desperately wanted to be.

But neither of them saw it—or could see it.

According to Jen, when Bobbi returned to her grandmother's house, Jen was upstairs waiting, watching *The Ren & Stimpy Show* on television.

(Bobbi does not recall this entire scene ever taking place in her life.)

"Don't move," Bobbi allegedly told Jen as she put her son down and jumped on top of Jen, straddling, pinning her down on the bed.

Jen froze. *What the hell?*

"[Abby's] underneath the bed," Bobbi said. She was messing with Jen, trying to "freak her out."

As Jen later explained, the moment took on a surreal vibe, as if they were taking hallucinogens (drugs Bobbi told me she has never taken). Perhaps it was another one of Jen's fairy-tale memories— or nightmares. She seemed to have several after the fact. As she and Bobbi lay on Bobbi's bed, Jen explained, with Bobbi's son playing on the floor nearby, she and Bobbi sat still as rocks "for hours." Not moving a muscle. Stiff. Like they were in a contest. Then, while staring at the ceiling, they imagined all of the "doors in the house . . . opening and closing," like something out of the *Amityville Horror* films.

They did this a lot, according to Jen's later

testimony (in court): "Well, first, we would—we would get—we would do drugs to get inside that state of mind. And then after that, we would just sit there and read each other's minds. We would just talk to each other without saying a word, you know, verbally. And it's—it's kind of, like, you know—you and someone say something at the same time. You know, y'all's minds are thinking alike."

Jen also claimed that during the late afternoon hours of April 28, 2004, things turned dangerous when Bobbi was certain she could understand her son's baby talk—that he was actually communicating with her and encouraging her to do something terrible.

"We've got to burn the whole place down," Bobbi said (according to Jen).

It was a sobering moment. *Burn the house down? Why? For what purpose?*

As Jen told it, Bobbi was worried Abby had cast a spell on the house and everything inside it. The only way for them to break the spell was to get rid of *everything*.

Jen said she told Bobbi, "You cannot do that."

They talked about it, or maybe the high wore off. Either way, Bobbi apparently came up with the idea of gathering anything in the house Abby might have touched. So they jumped off the bed and collected all of the weed, perfume, makeup, papers, and magazines that Abby had touched and had an old-fashioned backyard bonfire.

"There was some girl that Bobbi Jo met that was

into Wicca," Bobbi's mother, Tamey Hurley, later told me, saying how both Bobbi and Bob Dow had told her. "And supposedly this girl put a curse on the house, and it scared Bobbi so bad, she wanted to burn the house down. They were all high, of course. But Bobbi Jo was terrified."

Bobbi did not remember this.

Jen claimed she and Bobbi never did anything without first talking it through. They had a bond, Jen later testified. They shared an unbreakable, emotional connection on top of an oath etched in their own blood—and no one could come between it.

"We cut our fingers, the tips of our fingers," Jen said in court during her sentencing hearing, "and our blood connected to each other." From Jen's viewpoint, they were two lovers pledging the ultimate dedication to each other. "And from then on, that, right there, was supposed to symbolize unity," Jen observed, adding, "like a marriage, you might say."

This covenant, if you will, joined the two girls in DNA together for life.

I asked Bobbi Jo to explain this event to me.

She did not recall that blood oath ever taking place.

"Blood bond with Jennifer?" Bobbi questioned. "Huh? I've never made a blood bond with anyone, except my son's father, and that only came from our sex, not *cutting* each other up."

Jen claimed this blood oath took place merely days after she and Bobbi hooked up.

According to Jen, these weren't the only brushes they'd had with that "otherworld" of mind reading, Wicca, and black magic. And yet the following anecdote actually exemplifies a point that Bobbi disliked black magic of any kind.

According to Jen, sometime before Bobbi's birthday, she and Bobbi Jo had met up with Bobbi's cousin Grace (pseudonym) and another friend, Carmen (pseudonym), to have a little precelebration. They were at Dorothy Smith's house in Graford. At first, to Jen, it felt like a family gathering. Bobbi seemed happy. Everyone was having a good time.

Carmen was acting strange, however, Jen remembered. She didn't say if they had gone off and gotten high or not, but one has to believe, based on the life they shared, they had. In any event, at one point, Carmen said some weird things and talked about what Jen referred to later as voodoo.

It freaked Jen out when Carmen, still talking, walked up and "touched" Jen somewhere on her body. "And I started shaking," Jen said in a statement she gave police.

When Bobbi saw what Carmen was doing to Jen, she walked over and asked Carmen about it.

Carmen looked alarmed as Bobbi became livid, according to Jen, screaming, "Get . . . out! Take your voodoo shit with you."

Carmen "walked back to Mineral Wells," Jen explained.

CHAPTER 17

CRUISING THROUGH TEXAS, the girls talked. That electrifying *Thelma & Louise* effect, which Jen later talked about feeling as an adrenaline rush that pumped through her veins, and the thrill of taking off, on the run, after killing a man dwindled as the sun started its descent on the evening of May 5, 2004. For one, the sheer seriousness of what had taken place settled on the one adult in the group, Kathy Jones, as she thought about what the future had in store for her daughter. If the girls ran, they looked guilty, Kathy considered. If they went to the cops and pled that Bob had tried raping Jen (the story Jen was trying to sell at the current moment), that might be different. Maybe it would work? But heading into Mexico (as Kathy and Jen later said Bobbi wanted to do)—without passports, nonetheless—was probably not the best idea at this point.

Kathy stared at her daughter. Throughout Jen's

life, Kathy had never been the mother she had wanted to be. Guidance was not something Kathy had given to her daughters, especially Jen.

"I tried," she said later. "Sometimes we had . . . There was *some* guidance, and I believe it didn't take because of the actions I was showing her. I was telling her the right things, but I wasn't *showing* her."

Some might refer to that as "setting a bad example."

In deciding where to go next, one of the girls mentioned Walmart.

"Walmart?" Krystal asked.

Bobbi was driving.

"I need a calling card," Audrey said. Audrey had one of those pay-as-you-go Tracphones.

From Graford to Weatherford, where the girls decided to head next, Walmart was on the way. Bobbi stopped and Audrey went in; Krystal tagged along. She bought a calling card. Audrey needed to make a few calls. Audrey still wasn't sold on the notion that Bobbi and Jen had whacked Bob. It didn't seem possible. Two girls, higher than Mount Everest most of the time, killing a guy like Bob? It didn't add up for Audrey. Thus, Audrey explained to me, she wanted to stay in touch with a few friends back home while they were on the run so she could get a bead on what was being said around town and on the local news. She was determined to find out the truth about what had happened.

It was near seven in the evening, according to Krystal, when she and Audrey walked out of the Walmart. (Some of the girls claimed they stopped at Walmart before going to Weatherford, and some said after.)

From Graford, Weatherford was west, toward Fort Worth, Arlington, and Dallas. You could take the 337 southeast through Mineral Wells, or a more direct route on the 254 east. They needed to head west, toward Abilene and eventually Mexico, if they were sticking to the plan.

Why go to Weatherford?

Bob Dow had a trailer in Weatherford, where he had lived most of the time. Bobbi knew the trailer. She had spent plenty of time there with Bob and alone.

"A ring," Bobbi said. They needed money. (Bobbi had left her engagement ring inside the trailer, she later told me, and she wanted it. Going there wasn't about money for her; it was about getting that ring.)

As they drove, Kathy had a moment with her daughter. Kathy was interested in something— death, the taking of a life.

"How did it feel to kill someone?" Kathy asked Jen.

Jen thought about it. She looked her mother in the eyes, as serious as she had ever been. "Pretty fucking good," Jen bragged, sounding almost proud of what she had done.

CHAPTER 18

AUDREY, KATHY, JENNIFER, Bobbi Jo, and Krystal arrived at Bob Dow's Weatherford trailer home sometime during the evening hours of May 5, 2004, after leaving Graford and stopping at Walmart (or the other way around, depending on who is asked).

As the girls piled out of Bob's truck, the MWPD prepared a second APB to be broadcast statewide:

REF TO POSSIBLE HOMICIDE

OCCURRRED IN OUR CITY . . .

RED AND WHITE CREW CAB CHEV TRUCK OCCUPIED BY 5 W/F'S POSSIBLY ENROUTE TO MEXICO . . . ARMED AND EXTREMELY DANGEROUS [AND] POSSIBLY INVOLVED IN HOMICIDE . . . DECEASED SUBJ'S VEH TAKEN POSSIBLY . . .

It might have seemed strange that the MWPD did not notify the public about a band of criminals on the loose (some of whom were quite hardened, had done serious time in prison, and one of whom was wanted for murder). It was up to the chief of police to stand on a podium in front of a mish-mash of microphones and make that announcement, according to Detective Brian Boetz. But, the detective added, "[As we got] into the investigation, we were getting phone calls from the families. . . ."

So the MWPD decided to wait it out. After all, according to Boetz, they were gathering information on their main suspect and did not need to cause any sort of public panic. Announcing in the state of Texas that there was an armed and dangerous murderer on the loose might stir up some unneeded vigilante justice. They weren't there yet—at least that's what the MWPD later said about the situation. There was not a lot of concern about Bobbi going on a murder spree.

"We used . . . [the] state and nationwide communication between law enforcement agencies' systems," Detective Brian Boetz explained further. The MWPD was under the impression, Boetz reiterated, that sooner or later, as they put pressure on family members of the girls, the information they needed would come. Yet, those family members consisted of Dorothy Smith, the Cruzes, and Jerry Jones. The MWPD, as far as I could find out, contacted no one else.

At Bob Dow's trailer, Audrey flipped open her cell phone and tried calling a few friends back in town to see what was happening, to learn if there was any news. Audrey wanted to know what the local stations were saying. The girls had not heard anything on the radio in the truck. It was as if the murder had not occurred, which led Audrey to start thinking that her sister and Bobbi had lied about the entire event.

Out of all of the girls on the road trip, Audrey was confused the most, she later claimed.

"When we were at Bobbi Jo's grandmother's house, Bobbi Jo was tellin' them that she was the one that killed Bob," Audrey recalled. "In the truck, Jennifer was saying that *she* killed Bob. When they first came in the door back at the apartment, Bobbi Jo was sayin', '*We* killed Bob. . . .' I didn't understand what was going on or who did what."

At one point, Audrey had asked Bobbi, "What in the hell is going on?" Had they murdered Bob? And if so, why'd they do it?

"Well, he was raping Jennifer," Bobbi said (sticking to the plan she and Jen had come up with), according to Audrey.

"And that's all she said," Audrey told me. "She just kept saying, 'We gotta get out of town. . . . We gotta get out of town. We gotta leave. . . . Hurry!'

So we packed up some of our stuff and some of Jen's stuff and we done left."

"Wait a minute, Bobbi Jo just said that *she* killed [Bob]. . . . I thought you said that *you* killed him?" Kathy had asked Jen soon after they left Dorothy Smith's.

"Look, we were all thinking in our minds, if Jennifer didn't do this, then we ain't fixin' to go nowhere," Audrey later explained. They didn't want to stand behind Bobbi Jo, per se, and take off with her if Jen was not involved.

After Kathy asked her daughter who was responsible—and if this whole thing was some sort of prank—Jen got quiet and serious.

"Jennifer wasn't really saying much," Audrey remembered. "She was kind of, like, shaken. That's one of the reasons we all decided to go with them."

One of the girls searched through the keys on Bob's key chain, trying several in the lock, but she couldn't come up with the right key to get into the trailer.

"I wasn't giving them the key," Bobbi later told me. She didn't want them breaking into Bob's trailer and rummaging through his things. She had driven to the trailer so she could get her engagement ring. This way, if she needed money, at least she would have something to fall back on.

But the three of them—Kathy, Krystal, and

Jen—had different plans. Without Bobbi knowing, they walked around to the back of the trailer in search of a big window to smash. This way, one of them would be able to climb in and open the door.

Suspicious, Bobbi followed.

In the front yard, Bob had one of those dangerous trampolines that kids like to take the safety nets down from and horse around upon. It was one of those round, springy leg-breakers that adults like to make zany YouTube videos of themselves doing stupid-human tricks on. There was some other junk hanging around the yard, but Audrey spied the trampoline. As the others trekked into the backyard, she walked over to it.

Looks like fun.

Watching the others head toward the back of the trailer, Audrey thought, *I'm not going into that trailer to commit burglary. Y'all can do what y'all want. But not me.*

Robbing a dead man didn't seem like the right thing to do.

Krystal found a nice window in the back and pointed to it.

They had to be ultra-careful, Jen later testified. "We couldn't get inside. We couldn't find the right key. We were scared because the neighbors were outside. And we were thinking that they were going to call the cops . . . since Bob wasn't there."

(Jennifer never mentioned that Bobbi was a part of this in any way. And with Bobbi being the size of a young boy, was she about to try and stop three grown women from breaking in?)

Krystal took a rock and smashed the glass.

They were in.

According to Audrey, Kathy and Jen were under the impression Bob's late brother had left a stash of cash hidden somewhere inside Bob's trailer.

"And they wanted that money," Audrey said.

Audrey bounced up and down on the trampoline out front as the girls pillaged the inside of the trailer, lifting cushions, opening cupboards and drawers, searching underneath the bed, in the bathroom. As she sprang up and down, she felt the elastic bounce of the trampoline, which was making her stomach feel queasy, like she was on an amusement park ride. Bouncing, Audrey thought: *What is going on here? What in the hell am I doing with these people?*

"I was kind of in disbelief," Audrey remembered, thinking back to how strange that moment seemed. "I was like . . . thinking that this didn't really happen. It even seems that way today. You know, I wasn't there [when Bob was murdered], so it was easy for me not to believe it and think it was just all some sort of story they had made up."

Jumping and thinking, Audrey came to the realization that maybe they were full of nonsense. Perhaps Jen and Bobbi had gotten so high that they couldn't decipher reality from fantasy. Maybe they thought they'd killed Bob in one of their otherworld trips? Perhaps they had partied so hard, they were confusing a television movie with reality?

Inside the trailer, Bobbi searched for her engagement ring, while the others got busy thieving things.

Loading it into Bob's truck took some time, but after about a half hour inside the trailer, they managed to leave with, as Krystal later reported, a scavenger hunt's list of worthless, everyday items: a "twenty-seven-inch TV . . . a big, old fool's-gold rock, [and] a strobe light. Stupid stuff."

With the bed of Bob's truck filled with junk from his trailer, Bobbi hopped back into the driver's seat. She knew she couldn't stop them from burgling the place, so she waited for them to finish and then took off.

In town, Bobbi found a pawnshop, which Kathy had directed her to. Kathy was the one with the ID and the only bandit out of the bunch willing to use it to pawn a stolen television. So she went inside and sold the television for $75 as the others waited in the truck out front.

Later, Kathy told police: "Krystal told me it was *her* television. . . ." That, however, seems hardly possible to believe, seeing that Kathy was with them when they lifted it from Bob's trailer.

After selling the television, the gang was in the mood to get back to some serious partying.

"We stopped at a truck stop," Audrey said. "We got us some beer and then started smokin' some

weed. But I was the *only* one"—as if it mattered—
"that wasn't drinking."

Then Bobbi hit the 171 out of town and found
Interstate 20, some miles after that.

"Any idea where we're going?" Kathy asked,
taking a pull from a beer. She was wondering if
Bobbi was still thinking about Mexico. Or had another plan. They seemed to be making it up as
they went along.

"Mexico," Bobbi restated, according to Kathy.

"We'll go here, and then we'll go there," Jen
added. Then, an interesting piece of dialogue all
the girls agreed they heard Jen say: "I did this,
maybe I should drive."

"Maybe we stop back in Mineral Wells and ask
Jen's dad for some money," Bobbi suggested.

"They was just driving in the opposite direction," Audrey explained. "They didn't know *where*
the hell they was goin'."

No one pointed out that the quickest way to
Mexico wasn't west, but south, heading toward
Waco on the 77, into San Antonio, and then across
the border from there.

"I don't think [Bobbi] knew exactly where she
was driving," Krystal later said. "She was scatterbrained. I don't know. . . ."

As they traveled along the interstate, the drive
turned long and quiet and monotonous. They
pounded beers and smoked weed. The music
coming from the stereo was pure country, and

there were times when, Kathy and Jennifer later claimed, they all sang along to a popular tune.

Occasionally the conversation turned back to what had happened at Bob's. The girls were curious. They needed to know. So far, they'd heard several different versions of what was one truth: Bob Dow was dead.

"The story kind of changed a *lot*," Krystal remembered.

Audrey later told me Bobbi took on the role of leader quite aggressively and confidently, and was beginning to "piss everyone off" with her demands and the way she made the decisions about what they were going to do, where they were going, and when.

"My mom was going to knock her out a couple of times," Audrey said. "But Bobbi was the one with the gun."

Bobbi said that analysis by Audrey was a total fabrication. It wasn't as if she was driving with the gun tucked in her belt, threatening everyone with it, waving it around. There was a gun in the truck—yes. But no one in particular had it. Additionally, Bobbi explained, Kathy was the one telling her where to go, taking total control of the trip.

Tamey Hurley did not see her daughter as a leader. To the contrary, Tamey told me, "Bobbi was a follower. That was her trouble. It kind of freaked me out when Jennifer became so attached to her. Part of Bobbi's problem was always that she was so softhearted. She always wanted to make everyone happy. She'd do anything she can to please people. She was always taking the blame for other people so they wouldn't get into trouble. Her brothers, especially."

"Bobbi was definitely someone who would stand up and take a hand across the face for you," said a friend. "She would absolutely take on someone's pain. She would take responsibility for things she didn't do to protect a friend. That is Bobbi."

Heading down the 20 toward Odessa, about sixty miles from the Arizona border, two hundred miles from the closest crossing into Mexico, Kathy and Bobbi Jo got into an argument.

"And what the hell if we get pulled over?" Kathy snapped at Bobbi. What was the plan then? Here were five girls cruising through Texas in a stolen vehicle, a dead man left behind in Mineral Wells. They had drugs on them; Bobbi was knocking back beers and smoking weed as she drove; they had a loaded weapon; they were all supposedly laughing and yelling and screaming to the music blaring from the car stereo. Kathy was beginning to feel that there was no light at the end of this tunnel—that this was not going to end in a good way. Jen said in that *Texas Monthly* article that she and Bobbi were talking about going down in a hail of gunfire, busting through a barricade of police at the border as if they were outlaws. Bobbi was certain that the cops were onto them and there would, at some point, be a roadblock set up with their names on it—sheriffs and deputies and cops with rifles pointed at the windshield, surrounded by a band of reporters with cameras, pumping it all out live on the cable networks. This was their destiny. Their fifteen minutes.

(The problem with this memory, however, was that no one else along for the ride could later recall Bobbi and Jen talking about it, or acting out scenes like this from *Thelma & Louise*. The impression was that Jen had made all of this up later when she sat down with the magazine.)

Bobbi talked about killing herself and the others if they got stopped.

"I'll be damned, Bobbi. . . . That's what y'all got planned," Kathy apparently said. "No, no, no . . . this shit ain't about to go down like that."

The girls knew Kathy was a badass. Not too many people back home messed with Kathy Jones. She'd been stabbed, beaten, knocked out, done years in the joint, and was still standing. She'd taken on men and whupped her some Texas testosterone-fueled butt. Some chick the size of a twelve-year-old boy was not about to threaten Kathy and her daughters' lives in any way, Kathy claimed, and she had made this clear to Bobbi.

There was a second weapon in the vehicle (one that Jen had taken from a green trunk in Bob's bedroom). The plan was to pawn the weapon at some point to finance the trip.

So there were two weapons in the truck at the time, Kathy thought as they made their way out of state. The only problem Kathy could see then, which felt pretty significant to her at that moment, was that one weapon was loaded and one wasn't.

CHAPTER 19

AS SOON AS KRYSTAL, AUDREY, and Kathy walked into Bob Dow's party house on the night of April 28, 2004, they took one look at Bobbi and Jen and knew the night was going to be one hell of a bender. This was the first time Kathy met Bob, a guy she had heard a lot about.

"You want a drink?" Bob asked. He was tending bar. They were sitting around in the living room, smoking weed and drinking.

"I don't remember what kind of drinks they were, but Bob mixed me one," Kathy said. "And, anyway, we all got to drinking and, I believe, I did smoke weed that night, too."

Audrey and Kathy did not know it was Bobbi's birthday. Their mission going over there was to check up on Jen and, once again (according to them), try to talk her into leaving. They later claimed to have wanted to get Jen as far away from Bobbi (and Bob) as they could. And yet, within moments of walking into the house, they both had drinks in their hands and were partying with everyone.

Bob had his mother locked away in her room so she wouldn't disturb them.

Bob soon broke out what Kathy described as "a big bag" of dope. Bob was the medicine man. He had all the drugs. Bob reached down into the bag and, like Santa Claus at an office Christmas party, took out yellow and white bars of Xanax, along with blue "footballs" (more Xanax). Beyond that, he had "some hydrocodone [pills], too," Kathy recalled. Hydrocodone is an opiate prescribed to treat severe and chronic pain. As PubMed Health claims, *Hydrocodone is in a class of medications called opiate (narcotic) analgesics and in a class of medications called antitussives. Hydrocodone relieves pain by changing the way the brain and nervous system respond to pain.*

In other words, serious narcotics. You take a few of those and have a cocktail and you won't remember your own name.

"It was just like a big, old party all the time, whenever I went over there," Kathy said. "If there wasn't one, he was making one, you know. That's just the way it was."

As the night progressed, the girls got high until the moon began to burn its midnight oil and the early-morning haze arrived. They'd pop pills, drink hard liquor, dance a little bit, smoke some weed, pass out, get up, and do it all over again. No one later mentioned anything about Bob whipping out his camera and taking videos, or that they had some sort of orgy. The perversion that had become Bob's signature, and what he was known for within the circle of girls frequenting the house, had taken a backseat on this night to the celebration of Bobbi's birthday.

According to Jen, the filming parties took place during what was a normal, regular course of Bob's days and nights. And the way she described how these types of parties were different from, say, a get-together like they were having on the night of Bobbi's birthday, it appeared that it was consensual among the participants. Still, if minors were involved (which they were, according to the MWPD, Bobbi, Jen, and Audrey), even if the minors agreed with what had been going on, it was *never* consensual. *Never* okay. And certainly *never* legal. Bob was committing an evil, criminal act, stealing the innocence of girls who didn't know any better. Even worse, he was documenting it on film.

"People having a good time," Jen said later, talking about a typical night of partying and filming. "Not just with their clothes on, but with their clothes off. Sexually, there were . . . Ah, sometimes people would get photographed being intimate with each other."

Bob was the instigator, Jen claimed. Not Bobbi.

But as far as "who kind of directed the action," Jen later insisted, "Bob and Bobbi both did." (This was an accusation Bobbi readily admitted to when I asked. "Yes, I did those things for Bob.") Jen said she personally never got involved with "directing" (such an unusual choice of words here when describing what was going on inside that house).

"She would more just be, like, kind of the actor and director," Jen said in court, speaking of Bobbi's role. "And sit there and just tell you" what she and Bob needed. "And I would do whatever she asked me. If she asked me to pose for the camera, I would. If she asked me to take off my clothes, I would."

Sometimes the three of them would get high and sit around, put the tapes on, and watch, laughing and joking at the action. It seemed as if Bob was some sort of Svengali or David Koresh character, wielding his experience, conning much younger and inexperienced prey. Often the films involved Jen and Bobbi having oral sex with each other. Or Jen having some fun with Bobbi's breasts, and Bobbi reciprocating.

"It was just for fun," Jen claimed.

Some of the other "fun," Jen added, was a bit more risqué and dangerous.

"Sometimes we would just . . . just grab each other in the sexual body parts. Sometimes we would hold up items to each other, like a gun or a knife or something, and, you know, just pose for the camera."

It was all part of the game—the act of getting high and engaging in risky, aggressive, and salacious conduct. The girls saw a way out of their own reality within this sexual exploitation by a male old enough to be their father. They didn't think anything of it—especially Bobbi. It was simply what they did when they got high.

That is, until it became too much.

And then Bob Dow had to die.

CHAPTER 20

AS KRYSTAL LATER EXPLAINED, despite how fragmented and vague her words came across, the murder narrative of what happened back at Bob's changed frequently as they drove out of Texas. She and the others kept going back and forth, not knowing what to believe.

"Basically," Krystal recalled, "they said Bob was raping Jennifer and they got a gun. Basically, [they] had the gun loaded by somebody other than themselves, and [they] was going to go in and take care of it, and he (Bob) was not going to have [to rape] Jennifer at all. It was going to be taken care of."

Krystal never placed the blame on one girl or the other; to her, Jen and Bobbi were equally responsible.

According to one story Jen told on the road, Bob had become so overpowering, abusive, and domineering—sexually harassing her continuously while she was at the house—it became unbearable to be around the man. But that was Jen, not Bobbi.

As one source later observed, "They weren't in fear for their own lives at the time, right? I mean, they could have just moved away from Bob Dow. And if he pursued them, they could have gone to the cops and said, 'We have evidence that this guy is having sex with underage girls.' They could have gotten Bob Dow locked away for a long time. . . ."

Mike Burns, the prosecutor who later became involved in the case, reiterated this same point: "There's a lot of folklore in Texas about the 'he needed killing' defense, but the truth of the matter is, that's really not a fact in Texas. Regardless of the status, whether they're good guys, bad guys, whatever, a murder is a crime, and it's one of the most serious crimes we have. That defense is still tried in . . . courtrooms . . . of an unsavory character being killed. But it doesn't wash with the juries . . . because they understand, and it's part of our job to make them understand that taking a human life—regardless of the circumstance of the victim—is still against the law and needs to be dealt with accordingly."

The argument Jen presented to the girls on the road was, essentially, that she *and* Bobbi couldn't take it any longer. Bob Dow was constantly in Jen's face, constantly *asking* her to sleep with him, constantly *demanding* that she sleep with him, and constantly on Bobbi's case to *convince* Jen to have sex with him.

Bobbi, Jen later insisted, kept telling Bob no. But Bob kept pushing.

One thing led to another; and, well, after Bob made one final advance, Jen decided he needed killing.

As Jen sat in court during her sentencing hearing and retold this part of her story (the third version by then) about being on the road that first night, after stopping for a break somewhere before heading out of Texas, Bobbi fired up a cigarette, pulled her aside, and said, "Let's talk."

"What's up?" Jen asked.

"We need a plan."

"Yeah."

They discussed what to tell the police if they were caught. ("It was Bobbi's idea," Jen recalled. "We . . . we were thinking that if we did get caught, that that was, you know, the safest plan that we could come up with. That we . . . we both wouldn't get into trouble.")

The plan was, Jen explained, "that he was trying to rape me. And that I was—it was self-defense that I killed him. . . ."

Jen was in "a state of mind" at the time, she claimed, within the fog of her relationship with Bobbi, that didn't allow her to think on her own. Her feelings toward Bobbi were growing deeper every day; and now, from how she viewed the situation, they had this secret, evil act between

them. Jen truly believed that she was falling under
Bobbi's spell.

"They were strong," Jen remarked, talking
about how intense her feelings for Bobbi were.
"They were still in . . . a state of caring and loving
and showing affection. I felt like I was afraid of
losing her."

Instead of heading south into Mexico, a decision was made to head northwest toward Arizona.
The idea of crossing the Mexican border legally
(or even illegally) didn't seem so practical. There
was the likely chance that immigration and border
patrol had a description of the vehicle. Heading
into Mexico was more or less akin to a spiderweb;
whereas, heading into New Mexico and continuing west—the new plan—seemed to be a bit more
pragmatic as far as bettering their chances of getting away. As long as they could keep their noses
clean and obey some rather liberal speed-limit laws
throughout the southwest, they were going to be
fine. There had been no roadblock or army of law
enforcement waiting at the border as they passed
into New Mexico, near Ciudad Juárez, heading for
Las Cruces on Interstate 25. They were free and
clear to continue onto Interstate 10 and find their
way to Arizona.

The drive through New Mexico was quick. By
the early-morning hours of May 7, 2004, they
had traveled some six hundred miles or more.

After passing the border into New Mexico, Kathy suggested stopping somewhere to pawn the second gun.

"Bob gave the gun to Bobbi," Jen said later in court. (This was another important fact to highlight—the gun was Bobbi's to begin with, as Bobbi had later claimed.)

In town, after Kathy pawned the gun, they stopped for gas and something to eat. Kathy was growing increasingly impatient with Jen and Bobbi. She needed to know the truth about what had happened. Enough was enough.

"I need to know," Kathy announced.

Bobbi and Jen looked at each other.

Jen explained how it started the day before Bob was murdered. Jen said she needed a ride home. No one else would pick her up. Bob came. And for that ride, Jen told her mother, Bob said his "payment" would be having sex with her.

The way she first told this story, Jen implied that she was alone when Bob picked her up. And then, when they got back to the party house afterward, "Bobbi Jo walked in," Kathy said later, explaining how she had first heard the story from her daughter, "and [she] found Bob forcing himself on Jennifer. Bobbi Jo then knocked him away from Jennifer and he told them both to get their clothes and get out."

"So we took our stuff and spent the night in

Graford at Bobbi Jo's grandmother's," Jen told Kathy.

Kathy stared at the two of them. Something seemed off with the story. It had holes. Details were missing. It was too prepackaged. It felt as if they were trying to *sell it* more than *tell it*.

"The next day, we went back to the house and broke in by the window in the back," Jen continued.

Kathy believed this. She looked down as they drove and realized Jen "had small cuts on her hand."

"You did that breaking in?" Kathy asked.

Jen held up her hand. "Yes."

From there, Jen said, she and Bobbi walked into Bob's mother's house and found Bob "passed out on his bed."

"And what happened next?" Kathy pressed.

CHAPTER 21

THE MORNING AFTER BOBBI's birthday party, Thursday, April 29, turned out to be a fairly significant day by global standards—beyond, that is, the boundaries of Bobbi and Jen's Mineral Wells bubble. The fallout from several disturbing images of U.S. soldiers allegedly abusing Iraqi prisoners at a jail near Baghdad was fueling shock and anger around the globe. It was all over the news.

For Bobbi and Jen, both of whom were totally oblivious to what was happening in the world, the morning started late (around noon). After another night of partying at Bob's mother's house—this time with Jen's mother and sister—Bobbi and Jen wound up back in Graford at Bobbi's grandmother's house.

"Can you come up and get us?" Bobbi asked Bob over the phone.

"I guess," Bob said.

Bob Dow drove from Mineral Wells to Graford. From there, the girls went with Bob to his friend's house to have lunch.

After that, Bobbi asked, "Can you stop off at the store for us?"

In what seemed to be the normal course of the day for the past several weeks, Bob stopped at the liquor store and went in and bought the booze Jen and Bobbi needed to get through the day.

It was party time all over again.

They spent the afternoon at Bob's drinking.

"I took half a Soma and fell asleep," Jen said in one statement she later gave to police. Soma is the trade name for the prescription drug Cariso-prodol, a muscle relaxant designed to treat pain from muscle injuries and spasms; it's definitely not a good companion to alcohol. It's safe to say Jen passed out. She certainly had not fallen asleep.

Nevertheless, Jen didn't say what time, exactly, but she claimed to have opened her eyes to Bobbi standing bedside, staring down at her.

"Grace (pseudonym, Bobbi's cousin) and Charlie (pseudonym, a friend) are outside," Bobbi said, according to Jen's recollection. "Get up. Let's go." Bobbi shoved Jen's arm. "Come on."

Jen never argued with Bobbi. Plus, Jen wanted to be with Bobbi, wherever Bobbi went. When she talked about this day later (if we are to take any-thing Jennifer Jones says in her first statement to police as truth), Jen said she wanted out of Bob's house, regardless of whether Bobbi Jo left,

too. Bob had turned from a man who had been
providing the girls with drugs and alcohol into
this weird, forcefully perverted character who
creeped Jen out. Bobbi, by then, was used to his
antics. But Bob had been coming on to Jen since
she started staying at the house with Bobbi, especially
when Jen was alone with him. He was obsessed with
Jen—according to *only* Jen. Bob had gotten used
to having the women Bobbi brought home, but
Jen was different. There was something about her
that turned Bob on in a way Jen could not figure
out. Maybe it was the simple fact that he couldn't
have her. Either way, it was beginning to turn into
a problem for Jen, who said in court (her third
version of events) that Bobbi had become incensed
that Bob was making advances toward her.

I felt obligated to care for him and his needs, Bobbi
explained in a letter to me when I asked about
this. *I did bring all kinds of women to him in exchange
for money and drugs. Women loved me—how I looked,
how I was. I'd take them over to "party" and [Bob] would
do the rest. That went on for two years before I even* met
*Jennifer. . . . I have not cared less if Bob wanted Jennifer
or had sex with Jennifer. It didn't matter to me. I wanted
to drink and do drugs. If not with Jennifer, I'd find another girl.*

According to Jen (during her sentencing hearing, the third version), all Bobbi had asked in
return for those years of service to Bob was that he
stay away from Jen.

Bobbi vehemently disagreed with this statement,

saying that the relationship she had with Jen wasn't like that one bit. Jen was just one more in a long line of girls Bobbi slept (and partied) with at that time. If Jen developed a fixation on Bob Dow wanting her, it was in her own mind. Yes, Bobbi said, Bob had made comments about Jen and she and Jen agreed to try and make this alleged "rape" story fly; but no, it wasn't true. Bobbi didn't care what Jen did—least of all with Bob. Because if it wasn't Jen providing for Bobbi's sexual needs, it would have been another female. And, Bobbi insisted, Jen had had sex with Bob a few times, anyway, for money and for dope.

It was all part of Jennifer's fantasy that I would be angry with Bob for coming on to her, Bobbi concluded. *Jennifer . . . hated [Bob].*

Bobbi's friend Charlie lived in Millsap, a twenty-minute drive from the party house. There's some indication that Jen planned on moving into Charlie's house to get away from Bob; but in her first statement to police, she never finished explaining why she didn't, or how much thought she had actually put into the idea.

Bobbi and Jen wound up staying at Charlie's house, likely partying, until the following day, April 30, a Friday.

"Then they took me back to . . . get my clothes, so I would not have to go back over there [to the party house] alone," Jen said of Bobbi and Charlie.

If Jen wanted to move out of Bob's, so be it, Bobbi felt. Go for it. Bobbi didn't care if the girls she brought over to the party house hung around or left. There would always be others.

Bob Dow's sexual bombast, coupled with several overt sexual advances Jen later claimed he made toward her, had reached the point where Jen couldn't take it anymore. She was beginning to feel as though it wasn't safe being around Bob, with or without Bobbi (a factor that would become very important in Bob's murder).

Jen grabbed her clothes.

Bobbi Jo's family—grandmother, aunt, and uncle—were in Mexico, set to return on Saturday, May 1. In Jennifer's version of this day, the plan was to hang out in Graford at Bobbi's grandmother's house and wait for them to return. From there, Jen could decide where to go next.

Jen later claimed Bobbi wanted to stop by and pick up Kathy, Jen's mother, so Kathy could meet Bobbi's grandparents.

"Not true," Bobbi later said. "The last person in the world I would want to introduce my grandparents to was Kathy Jones."

"I don't recall this taking place," Kathy later told me when I asked her about the day and Jen's recollection of a plan to meet Bobbi's grandparents.

* * *

A few weeks before, on April 6, 2004, Bob Dow stood on the porch outside his mother's house and talked with ex-wife Elizabeth Smith. Elizabeth and Bob had had casual conversations in the past. On this day, though, according to Elizabeth's memory, Bob was in one of his moods, feeling sorry for himself. The girls, he explained, were getting to him. They were becoming a pain in the ass. Bob didn't know what to do.

"I like Bobbi Jo," Bob told Elizabeth. "She's a chick magnet, you know. I can have all the young women I want, as long as I keep her happy. She'll bring in lines of them, as long as she's taken care of."

Elizabeth didn't know what to think, or how to respond. She knew Bobbi was a lesbian, and she said she didn't have a problem with it. However, Elizabeth had never really met any of the girls Bob was referring to (so she claimed). Elizabeth would leave the house before the "parties" started, she later testified. She'd call Bob and hear loud music in the background, lots of girls talking and laughing and making a racket, and he'd explain what was going on. To her, it was wrong; though, she said, what went on inside the house was "Bob's business." She had no idea Bob was exploiting underage girls. She assumed they were all consensual adults.

In addition, Elizabeth wasn't close to Bobbi and later claimed she had never even met Jen. Not once. (A comment that lends itself to Bobbi's version of the relationship she had with Jen.) Elizabeth had heard a lot about Jen while at Bob's, but she had never been introduced. And

Elizabeth was no dummy. Bob had what Elizabeth later described as "a weakness for the flesh." She learned this firsthand while married to the guy. However, she stayed out of the way when it came to what he did when she wasn't around.

"That was him," Elizabeth said. "I mean, Robert wasn't perfect, and my belief is, none of us are, if we really looked in the closet."

As they stood on the porch, this "worried" look came over Bob.

"What is it, Bob?"

"Tell [my son] that I've always known that he was mine and that I loved him, and I hope that I've been the best father I could possibly be to him."

Elizabeth was confused. Why couldn't Bob deliver the message himself? Was he planning on leaving?

It was no secret between them that Bob's son had not been given his father's surname. There was an issue with maybe Bob not being the boy's father and a DNA test had been conducted after the boy requested it.

"What's going on, Bob?" Elizabeth asked.

"I have messages for you to deliver, and I need you to do that for me," he said.

Later, Elizabeth talked about this moment, making the claim: "He knew something was going to happen, and he gave me all these messages to tell everybody. . . . I'll never forget them."

"I wanted to apologize to you, Elizabeth," Bob

continued. He didn't go into specifics; it was something between them that neither had to talk about in detail. Bob had messed up a good thing with Elizabeth by cheating on her. He had always wanted to say that. He needed to take this moment, he explained, and acknowledge he'd done wrong. He was sorry for it.

"Bob—"

"Listen . . . I have a message for all of my friends and daughter." Bob had a six-year-old child out of wedlock. He didn't spend much time with her. "Tell them all not to be sad. . . ."

"What are you talking about?"

It sounded as though Bob was going to kill himself, or he had a feeling he was about to die.

What Bob was alluding to, Elizabeth soon realized, was that he'd had a premonition that his number had come up. Elizabeth took it as Bob thinking that his heart was going to give out at any moment. He felt tired and sickly. All the partying, acting like he was still in his twenties. Not following doctor's orders. Not eating right. Not sleeping. It was adding up.

"At my funeral, I want you to throw a big party. And just tell them all, you know, not to be sad for me. Just be happy, because that's the way they would have been with me. Tell them to go on with life and be happy. Have a party."

About ten minutes into the conversation, Bob's cell phone rang.

"Yeah . . . hello?"

Elizabeth could hear Bobbi's muffled voice through the earpiece. "Can you come get me?"

"Okay. I'll be there." Bob looked at Elizabeth. "Gotta go."

CHAPTER 22

KRYSTAL BAILEY WAS GETTING worried about the situation she now found herself in, riding shotgun with two potential murderers, along with two family members, who seemed to be in this thing for the long haul. This was not how Krystal had envisioned the past few days going as she drove over to Audrey's two days before to pick up her things and hopefully talk Audrey into a reunion. Here, as they came upon Tucson, in the early-morning hours of May 7, 2004, Krystal thought she needed to get away from the girls and get her bum back to Mineral Wells.

"It was just getting crazy," Krystal said later in court. "I didn't want to be involved any longer."

She wanted out.

Krystal Bailey might have been considered a bad girl, but she was not like the rest of them. Much like Bobbi, Krystal had never been "in trouble with the law," or "convicted of a felony."

And up until this point, she hadn't put much thought into the girls killing Bob. She didn't believe them. But now, as the sun rose, scorching the cactuses and desert sand of Arizona, Krystal was more certain than ever that Jen and Bobbi together—or one of them alone—had committed murder. They were one thousand miles from home and not talking about turning around. If this was some sort of joke, Krystal reflected, they had taken it to extremes.

Bobbi stopped at a rest stop so they could take a break and use the bathroom. It was time to regroup and reevaluate, to see what everyone wanted to do.

As the others stretched and smoked, Krystal made a call home from a payphone.

"Mom?"

"Krystal! Where are you? What in the hell is going on?"

"Calm down . . . Mom . . . just clam down." Krystal's mother was nervous. She had been talking to people in town.

"Did you kill Bob?"

"What? Are you kidding? . . . No, Mom. No, I didn't." A sound of relief echoed on the end of the line. Krystal's mother took a deep breath. "Why? Why are you asking?" Krystal knew at that moment the girls weren't kidding. Bob Dow was dead.

Krystal's mother explained that she had spoken to the MWPD. Detective Brian Boetz had asked where Krystal had run off to; he explained why they wanted to talk to her. Through that conversation, Krystal's mother had put two and two together and thought maybe Krystal had been involved in some way because she was so close to Audrey and Jen.

"Are you okay?" Krystal's mother asked her daughter.

"Mom, so the rumors are true?" Krystal wanted to know. "This really *did* happen?"

"Yes . . . Bob Dow was murdered."

Krystal paused. She stared at the others, who were hanging around the truck. Krystal realized she was possibly traveling with a band of murderers. It became very real. She could be charged herself.

"Where are you?"

"Arizona."

"Stay right where you are and I'll come and get you."

"Gotta go, Mom." The others were ready to take off. "I'll call you back."

CHAPTER 23

WHILE BOBBI AND JEN stayed at Bobbi's grandmother's house during those days following Bobbi's birthday bash, Bob called. He had gotten home and realized Bobbi had left the house. Maybe for good this time. He was upset. He wanted Bobbi to come back.

"Let me come and pick you up," Bob told Bobbi.

"I don't know," Bobbi said. She felt conflicted. It was easy, Bobbi later explained to me, to give in to a guy who had essentially been her keeper for so many years. Bobbi wasn't necessarily implying there was a Stockholm syndrome element to her relationship with Bob Dow. But then, looking at it from an objective point of view, here was a teenage girl, addicted to drugs, deeply involved in an abusive relationship with a much older man. Bobbi did not have the emotional faculties to address the clinical side of what was happening to (or around) her.

Stockholm syndrome is when the victim of a

kidnapping becomes oblivious to the crimes of her captor and ends up feeling sympathy toward him. She cannot escape. In some cases, he has threatened her with death if she tries. And yet, at the same time, the Stockholm syndrome victim has been taken in by her captor's contrived acts of kindness and goodwill. It's a psychological game of chess orchestrated by the captor; his victim is not allowed (and is certainly afraid) to move a pawn without his consent. This was not the type of relationship Bob had developed with Bobbi. However, if what Bobbi said is true, he had convinced her, through lies and manipulation, that she was dependent upon him. Bobbi explained that she never realized how "low" she'd "come" until much later, after being removed from the situation and looking at it soberly, from afar.

"We [Bob and I] had sex with the same women," Bobbi told me. "I never *willingly* had sex with Robert. He would get me so high that I'd fall asleep. Jennifer told me that he was having sex with me while I was passed out and lifeless. Whenever I tried to leave, he'd come and get me. Or look for me."

No one involved ever mentioned that there were any videotapes or photographs of Bob and Bobbi having sex.

For Bobbi, going back to Bob always seemed like the right thing to do. She needed to work. She needed—was dependent upon—drugs. She was addicted to promiscuous sex with different partners.

In a rather eye-opening 2012 article in *Time* magazine, "Understanding Psychopathic and Sadistic Minds," reporter Maia Szalavitz hit on the psychological makeup of a teenager in Bobbi's situation, writing: *When young children, who are dependent on their caregivers, are abused, they have little choice but to love the people who are hurting them. "If the caregiver is inflicting pain and you also love that person, a weird relationship can develop where pain becomes pleasurable," said Jean Decety,* a professor of psychology and psychiatry at the University of Chicago.

It's the *"pathways in the brain that are involved in pain processing and the pathways involved in pleasure,"* Decety went on to note, that are linked. *"They have to overlap to some extent. That's why if in development something goes wrong and you mix the two, you [may] seek pleasure from pain."*

Without Bobbi realizing it, Bobbi's emotional state was in a holding pattern when she met Bob, which made her the perfect victim to the future madness she would endure under the direction and influence of this man. The setup started for Bobbi when "my mother abandoned me," she said (her mother later agreeing with this statement during one of our interviews). "She left me with my grandma." (Both Tamey Hurley and Dorothy Smith verified this.) "I bounced from house to house, family member to family member." In hopping from one home to another, Bobbi explained, she'd end up spending a night or two with one particular family member. It was an older person in that household, Bobbi said, who would rape her. The sexual abuse began early. "He did it for so long—I thought it was okay. And being so little, I was caught in mixed emotions." She didn't know if it was right, wrong, or within the normal course of a day for a kid her age. "I didn't speak of it." And when Bobbi finally dredged up the courage to go to her mother (years after the abuse, which had started when Bobbi was nine), she claimed her mother "blamed me, saying it was me 'making him want me.' I didn't understand. [My rapist] was seven years older [than me]." This went on, Bobbi said, until she met her child's father. Through him, she met Bob Dow.

Based on her upbringing, in addition to a drug/alcohol addiction Bobbi developed while with her son's father, one could argue that when Bobbi left her fiancé and moved in with Bob, she was at the lowest point of her life, emotionally weaker than she had ever been. She didn't know right from wrong, in the sense of what a codependent relationship could do to her evolving psyche, not to mention her spirit. Most of the males in her life had let Bobbi down and had abused her in some form or fashion, according to the way Bobbi remembered it. And here was Bob Dow, a much older and more well-groomed abuser, a man she trusted, taking her in, plying her with the essentials of food and shelter, and then providing all the drugs and alcohol she wanted to consume. Bob became a savior in Bobbi's skewed way of looking at life.

Bob Dow cried on the telephone that day, Bobbi told me, when he realized Bobbi had left the party house for good and didn't want to return.

"I'm so sorry," Bob said. "Please, please forgive me. . . ."

"I don't know." Bobbi was fed up with the life.

"Please come back, Bobbi. Please." Bob begged her to reconsider his apology, and he promised that he'd be nicer. "Please, Bobbi."

Bobbi Jo thought about it.

"Okay, come and get us."

As things would soon turn out, going back over to Bob's was a decision she made that would change the course of her life forever.

CHAPTER 24

THE GIRLS HEADED northwest from Tucson to Phoenix. That stop along the way, after a long night of driving, didn't do much for what were now severe hunger issues. They needed something substantial. By now, they were just about out of money.

"We went into Phoenix and got something to eat," Krystal later explained. "We really didn't have any money, so we were kind of bummed."

They hit the streets and begged in the city square.

"Some people gave us money."

One guy running a food cart downtown saw the girls begging and called them over.

"I've got a few extra burritos," he said. He handed Bobbi four.

"There were five of us," Krystal said later. "So I didn't eat."

Audrey worked the phones, hoping to see, as

Jen later told it, "if anybody was onto us yet." There was also the chance that Jerry Jones, with whom they had been in constant contact throughout the trip, could wire them money.

They drove out of Phoenix and headed toward Buckeye, Arizona, about an hour's drive directly west of the big city. The new plan was to continue west into California. As they looked for a place to stop along the way, Bobbi realized how hot it was getting. The temperature was a scorching 98 degrees Fahrenheit by noon, with dips only down into the high 80s, spikes as high as 100 degrees. Coupled with hunger, Bobbi was tired of listening to Kathy and Audrey, she later said, both of whom now blamed her for everything.

"I do know that when I went back to my grandmother's house," Bobbi told me, "after the murder and after picking [them] up, I was trying to take up for Jennifer. I felt obligated [to take the blame for the murder] because I felt it was all my fault. Her mom and sister were telling me it was all my fault and I'd love being in prison because I was gay."

Bobbi claimed she was confused and "only trying to be loyal to Jennifer." In Audrey and Kathy's view, Bobbi was a great scapegoat. And because of that, Audrey and Kathy tried to convince Bobbi to take the rap and admit to killing Bob so Jen could get out of it.

"Kathy kept saying, 'You're gay. You'll love prison,'" Bobbi told me.

Outside Phoenix, Bobbi spied a new housing development and stopped for a break. It was midafternoon and hotter than a cowboy's armpit. The dry air and the heat and the malnourishment were getting to everyone. They needed to collect their senses, maybe find a spot to cool off, and come up with a good plan.

"Call Jerry," someone suggested to Audrey.

It wasn't that easy. They needed to find a Western Union first, or someplace where Jerry could wire the money. Plus, Krystal wanted to return home.

There was a water pond in the development. It didn't appear, at first glance, that anyone was around.

"Let's go for a swim," someone yelled, pointing to the water.

Bobbi pulled over by the water and parked. They were "right by the freeway," Audrey recalled. "It was a pond with a little waterfall."

Some of the girls stripped down to their skivvies, while Audrey and Kathy changed into bathing suits, which they'd taken on the trip. They hopped into the water, splashing and frolicking, like little children on a summer afternoon playing in a sprinkler.

"It was hot, so we were just cooling off," Audrey explained to me with a laugh.

After a romp in the pond, the girls headed back out on the open road and wound up in Chandler, Arizona—in the opposite direction they had wanted to drive. They had gotten lost and headed the wrong way for miles on the interstate. "We had been driving around in circles," Jen said in court. They were still outside Phoenix and had not made any progress. In fact, as Bobbi figured out where they were, she saw a sign, which put them south of Mesa, now southeast of Phoenix.

"We went the opposite way," Bobbi said.

"I want to go back to Texas," Krystal said.

"I don't want you here with us, anyway," Audrey told her. ("She was wanting to get back with me, and I didn't want nothing to do with her . . . ," Audrey explained. "I didn't want her with us. Krystal and me, we was broken up.")

Audrey told Bobbi.

Maybe now was as good a time as ever, Bobbi thought.

Bobbi found a convenience store in Chandler and pulled in.

Krystal and the others got out.

"They went into the store," Audrey said, "and stole some stuff."

On a pay phone, Krystal dialed her mother.

"It's me, Ma."

"Where are you?"

"I don't really know," Krystal said, looking around. Then she asked someone. "Chandler, Arizona," she said.

"Sit tight. I'll be out there to get you."

Krystal gave her mother the name of the convenience store. They exchanged a few more words and hung up.

"So [I grabbed] my basket of clothes, my bag of hygiene stuff, got out, and we parted ways," Krystal later said.

Bobbi and the others didn't care one way or the other whether Krystal stayed. If Krystal wanted to go, she should get out and head home. The entire trip for Audrey and Kathy never had that "we're running from the cops" feel to it, they later explained. It was more of a road trip. The talk now was that perhaps Jen and Bobbi had done the world a favor by ridding it of a man who used and abused women. Perhaps it would all go away. Maybe they'd explain how Bob was coming on to Jen and that it had gotten to be too much for her and so she shot him.

He needed killin'.

It's important to point out here that throughout this trip, there had been no mention of Bobbi being the aggressor and having anything to do with asking Jen to kill Bob Dow. If you read through the transcripts and interviews and all of the documentation surrounding this part of the case, you get a feeling that Audrey and Kathy and Bobbi were trying to come up with a way to protect Jen. It appeared that they traveled with the idea that at some point they would be back in Mineral Wells and they had better have a story ready to make sure Jen did not go down for committing this crime.

Meanwhile, Bobbi and Jen got to talking while Kathy and Audrey were inside the store. Jen was paranoid the cops were going to be waiting around every corner, weapons drawn. She was shocked they had gotten this far already.

"We get us a hotel room. Maybe Jerry wires us some money for it," Bobbi suggested, per Jen's claim.

"Yeah, sounds good."

Jen later admitted she felt "people were out to get us." She meant her sister and mother. She wanted to be alone with Bobbi. It was kind of like that fantasy of Bonnie and Clyde that Jen had talked about: Here it was, her chance to live it out.

"What do you think of Ma and Audrey?" Bobbi asked.

Jen took a pull from a cigarette she'd fired up. "Maybe they're trying to turn us in?"

After saying their good-byes to Krystal, Bobbi found her way back onto the freeway, heading in the direction they wanted to go from Phoenix earlier. In the back of her mind, Bobbi was worried about Bob Dow's truck. She knew it had trouble running in hot weather. The engine had a tendency to overheat. They'd been good about stopping and replenishing the water in the radiator so far and hadn't run into much trouble. But as they drove toward Buckeye on the 10, the truck made a funny noise. It started bucking, too, like they were running out of fuel.

"Shit," Bobbi said.

"What is it?" Kathy asked.

"The truck . . ."

Bobbi pulled over and popped the hood. The radiator was making a hot, hissing noise. Steam rose from the top and sides.

The rest of them got out. Bobbi had the hood up, with her head buried in the engine.

"We need some water. We'll have to let it cool down," Bobbi explained. They were close to Buckeye. There was a hotel nearby.

Just then, one of the girls spied a truck with red and blue lights coming down the road. It looked to be a sheriff or a cop. He was heading straight for them.

CHAPTER 25

ON MAY 7, 2004, DETECTIVE BRIAN Boetz got a tip. Boetz felt patience was going to solve this case more than an aggressive, predatory trek out into the wilds of Texas, on a manhunt (although, one could argue with this sexist term, considering that all of these suspects were women), searching for a band of inexperienced, mainly drug-fueled females. In short, the detective knew that in time they would give themselves away. Still, one had to ask: Would an innocent bystander get hurt in the process? Of course, that was the last thing Boetz and the MWPD wanted to see happen.

Earlier, Boetz had gotten hold of Krystal Bailey's grandmother and heard that Krystal had called and said she wanted to come home. Krystal didn't want any part in what was going on.

"They dropped her off somewhere out there," Krystal's grandmother explained to Boetz.

"You don't know where?"

"No, but her mother is on her way to go get her."

Boetz was interested in chatting with Krystal. For all he knew, she could have taken part in the murder, too. There had to be the question of whether Bobbi had acted alone, or if all of the women had participated.

"Can I get a phone number for your daughter?"

The grandmother gave it to the detective.

Boetz called Krystal's mother, who explained that she and Krystal were on the road, heading back to Texas. Krystal said she would call Boetz as soon as she returned; Krystal added that she was prepared to do whatever she could to help.

Boetz asked if she had heard anyone talking about what had happened to Bob.

"Yes," she said. Then Krystal told the detective how Jen and Bobbi were taking credit for the murder, but she was confused as to who actually committed the crime.

After talking with Krystal, Boetz went back to his office and typed up a second probable cause affidavit, now requesting a warrant for Jennifer Jones's arrest on murder charges (based on that *one* conversation with Krystal). What Boetz really needed to do, however, was speak with Krystal in person before he could go back and rattle the cage of the judge to sign off on the warrant.

So, once again, Detective Boetz could do nothing more than wait.

CHAPTER 26

BOBBI, AUDREY, JEN, AND KATHY looked on as what appeared to be a cop rolled up on them. They stood on the side of the road just outside Buckeye, Arizona, waiting for Bob Dow's crappy truck to cool off enough so they could get back on the road.

Later reports claimed this was a police officer. But according to Audrey's recollection, it was one of those road patrol vehicles out and about, stopping off to see if the girls needed a hand. Bobbi didn't believe it was a cop, either. (I could never locate a report that the MWPD or the prosecutor in this case tracked down to see what this so-called officer had to say.)

"Do y'all need any help here?" the patrol officer reportedly asked, pulling up, leaning over the seat, speaking through a rolled-down passenger-side window. "Is everything okay?"

"Our truck overheated," Bobbi said as the others looked on. "We could use some water."

"All right."

The officer took off. Then, a few minutes later, he returned with several gallons of water, saying, "Y'all gotta be careful. Look out." He got out of his vehicle and unloosened the radiator cap. According to Audrey, hot water from inside the radiator, from under all of that pressure, shot straight up into the air like Old Faithful.

"Wow!" Bobbi yelled.

The patrol officer helped them get the truck running again. "You should be fine now."

Then he took off.

They headed toward a nearby hotel that Bobbi had spotted along the way. It was time to call Jerry and have him wire some money so they could hole up for the night.

"We weren't really worried about the cops catching us," Audrey remembered. Even that close call didn't faze Kathy or Audrey. "We just weren't thinking straight."

Audrey made a call to a friend in Mineral Wells. The guy had helped Audrey out from time to time. She had spoken to him several times during the trip and he said he would send some money as soon as he could.

"He was a preacher, but I guess . . . well, he wasn't really a good one," Audrey explained to me. "Me and him used to date. We used to smoke weed together and talk. In fact, he was the guy who confirmed for me that it (the murder) really happened."

How?

Audrey had asked the preacher to take a drive by Bob's the day after the murder when they first took off. He called Audrey back and told her there were cops all over the place; there was yellow crime-scene tape cordoning the house.

"I guess he's really dead," the preacher had told Audrey.

The day before the truck broke down, the preacher had promised to wire some money. They found a Western Union along the road and he made good on the promise. But they were out of funds once again. They had stopped at a truck stop, and for $6, they had taken showers. But now they were hungry, tired, and just about out of fuel.

As they pulled into the Days Inn, which Bobbi had spotted, Audrey noticed a truck stop up the road. They couldn't get a room without funds. So Audrey said, "I'll call the preacher and Jerry and see if we can't get us some money." The truck stop had a Western Union. "I'll be back."

Some time passed. Bobbi wandered into the pool area of the hotel, waiting. There was a shady-looking dude sitting poolside, sipping beers. The guy was grimy and unkempt.

The others looked on and watched as Bobbi spoke to him.

When she returned to the truck, Audrey was back.

"It's going to take a while," Audrey explained, "but Jerry's sending us some money for a room."

"Good," Bobbi said. "That guy over there said we could hang with him in his room until we get our own."

When they got settled inside the guy's room, Bobbi took a moment and called her mother. Kathy and Audrey were outside with the guy. Bobbi didn't know where Jen was, but she assumed she was with Kathy and Audrey.

Bobbi was confused. She didn't know what to do. She was concerned about Kathy and Jen.

"Mamma?"

"Yeah, baby, what is it?" (Tamey recalled Bobbi sounding "very scared . . . whispering into the phone.")

"Mamma, they won't let me talk to you," Bobbi explained, meaning Kathy in particular. "I'll call you back."

Tamey felt Kathy was leading the group and Bobbi was terrified of crossing her. Bobbi was going along with some of what Kathy had suggested, just to keep peace. She didn't want to upset Kathy in any way.

Bobbi called back later that night. She was whispering again. She sounded even more frightened than she had previously. She said Jen had woken her up out of a deep sleep and said that something was going to happen to her. "I think my mother and sister want to kill you, Bobbi," Jen told Bobbi that night. "So you can take the blame for the whole thing."

Tamey told Bobbi to get rid of them as soon as she could and call her when she was alone with Jen.

"The way I took it," Tamey said later, "was that they was all gonna kill Bobbi Jo and put the blame on her for everything so they could get out of it."

Back in Mineral Wells, near midnight, Krystal Bailey arrived at the MWPD. Brian Boetz was waiting.

"Sit down, get yourself comfortable," the detective said. Krystal looked beat from her time on the road. The miles had not been good to her.

Krystal explained how she had waited five hours for her mother to arrive; she had to sit on top of a garbage can at a truck stop. She had no money, but it had been worth it. It felt good to be home.

Boetz's first major witness started with a detailed description of the night of Bobbi's birthday celebration, April 28, at the party house.

"I've been to parties over there before."

"What goes on at these parties, Krystal?" Boetz asked.

"Usually, we smoke marijuana, take some pills—these Xanax bars—and drink beer."

"That all?"

"Bob was usually the one that supplied all the drugs for us."

"What'd y'all do at Bobbi Jo's birthday party?"

"Same," Krystal said, explaining how they had smoked weed and drank. "Took the Xanax pills and had some beer." Then, contradicting what Kathy would later say, "Bob also took photos of everyone. We posed for Bob. I think Jennifer and Audrey pulled up their shirts and showed their tits. Jennifer and Bobbi Jo were making out. . . ."

"How long did the party last?"

"I don't remember."

Krystal gave Boetz a narrative of what she had heard had happened to Bob Dow. Although complete hearsay, it was the MWPD's first glance into what might have occurred at the party house on the night Bob was murdered. It wasn't a long, detailed statement, but Krystal was able to pull together the first account of the murder from what was a third-party perspective.

"Jennifer [told] Kathy that she shot Bob." Krystal said she had heard the conversation several times while on the road. "I don't remember who asked why, but someone asked them (Bobbi and Jen) why Bob was shot."

"What did they say?"

"Jennifer told us that Bob was forcing himself on her. Jennifer said she had tried getting him off of her and then she grabbed a gun and started pulling the trigger—that she 'just kept pulling the trigger.'"

According to Krystal's recollection of what was said about the actual murder, Bobbi didn't have anything to do with either murdering Bob or convincing Jen that Bob needed killing. From what she had heard, Krystal was certain Jen murdered Bob Dow on her own. That name kept coming up in her conversation with Boetz: *Jennifer, Jennifer, Jennifer.* Krystal never mentioned that Bobbi had asked Jen to kill Bob, or that Bobbi provided the weapon.

It was all Jen.

"She turned on me," Bobbi explained to me when I asked about the plan she and Jen had designed. "That hurt. I never killed *anyone*—nor had anything to do with it. I was lost within drugs and guns and sex with all types of women, but I'm not a murderer. I do not hate Jennifer. Deep down, she knows she lied on me. . . ."

What Krystal had reported was enough, Boetz figured, to fill in the blanks of his probable cause affidavit and rustle up the judge to sign it.

It was well after midnight when Boetz finished with Krystal and knocked on the judge's door.

After getting the warrant signed, Boetz called Jerry Jones to see if he had made contact with the girls again.

"I have heard from them," Jerry said.

"Where are they?"

"Buckeye, Arizona. They're at a motel room and want me to come and pick them up and bring them back." Jerry was referring to Audrey and Kathy, although he didn't say it.

Boetz got off the phone, called the Buckeye

Robert "Bob" Dow's mother, Lila Dow, was elderly and ailing when Bob started to spend time at her Mineral Wells, Texas, home in early 2004.

The rundown home that Bob Dow turned into a party house also served as a set for his amateur porn filming sessions. His videos featured underage girls, booze, drugs, and sex parties.

(Courtesy of the author)

This photo of Bob Dow was taken shortly before he was murdered at age 49.

THE SOUTHWESTERN INSTITUTE OF FORENSIC SCIENCES
AT DALLAS

Name Dow, Robert   Case No. JP 1588-04

Age 49   Date 5/6/04

COPY

DALLAS COUNTY
INSTITUTE OF FORENSIC SCIENCES

#2

#1

#3

#4

o = Gunshot
wound
Entrance

This diagram shows the areas of the body where Bob Dow was shot on the night of May 4, 2005.
(Courtesy of the Mineral Wells Police Department)

A - 1 (Rev. 7-84)

The Baker Hotel was an iconic tourist destination in Mineral Wells, Texas, in its heyday. Celebrities and visitors came from around the world to enjoy the "healing water" baths on the top floor. Today, the hotel is rundown and nothing more than a memory of what Mineral Wells once was. *(Courtesy of Gerard Selby)*

Before she became a party girl and realized she was a lesbian, Jennifer Jones was a child trying to find her place in the world. *(Courtesy of Melanie and Robert Brownigg)*

As a teen, Jennifer enjoyed dressing up for Halloween (left) and going on a cruise with her aunt and uncle (right).
(Courtesy of Melanie and Robert Brownigg)

Bobbi Jo Smith says her life was shattered by the sexual abuse she experienced as a child.

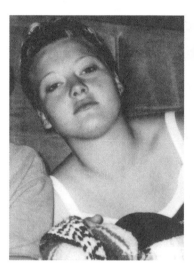

As a youngster Bobbi Jo was a tomboy, growing up with all brothers.

Although she was engaged to a man and became pregnant at sixteen, Bobbi Jo said she hid an attraction to females.

Bobbi Jo's son is the love of her life. The birthdays she celebrated with him are memories she holds closest today.

Today Bobbi Jo dreams of such normal, everyday pleasures as talking to friends on the phone and laughing.

Jennifer had never been involved with a female before meeting Bobbi Jo Smith and becoming obsessed with her.

When detectives searched Bob Dow's computer, they found a variety of photos of underage girls in poses that ranged from suggestive to pornographic.

Bobbi Jo loved to take photos of the women she was involved with, like this one of Jennifer.

Bob Dow would get wasted on booze, pills, and weed, then put Bobbi Jo in charge of taking photos and directing his films.

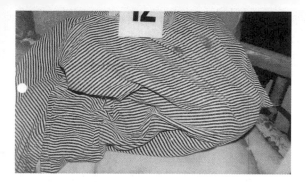

Often mistaken—even by police—for a pillow case, this laundry bag was placed over Bob Dow's head and upper body by his killer before she shot him.
(Courtesy of the Mineral Wells Police Department)

Detective Brian Boetz found Bob Dow's pants and wallet on the floor of the room where he was killed.
(Courtesy of the Mineral Wells Police Department)

This green trunk would become a talking point in the prosecution's case against Bobbi Jo Smith.
(Courtesy of the Mineral Wells Police Department)

Mineral Wells PD Detective Brian Boetz was one of the first investigators on the scene of Bob Dow's murder. *(Courtesy of Gerard Selby)*

After the murder of Bob Dow, Jennifer Jones and Bobbi Jo Smith drove to the Spanish Trace apartment complex, where they picked up a friend, and Jennifer's sister and mother. *(Courtesy of the author)*

It was said that Bobbi Jo tossed the gun that killed Bob Dow out of the window here on the Farm to Market Road (Route 1821 North) after she'd wiped it clean of prints. *(Courtesy of the author)*

After being caught in Blythe, California, at the end of a four-day run across the Southwest with two other women, Bobbi Jo and Jennifer were booked by the Mineral Wells Police Department. *(Courtesy of the Mineral Wells Police Department)*

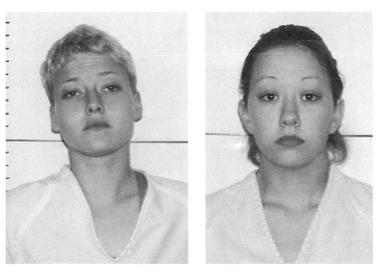

Kathy Jones (top) and Audrey Sawyer (bottom) were questioned on videotape after Bobbi Jo and Jennifer left them in Arizona and took off to California. *(Courtesy of the Mineral Wells Police Department)*

Special Prosecuting Attorney Mike Burns charged Bobbi Jo with murder after Jennifer pled guilty.
(Courtesy of Gerard Selby)

Bobbi Jo's trial was held at the Palo Pinto County Courthouse in Palo Pinto, Texas.
(Courtesy of Gerard Selby)

Bobbi Jo Smith in 2012, standing inside Texas's infamous Gatesville Prison, where she is serving a sentence of 50 years for a crime she claims to have taken no part in.

Police Department, and explained the situation. He said he'd fax them the warrant.

"Well go check it out," the Buckeye cop told him. "Let you know what we find."

What Boetz didn't know, however, was that there was trouble brewing among the four women. There was the chance that the Buckeye PD officers were going to drive out to the Days Inn and find that the seam holding the women together had torn apart.

CHAPTER 27

JERRY JONES WIRED the girls some cash on the evening of May 7, 2004, but it took some time to go through. Bobbi had met a man at the pool who had invited them to stay in his room as long as they needed. As it turned out, the guy, Mike Depardi (pseudonym), was cooking meth inside his room.

Thus, it was time to, once again, *par-tay*!

"When we stopped in Buckeye at the motel," Bobbi Jo told me, "a Mexican man came up to me. He thought I was a dude. He was with his woman. He said nothing about dope. He offered me a beer. Kathy . . . was hounding him about dope. . . ."

The dude was creepy; he was like a character straight out of a Quentin Tarantino film. It all seemed surreal to Bobbi. Audrey later said she wanted no part in partying with this guy and didn't. She admitted drinking and smoking some weed, but meth? Especially being cooked inside a hotel room by some guy nobody knew?

No way. (Incidentally, Bobbi Jo later vehemently disagreed with Audrey on her recollection.)

Before they hooked up with Mike, Bobbi and Jen were cooking up something of their own: an idea. As they stood outside in the parking lot of the hotel, waiting on Jerry's money to come through, "They was talking," Audrey said, "about getting married."

(There is much dispute regarding who came up with this idea. Audrey first told me it was Jen and Bobbi. Then she changed and said it was Jen and Kathy. Bobbi didn't even recall most of it, better yet dreaming up the idea with Jen. So once again, the truth of how this scene transpired—or if it even happened the way Jen later remembered—remains a mystery.)

The conversation (mostly coming out of Kathy Jones's mouth) was centered on the premise that if Bobbi and Jen got married, they wouldn't be forced to testify against each other. A wife cannot testify against her husband, or vice versa. It worked the same, the girls thought, if a wife testified against her wife.

This was certainly true in the case of Arizona law and a marriage between a man and a woman, Title 13 Criminal Code, section 13-4062, the "anti-marital fact privilege." As the statute reads, however: *A husband [cannot testify] for or against his wife without her consent, nor a wife for or against her husband without his consent, as to events occurring during the marriage, nor can either, during the marriage or afterwards, without consent of the other, be examined as to any communication made by one to the other during the marriage. . . .*

The key phrase is "during the marriage." What happened before and after was fair game. On top of that, you could bet the girls had not Googled the law and were totally oblivious as to what it actually stated. Not to mention that Arizona's Constitution "explicitly" denied the "recognition of same-sex marriage."

Audrey, at first, thought the girls were kidding.

"I'll grab a Bible from one of the rooms," Kathy suggested. "I can be the preacher."

First, the girls "got really, really high" with Mike, Audrey claimed, and then smoked some of the weed they had left over.

"It was my mom's idea," Audrey said, changing her mind. "Bobbi and Jen were talking about getting married and not having to testify against each other, and my mom decided she could marry them right then and there."

"Look," Bobbi said, barely recalling what amounted to a mock wedding, "I was traumatized and coming off (down from) a high I'd been on for almost two and half weeks. I do not recall any of this."

So, according to Kathy and Audrey, they had a wedding ceremony in back of the hotel, in a field, as cars and trucks whizzed by on the nearby freeway. One report claimed Kathy read I Corinthians, 13:4–8:

4. Charity suffereth long, and is kind; charity envieth not; charity vaunteth not itself, is not puffed up,
5. Doth not behave itself unseemly, seeketh not her own, is not easily provoked, thinketh no evil;
6. Rejoiceth not in iniquity, but rejoiceth in the truth;
7. Beareth all things, believeth all things, hopeth all things, endureth all things.
8. Charity never faileth: but whether there be prophecies, they shall fail; whether there be tongues, they shall cease; whether there be knowledge, it shall vanish away.

Whatever the case, the girls gathered some wildflowers from the field and, with cigarettes dangling from their mouths, Bobbi and Jen were "married" by stand-in preacher Kathy Jones. As Audrey recalled the scene, Jen wore a swimsuit and tank top. She was barefoot. Bobbi donned a black hoodie sweatshirt pullover, with the sleeves cut off, and white sweatpants, with black stripes on the sides. Before the ceremony, Audrey recalled, Jen and Bobbi ran over to the truck stop and bought a few penny-candy, gumball-machine rings.

"It was kind of, you know, stupid," Audrey said, thinking back to the moment. "But it was entertaining and they thought it was real."

(Audrey told me she had photos of all this—but she could never produce them.)

The reception was held inside Mike's room: more dope smoking and beer guzzling. After getting a good buzz on, Audrey, Jen, and Bobbi went out and sat by the pool. Kathy stayed in the room with Mike and his girl.

At some point, Bobbi fell down on the ground and had a seizure on the pool deck, twitching and shaking and flopping around.

"Shit, help me here, Audrey," Jen said, jumping up, running over to Bobbi.

Audrey didn't believe Bobbi was for real. She'd had several "seizures" since they had known each other, Audrey recalled, believing the seizures were a way for Bobbi to draw attention to herself.

But Jen obviously thought different.

Jen knelt down next to Bobbi. She stuck her finger in Bobbi's mouth, afraid Bobbi would swallow her tongue and choke to death.

"She's faking that shit," Audrey said, walking over, staring down at the two of them. "She ain't havin' no seizure."

"Help me out here," Jen pled.

Jen finally got Bobbi calmed down. Then she went inside the room to get Bobbi some water. Now Audrey and Bobbi were alone.

"And she leaned over and she tried to kiss me, and shit," Audrey claimed.

(Bobbi said Audrey was a liar. Bobbi already had Audrey and had dumped her. She didn't want her anymore. And why would she do this at this time? It didn't fit.)

When Jen came back, Audrey said something about Bobbi coming on to her.

Jen snapped, "mouthing off," Audrey remembered. "We got into it something good."

But Jen kept running away, playing ring-around-the-rosy, using the pool as a shield, not allowing Audrey to get to her.

"What the hell you doin' here, Jen?" Audrey yelled across the pool. "All this—it's crazy."

"Shut up, bitch."

Audrey gave up.

Kathy came out.

"Let's go to that truck stop over there, Ma," Audrey said. "Leave these two here."

Bobbi's seizures began in her early teens, she explained. It started after suffering a concussion. They are documented. Bobbi had no idea what a seizure actually was, when she first started having them. Today, however, Bobbi is forced to take seizure medication.

"At first, I didn't even know what was going on," Bobbi explained. "I'd wake up unable to move— piss all over me."

As for that faked seizure by the pool, Bobbi said: "I *never* had a seizure during the *entire* time we were running. . . . And just a little insight? Every single one of them (Audrey, Kathy, and Jennifer) are dopeheads. . . . They lie."

The plan Audrey and Kathy had come up with after leaving the hotel was for Kathy to try and finagle money out of a truck driver, so they could get back home. Audrey didn't want to continue onto the next stop. The road trip, apparently, was over.

"Me and my mom planned to grab Jennifer when Jerry showed up and take her back home with us," Audrey recalled. "We was gonna leave Bobbi there, but we didn't want to tell Jennifer what we were doing. We wanted to take Jennifer back to find out what was going on. We knew Jerry was talking to the cops. It was sort of a plan to get Jennifer in to speak with the cops. We knew that the cops knew where we were. Jerry told us, 'The cops said to come in and we can talk about it. If it was self-defense, fine . . . but with y'all running, they say it makes her look more guilty.'"

So Kathy and Audrey headed over to the truck stop, and Bobbi and Jen went back to the hotel room.

CHAPTER 28

BOBBI WAS ANXIOUS. Stewing might be a better way to describe Bobbi's demeanor at this time. She was scared. Bobbi believed Kathy and Audrey were going to pin the murder on her; they had some sort of plan to set her up to take the fall for Jen. After spending a few minutes inside the hotel room, Bobbi took Jen and went back to sit poolside. Jen tried to calm Bobbi down.

Bobbi paced.

Jen suggested they go for a swim and wait it out.

"Where'd they go?" Bobbi asked. She was looking around the parking lot of the hotel, bugging out a little. Kathy and Audrey had been gone for a while. Bobbi was concerned.

"They'll be back," Jen said. "Come in the water."

"They been gone a long time."

"It's okay," Jen tried explaining. She got out of the pool.

Bobbi was concerned that Audrey and Kathy

had run off to the cops to give her up. Thinking back, Bobbi wondered how her life had come to this—another mess she was trying to find her way out of. There was a time, not long ago, when Bobbi had wanted to die. She had separated from her son's father and, she told me, "I became more strung out on drugs and went into a depression." Not seeing her child, she felt her life had become nothing but a twisted clutter of addictions and let-downs, before she was even old enough to vote. "I could not care for my son. . . ." To Bobbi, neglecting her child was the final blow, the one that hurt the most. Not being able to be a mother, Bobbi "took over one hundred eighty Xanax and went to sleep." She thought that would do it. Put a peaceful bow on it all. Wipe away the pain.

But it didn't.

"I woke up in the hospital. I hated myself. I was just like my mother." It was not long after, Bobbi said, when "Robert [Dow] offered me a job working with him." What seemed like a lifeline, a rope tossed down into the well, became another obstacle to overcome. "Bob only pulled me farther down."

Still standing poolside, Bobbi said to Jen, "They've been gone over an hour."

"Let's go look for them," Jen suggested.

Bobbi and Jen went back to the room and cleaned up. Then they hopped into Bob's truck and drove to that nearby truck stop. As Bobbi slowly drove around the parking lot, both she and Jen looking in all directions, Bobbi saw Kathy talking to a man.

There was a cop car parked in the lot, not too far away from where Kathy stood and leaned into the window of a truck. Audrey was close by, nervously smoking a cigarette.

Bobbi and Jen drove back to the hotel. Bobbi got Kathy's and Audrey's stuff together, asked Jen to pack up their belongings, and then packed everything into the truck.

"Over there," Jen said.

"What?"

Jen motioned for Bobbi to put Kathy's and Audrey's possessions by a telephone pole, out in the open, so they'd see it.

Bobbi and Jen then hopped on the highway, putting Buckeye, Arizona, along with Audrey and Kathy, in their rearview mirror.

"We thought [Kathy] and Audrey were talking to the cops, so we dropped off their clothes . . . [and] we drove west," Jen later said in court.

CHAPTER 29

DETECTIVE BRIAN BOETZ WOULDN'T allow Jerry Jones to drive to Arizona and pick up the girls.

"I didn't know what would happen if he went," Boetz recalled. "So that's why we called on the local authorities in Arizona."

Audrey and Kathy didn't have any luck convincing a trucker to give them enough cash to get back home. Frustrated, they walked back to the hotel.

As soon as they entered the room, however, they realized something was up.

Kathy ran out into the parking lot to check on Bob's truck.

"Shit . . . they're gone," Kathy said after returning to the room.

"What? The truck's gone?"

"Yup."

"All of our shit was in that truck."

They walked out of the room and soon found

their belongings by that telephone pole, Audrey said. Then they went back to the hotel room and waited.

"What now?" Audrey asked.

Kathy suggested they hook up with Mike. When they got over to his room, Audrey admitted, "he was cooking some more meth, so we ended up smoking it with him."

After getting high, Audrey went out by the swimming pool and sat down. Before long, she went back to the hotel room. As they fired up the tinfoil for a second time, Audrey explained, heating up the meth to inhale the smoke, Mike's hotel room phone rang.

"Yeah?" Mike asked. He listened; then he put his hand over the receiver. "They's asking if anyone in here is from Texas, and if so, they want y'all to step out of the room."

Kathy and Audrey looked at each other.

Mike spoke again: "The cops are here."

After about five minutes, contemplating what they should do next, Mike walked out of the room with his hands up.

Audrey and Kathy had no choice, really. What could they do? So Audrey walked out five minutes later and Kathy followed right after.

"The place was swarmed with cops," Audrey remembered. "There were guns pointed on us."

Buckeye PD officers grabbed Kathy and Audrey. "Get up against that wall there. . . ." They were held, according to Audrey, at gunpoint.

Several officers went into the room, guns drawn, in search of Bobbi and Jen.

"Where are they?" an officer asked the women. "Where are Bobbi Jo Smith and Jennifer Jones?"

"We don't know. . . . We don't know. . . ."

Mike had a warrant against him, so they busted him and took Audrey and Kathy down to the Buckeye PD.

"They didn't handcuff us or anything," Audrey said. "But they sure wanted statements."

When Boetz finally got hold of the Buckeye PD, somewhere around one in the morning on May 8, checking to see how they had made out at the Days Inn, he got a surprise.

"We have Kathy Jones and Audrey Sawyer. But the two other females, Jennifer and Bobbi, they ain't here. They left the area before we got up there."

Kathy wore a dark-colored tank top, jeans, no shoes, just socks. At times, she sat with her legs crossed and her head down. She was placed inside a small Buckeye PD interrogation room. Kathy appeared nervous and fidgety; her legs were shaking, her arms waving in all directions. It was near 4:00 A.M. when they began. Kathy had been up all night, yet she seemed wide-awake.

"You understand you're not a suspect," the detective explained. A second cop, a female, sat directly across from Kathy and stared at her the entire time, not saying a word, and barely moving. "I'm here interviewing you for the Texas police there—"

"Yeah, yeah," Kathy interrupted.

After she signed a waiver, which allowed Kathy the right to speak without an attorney, Kathy told her story of what had happened. It took Jen's mother some time to find her bearings, and she really never did. As she spoke, Kathy Jones's narrative was all over the place.

When she got around to talking about Bob Dow, Kathy said, "He was whacked-out. He was always taking pictures and stuff. . . . He had a lot of guns. We was always taking pictures with the guns, you know, fooling around and stuff. But Bobbi Jo, she . . . she . . . she was like fascinated with the guns."

Kathy explained how the girls had barged into Jerry's Spanish Trace apartment and said (together), "We killed Bob." Then, as she talked through the story in more detail, Kathy explained that it was actually Jen who said, "'Momma, I killed Bob.' And I said to her, 'What do you mean, *you* killed Bob?' And she said, 'I shot him.'"

"Who said this?" the detective asked, stopping Kathy there.

"My daughter Jennifer."

From there, Kathy then related what was to become a familiar tale—at least for the time being. "I asked her why she shot Bob and she told me, 'He tried to rape me, Momma.'"

Kathy had a rough go with times, dates, days, who was driving, who did what, when, and where. She recalled the major events with ease, but the smaller details troubled her. Kathy couldn't remember, for example, which day the girls had come by Spanish Trace. It took her some time to try to pin the day down, and she never really could.

When Kathy described the gun being tossed out the window, she said, "Jennifer reached back and grabbed a blanket and unfolded it and there was the gun." Interestingly, she then added, without hesitation, as if certain: "It was a revolver, a twenty-two." But then, rethinking that statement, she abruptly changed her mind. "It looked like, I mean. To me, it did . . . I don't know that much about guns, you know."

"What color was it?"

"It was black."

"It had a big, long barrel, or one of those short ones?" the detective asked, using his hands to establish the size, as if describing a fish he had caught.

"It was long," Kathy explained.

"Really?"

As they talked, Kathy bounced around. "I kept looking over at Jennifer and asking, 'How does it feel?' And she said, 'What, Momma?' And I said, 'To kill someone?' And, you know, she said, 'It feels real good. . . .'" But then, after realizing what she had said, and that perhaps she was burying her daughter, Kathy tried to put the statement into context, adding, "I mean, I *think* she was showing off for Bobbi Jo. . . ."

At one point, in a muddle of blurred speech,

Kathy speedily told the detective, "Bob's mother, she was . . . she was done dead three days in the house before Bob was killed. . . . He really didn't care about her. I was over there and walking to the bathroom one day and . . . I . . . I knew I done smelled something. . . . It was coming from that room. . . . I could hear Bob go in the room and ask her if she wanted something to eat, 'Are you okay?' . . . but she never said anything. I mean, this is really weird. I mean . . ."

"Wow," the detective replied as Kathy continued. It was clear Kathy had no idea that Bob's mother had been found alive.

Kathy talked her way through, trying to recall where the gun was tossed. At one point, the second officer in the room asked, "Is that Mineral Wells you're talking about?"

"'Miserable Wells,'" Kathy responded, wiping away tears, chuckling at her little joke. "That's what we call it. 'Miserable Wells, Texas.'"

The lead detective asking the questions had to leave the room for a moment to take a phone call. With him gone, Kathy spoke to the female. Most of what she said was a jumble of words. It was clear Kathy was coming down from whatever bender she had been on.

"These girls have got my head so messed up," Kathy said. "I still can't believe Jennifer shot"—but she stopped herself from finishing that part of her statement—"I think Bobbi Jo did almost talk her into it, like brainwashing her. . . ." Then it sounded

as if Kathy said, "My ex-husband told me that the
police in Mineral Wells told him they got proof
that Bobbi Jo did it . . . that Bob was touching on
Jennifer and she (Bobbi) went off. . . ."

Kathy was cut loose after a few more inconsequential questions. Then they brought Audrey in.

Audrey wore a lime green T-shirt, blue jeans,
and flip-flops. Her hair was pulled back, tied in a
bun. Oddly enough, she seemed in good spirits,
actually laughing and joking around with the detective as they got settled.

As the interview began, there was an obvious
agenda on law enforcement's part. The detective
asked immediately, "One of the main questions I
need to know is, how long have you known
Bobbi Jo?"

Barely audible, Audrey said, "A few months."

It became clear that Audrey and the detective
had started the interview earlier; but for some
reason they had stopped and were now continuing
on videotape. After that initial question, Audrey
described how the girls showed up at the apartment. Her take was that Jen and Bobbi, "crying,"
rushed in saying, "We killed Bob." Then, "When
we got to Bobbi's grandmother's house, she
(Bobbi) had told her (Bobbi's grandma) that *she*
had killed him, while they had been telling us that
Jennifer had killed him."

Audrey spoke fast. She said Jen told her that

after she and Bobbi were released from jail on a shoplifting charge, they went over to Bob's house and "he wanted them out . . . but he needed to have something in return, so he wanted Jen [as payment]. Bobbi didn't want her to, so they just got drunk and high, whatever, and Bob tried to rape Jennifer, pulling off her clothes and stuff . . . and Bobbi Jo came in and pushed Bob away. So Bob then told them to get all their stuff and leave. So they went to Graford. The next day, they come in . . . went in Bob's house . . . and Bobbi Jo was telling Jennifer 'put a pillow over the gun so nobody can hear it.' 'Cause he was trying to rape her and they was trying to get back at him. And Bobbi Jo told Jennifer to go in there and try to seduce him, or whatever . . . so Jennifer went in there. Bob was naked. She was sitting on top of him. She told him, 'Cover your face with a pillow so I can imagine that you're Bobbi Jo.' He grabbed a pillow, put it over his head. She grabbed the gun off the nightstand and shot him the first time underneath the pillow . . . and Bobbi Jo heard it—she was, like, waiting outside [the room]—and she walked in and then Jennifer just unloaded the gun. . . . And Bob was shaking, he was not dead . . . and so Jennifer started choking him. Then they stole his money and his weed . . . and they left, and that's when they came to our house."

"What would provoke your sister to do something like this?" the detective wondered.

"I don't know. . . . I still can't believe she done it. I can't picture her doin' it. Even though I know that she done it. That's why I was thinking at first that it was Bobbi Jo and Jennifer was trying to take it up for her—until Jennifer started talking today."

"Why?"

"Oh, the way that she (Jennifer) was talkin', I *know* she did it."

"I bet especially when she started talking about choking this guy (Bob Dow) to death—wow!"

"Yeah, she choked me today when we got into a fight."

"Oh, you guys got into a fight?"

"Yeah . . . ," Audrey said, explaining how it started with Jen saying she believed Audrey and Kathy were going to turn them all in. "And I pushed her," Audrey said after describing how *she* had taken all of her belongings out of the truck and was going leave the group. "And she pushed me right away. And then we started fighting. And then she grabbed me by the neck right here"—Audrey put her hand up to her neck to show how Jen had put her hand on her trachea and squeezed—"she said, 'I killed somebody before. . . .'" Audrey had a hard time breathing, she explained, as though Jen knew exactly what she was doing.

"Bobbi Jo and my mom had to break us up. . . . After she did that to me, I know, you know . . . she's always had this in her. She was always so evil.

I walked in the door one time and she had my sister Stephanie with a choke hold up against the wall—this was about three or four years ago. . . . And she's always had anger built up inside of her and she has said she always wanted to do this (kill somebody)."

Nowhere in that statement did Audrey mention anything about Bobbi having a seizure or Bobbi coming on to her. The way Audrey made it sound, Jen had had a death wish since a young age, a strong desire to take a life, and anybody who might get in the way of that was going to experience her wrath.

The statements that Kathy and Audrey gave somewhat explained what went on during the road trip. Neither woman had offered the MWPD anything more than they already had—which, in the totality of the crime, was effectively nothing more than a number of statements that caused more confusion than anything else. These were contradictory statements, extremely inconsistent. Both Bobbi and Jen seemed to be taking the blame at various times.

After giving statements, Kathy and Audrey were dropped off back at the Days Inn, where they waited for Jerry Jones, who had gotten the go-ahead from Brian Boetz to pick up the women and drive them back home.

CHAPTER 30

THE NEW PLAN was California, the Golden State. The border was about an hour away if they traveled fast. One of the first towns over the border on the 10 is Blythe, which resides in Riverside County. Blythe is located, essentially, just over the Colorado River, where the 10 crosses into the state. It's desert country. You don't want to be around this area in the summer, when the average temperature ranges from about 101 to 110 degrees Fahrenheit. Dry heat or not, those temps will kill you if you're not careful. Moreover, if your vehicle is prone to overheating, Blythe is probably not the best place to be heading.

Bobbi and Jen had nothing: no money, no food, no idea what to do. All they had was a truck running low on petrol—and each other.

Pulling into Blythe on West Hobsonway, the main drag off the 10, the girls looked for a place to park the truck and sleep. It was late. Out here, the sky turns as black as tar when the sun goes down, and the stars shine like silver rocks on the bottom of a riverbed.

Bobbi was beginning to feel the effects of the trip and what she had gotten herself mixed up in. Why in the world, Bobbi considered, would she cover for a girl she knew only twenty-seven days, a little over three weeks? Did she really want to get involved in some sort of shoot-out with police over a crime she'd had nothing to do with? And Bob—although Bobbi knew the guy was no good for her and was not the most stand-up citizen—"a perv," on top of it all—a guy who exploited females at the expense of Bobbi bringing them over . . . still, in no way, did Bobbi want to see him dead.

"As I began to come out of a fog, I realized Bob was dead and that Jennifer had killed him."

It was a surreal thought.

Jen was driving this time. And, according to the story she told in *Texas Monthly,* her legs were all burned up from sitting in the truck—the sun beating down on her bare skin all that day as they drove from the Days Inn to California.

When they crossed the border, Jen claimed, she turned to Bobbi and said, "We can't run forever."

And so they found a place to park for the night.

Jen also told the magazine that she was disappointed there was no roadblock along the California border, along with troops of cops waiting

for them. It had felt kind of glamorous being on
the run with Bobbi, Jen thought. Likewise, there
had been nothing in the newspapers or on the
radio/television about Bob's murder. Jen had
expected the idea of two "killers," armed and dangerous and on the run, to be a national story. She
said she had been looking at newspapers, hoping
to see something about the crime, but she never
did. As it happened, Jen realized they weren't
going to be famous. They wouldn't be doing any
televised perp walk on CNN, or sitting down with
Anderson Cooper or *Dateline* in the coming
months. They were two girls, broke and tired—
and out of fuel and fervor—pulling into the back
parking lot of a pool hall in Blythe, California, feeling the entire episode now grating on their fragile
psyches.

It was over.

The way Jen told it, after parking the truck near
a field somewhere near the pool hall, she spread
out a blanket on the ground as if they were at the
beach. Then she invited Bobbi to lie down next
to her.

"Let's look at the stars."

As they lay on their backs, staring up into the
night, Jen claimed (in what sounded more like
that fairy-tale fantasy she had dreamed up), she
said they listened to the song "I Cross My Heart"
by country crooner George Strait.

"You want to dance?" Jen said she asked Bobbi.
They "wrapped their arms" around each other

and "slow-danced" to George Strait, reported *Texas Monthly*.

With the night came that cool desert air, crisp, dry, and chilly. Jen was getting cold.

"Let's get back in the truck," Jen suggested.

("Wow," Bobbi said when I confronted her with this story. "Jennifer really thinks this is all a joke, a game, a movie. When is she going to realize it's *not* a fantasy—we are *really* in prison." That entire story—lying under the stars and cuddling up to one another—was nothing more than a carefully constructed fantastical lie on Jen's part, Bobbi said. "Jennifer was asleep in the truck [mostly]. There was no dance. No music. Geez.")

With the blanket over them, Bobbi and Jen cuddled in the front seat for a time. Then, at some point, Bobbi decided she needed to call her grandmother. There was a pay phone out in front of the building they were parked behind. Bobbi could call collect.

This would be an odd choice, if Bobbi's plan was to get away and escape the iron fist of the law (as Jen repeatedly had stated later). Calling home would most certainly put their location at risk. And yet, this scenario aligned more with what Bobbi later told me: "I was tired of running."

Before calling Dorothy, Bobbi called her mother, Tamey Hurley. The last time they spoke in person, Bobbi and Jen were at Dorothy's. Tamey had dropped them off.

"I love you, Mom," Bobbi had said that day before Tamey drove away.

"I love you, too, baby," Tamey responded. "Y'all stay out of trouble now, you hear me."

Bobbi and Tamey were trying to make up for lost time. Forget about the past. Forgive and move on.

"Hey, Mamma," Bobbi said on that night she gave up and wanted to return home. Tamey knew her daughter. Bobbi sounded different from the previous day and night, after calling and whispering into the phone how terrified she was of Kathy.

"Bobbi, you need to tell me what's going on."

"I'm scared, Mamma." Bobbi was crying. "I need you to come and get me so I can turn myself in."

"Tell me where you're at."

Bobbi explained.

Tamey had been told earlier that night from a family friend (a Texas Ranger, in fact) that there was a warrant out for Bobbi and Jen. "He told me it was a 'shoot to kill' warrant," Tamey stated. (I never saw it.)

As Bobbi and Tamey talked, Bobbi became so overcome with emotion that she couldn't speak. The gravity of the situation was pulling Bobbi down. She wanted out.

"Let me talk to Jennifer," Tamey said.

Bobbi handed off the phone.

"Yeah?"

"Jennifer, now listen to me. You need to tell me what in the name of hell is going on here. I need the truth. Did Bobbi pull the trigger—did she kill Bob?"

"No, Tamey. She wasn't even there. I did it. I tell you that. Bobbi wasn't there. She's saying she wants to take the blame because she doesn't want me to get in trouble."

After they got off the phone, Bobbi collected herself.

"I'm calling my grandma," Bobbi told Jen.

Jen stood beside Bobbi as Bobbi spoke: "We're tired of running, Grandma. We just want to come home."

Dorothy asked Bobbi where they were.

Bobbi told her. Then: "You need to call the cops. . . . [Bob] is dead and his mother is in the next room, all alone, bedridden. . . ."

At this point, Bobbi explained to me, she was concerned about Lila and what happened back in Mineral Wells. "I am sure my grandmother flipped," Bobbi said. "We've never had to face any situation like this. She told my uncle Rick to call the cops, because she was in disbelief. I didn't want Bob's mother to die in there. I knew she would, because no one ever knew she was in there—nor did I think anyone knew [Bob] was dead."

According to Jen, it was Richard and Kathy Cruz whom Bobbi called, not Dorothy Smith, Bobbi's grandmother. Yet, it was Bobbi's grandmother, Dorothy Smith, who called the MWPD that night and reported that she had heard from the girls. Richard Cruz never mentioned that Bobbi had phoned him on that night.

"Jennifer and Bobbi are parked behind a pool hall in Blythe, California, just over the border," Dorothy told the MWPD on the night of May 8, 2004.

Finished with the phone call, Jen and Bobbi went back to the truck and fell asleep.

It was not long after they dozed off that Bobbi awoke to the sound of a radio. Not George Strait this time, singing the blues of love gone wrong, but the static of a Blythe Police Department officer communicating with a colleague.

According to reports of the arrest, there were three Blythe PD officers surrounding the truck, weapons drawn.

If Jen and Bobbi were going to go down in a blaze of gunfire, like two wild chicks out of a Hollywood film, this was their chance. They could jump up and try to run.

Bobbi nudged Jen, whispering, "Hey . . ."

Jen opened her eyes.

The game was over.

PART THREE

◆

SO MANY STORIES

CHAPTER 31

BOBBI JO SMITH AND Jennifer Jones later agreed on a few things that happened in the days leading up to Bob Dow's murder. It could be reckoned that May 1, 2004, was the beginning of the end for Bob Dow. The girls were with Bob at the Ridgmar Mall in Fort Worth that day. Ridgmar is one of those cookie-cutter corporate malls found in every major suburb throughout America: JCPenney, LensCrafters, a super cinema, the pretzel and cookie kiosks, the vendors lined down the center aisle pimping cheap sunglasses and crappy plastic flying helicopters and smelly "handwoven" blankets and second-rate jewelry.

Jen and Bobbi were walking around the mall, holding hands, kissing, laughing, having a pleasant time on May 1, 2004. The day was fairly normal—that is, in the course of their unhealthy, unbalanced, and imminently ruinous relationship. To passersby, they looked like nothing more than two teenagers enjoying their sexuality, sharing a day at the mall together. However, there was some "old" man, flanking them in the background, holding a camera, at times snapping photos like a paparazzo.

"I was enjoying this new chick," Bobbi told me. "It was fun."

Indeed, Bobbi was feeding several addictions all at once.

As the photographs left behind by Bob would later prove, he and the girls enjoyed several of these adventuresome days. According to Special Prosecutor Mike Burns, who would later prosecute Bobbi and Jen, Bob had taken Jen and Bobbi (along with Bobbi and other females Bobbi had brought home to sleep and party with) to Sea-World, Six Flags, Disney, and several other luxurious, touristy destinations. Bob had documented the trips with his camera. Although a large percentage of the hundreds of photographs Bob snapped were pornographic, there were plenty of photographs depicting Bob, Bobbi, and other females out and about, like a father enjoying life with his daughters.

Bobbi had some money on her from birthday gifts, which she'd received a few days before. ("I was birthday shopping for myself," she told me. "I never asked Jennifer to steal anything for me. I had my own money.")

"I want a new wallet," Bobbi proclaimed as they walked around the mall.

"Let's go," Jen said. She pointed to Hot Topic. Bobbi wanted a nice leather model with a chain, a reflection of how she felt during those days: rough, the alpha to the more laid-back, effeminate omega girls she hung with. According to Bobbi, this "thing" with Jen was not a love affair. The relationship was a fling, like scores of others she'd had before and during the time she spent with Jen. Bobbi was not exclusive to anyone. She liked to live her life carefree. She'd hid the lifestyle she had desired for a long time. Once she stepped out from behind that curtain, dating became a free-for-all. Jen was just one more in a long line of girls Bobbi was seeing and sleeping with.

"I wasn't 'in love' with Jennifer," Bobbi later told me. "You must understand. I liked her, but I didn't even *know* her. I was still in love with my son's father. Yes, I had sex with many different women all the time. But Jennifer was involved with someone else herself [while we were hanging out together]. Some dude who sold crack."

A former boyfriend.

It wasn't as though Bobbi didn't know what loving another female was like. Tamey Hurley told me about Bobbi's first relationship, although one might wonder if Bobbi, so young and naïve at the time, saw it as an affair or, like some girls that age, an experimental part of growing up. It happened before Bobbi met the father of her child. Tamey had worked with a young woman and Bobbi started hanging around with the girl. "I thought they were just friends, at first," Tamey remembered. "But she was messing around with Bobbi Jo, and what she did to Bobbi—Bobbi Jo thought she was in love with her. It was one of those things . . . where, I was there, you know, and I saw it. But when you were around them, it didn't seem like anything was going on. It seemed like friendship. Bobbi Jo still loves this girl to this day, deep in her heart, because it was the first person she was really ever *in love* with."

Back at the mall, Bob drifted off somewhere by himself as the girls walked into Hot Topic. Then they all met up inside JCPenney.

"Listen, I'm tired," Bob explained. "I'll meet you outside after you're done."

Bob left the mall and waited inside his truck in the parking lot.

As Bobbi and Jen walked the aisles of JCPenney, Jen spied a watch. Looking in all directions, when she thought the coast was clear, Jen slipped the watch into her purse.

Bobbi didn't realize what Jen had done.

They continued shopping.

When it came time to leave the store, as Jen and Bobbi walked out, two security guards approached.

("All I know," Bobbi told me later, "was people chased me and her out of the mall, some 'undercover cops.'")

"Do you have anything from this store on you?" one of the guards asked the girls. Obviously, they had Jen on video.

Jennifer said no.

Bobbi looked at them, confused. What were they talking about?

"We need you two to come back into the store."

Bobbi and Jen followed the security guards.

Bobbi had purchased several items from the store: a pair of pants and a few other things. The guards asked to see the bag.

"Do you have receipts for all this stuff?"

Bobbi pulled out her receipts. No problem. She could prove she had bought all of the stuff in her bag.

"I tried to plead with them and give them my receipts," Bobbi recalled. But unbeknownst to her, Jen had "placed the [stolen] items in my bag at some point when she went to hold my hand."

"What about this watch?" the guard asked. "There's no match to it on your receipt."

The guards made Jen and Bobbi sit and wait for the cops. This was alarming to Bobbi. "I didn't say anything. I'd *never* even had a traffic ticket before this."

Next thing the girls knew, they were sitting in a cell inside the Tarrant County Jail in downtown Fort Worth on charges of shoplifting items worth more than $50.

CHAPTER 32

JERRY JONES CALLED his sister one day and said he was getting married. The call came as somewhat of a shock to Melanie Brownrigg. The disbelief wasn't that Jerry wanted to get hitched; rather, it was the fact that the wedding was going to be held in just a few days. Jerry's sister was not even aware that her brother had been dating anyone. Now Melanie and her husband were summoned to a wedding?

The Brownriggs knew there had to be a catch.

As they stood in the pews, waiting for Jerry and his bride to walk down the aisle, Melanie and her husband turned to see who the bride was.

"And here comes Kathy," Melanie explained, "pregnant as ever."

The wedding took place on November 11, 1985. Jen was born weeks later in December.

"And," Melanie continued, "it was also a surprise

[to us] that Kathy had two girls (Audrey and Emily)" of her own.

That was how Jen's life began.

Not long after Jerry, Kathy, Jen, Audrey, Stephanie (born after Jen), and Emily became a blended family, Melanie's mother and stepfather pledged some money to help the rather large family get a van so Jerry had the room to tote them around.

"Kathy managed to get that confiscated due to a drug search, and the five-thousand-dollar [pledge] ended up being lost," Melanie explained.

When the girls were little, Jerry went off to work and Kathy was supposed to stay at home. One day, Melanie's sister was doing a drive-by to check up on the kids when she realized Kathy was not around. She found all of the girls home alone. Jen was baking brownies. At the time, she was five years old. The kids had lit the gas stove by themselves.

Kathy Jones's road to parenthood certainly was not paved with Mother of the Year accomplishments and PTA gatherings. When she was on the witness stand during Jen's sentencing hearing, pressed by sets of lawyers, Kathy was the first to admit she was a terrible mother. At one time a beautiful woman, with golden hair and arresting eyes, Kathy struggled as a young mother—not so much with caring for her girls, but caring for herself. Kathy was a tough woman—no one can take that from her. She had escaped death, by most everyone's count, at least four times. She OD'd on pills several times. But when Kathy's life is looked at as a whole, drugs became the focal point. She was in and out of rehab, as well as being a popular guest at the local jail, incarcerated on a bevy of charges ranging from solicitation to drug possession. The kids, as they grew into their teens, ran away and stayed at friends' houses to escape the madness. Melanie Brownrigg and her husband had always been there, as well as Jen's other aunt. As Jen experimented with drugs herself, no doubt mimicking what she saw at home, her siblings often reminded her that she was heading down that path their mother had already taken. She was warned to watch out. It was a road paved with misery and darkness. There was no returning.

"My brother, Jerry, tried his best at being a father," Melanie recalled. "He failed to keep Kathy out of Jennifer's life, which was a big mistake. But I have to say that Jennifer *did* have a chance. She was living with my husband and myself and we were promising her the sun, the moon, and the stars. She just threw it away. Jennifer and Stephanie (Jennifer's younger sister) were major in our lives, starting at about the age of ten and eleven. They spent summers, weekends and vacations with us, and ultimately came to live with us. Stephanie turned out wonderful. Jennifer just liked the 'bad' side better."

During that week before Bob Dow's murder, Kathy and Audrey told me they were trying to get

Jen to leave the party house and move back into
Spanish Trace. Although Kathy and Audrey generally wound up partying with Bob after heading
over, Jen wanted nothing to do with her sister and
mother telling her how to live her life. Jen was obsessed with Bobbi, both Kathy and Audrey told me.
Jen was totally taken in by that lifestyle at Bob
Dow's party house and this new girl she had met
and started sleeping with. Jerry had been putting
pressure on Jen to shape up. Jen balked. She
wanted to do what she wanted to do. Hanging out
at the party house allowed her that freedom.

Codependent might be a better way to describe
what was happening. Jen had found someone who
thought like her, felt like her, "understood" her.
She had discovered a lover who told her everything she wanted to hear and delivered on
promises. Jen had never had that before. The
lovers Jen had in the past—they had always let
her down. They had all wanted something from
her. In Bobbi, Jen found a carefree spirit, loving
and gentle, who also liked to party and have a
good time.

One day, Kathy drove to Bob's unannounced.
She was either in the mood to have another chat
with her daughter about leaving the party house,
was in the mood to party herself, or a combination
of the two.

After walking in, Kathy went directly to the
room where Bob would later be killed in to see if
Jen was asleep, passed out, or hiding.

But Kathy found Bobbi, instead. She was in bed. There was obviously, Kathy could tell, someone else under the covers.

"Tell Jen I want to speak with her," Kathy demanded.

Bobbi didn't answer.

"Jennifer? Jennifer!" Kathy yelled.

Nothing.

The person under the covers moved. So Kathy walked over, figuring Jen was trying to avoid her once again, and pulled off the covers.

Bobbi was naked—and so was the other girl.

Except it wasn't Jen. Bobbi Jo (in keeping with what she later told me numerous times) was having sex with a girl she'd just met.

("I was not exclusive to *anyone*," Bobbi said. "Certainly not Jennifer.")

Plastered all over the room were pictures of Bobbi and Jen, which Jen had put up. There were other photos of Bobbi's son. They were stapled and taped to the walls. Bobbi shared this room— two different beds—with Bob.

Kathy went around the room and tore the photos off the walls. Bobbi felt that Kathy believed she was leading Jen on. Bobbi had just assumed that everyone knew she was a free girl, not exclusive to anyone. When a visitor came over to Bob's and walked into the house, there was an unspoken rule of thumb that it was party city, and that meant the sex, too.

"Stay away from her," Kathy warned Bobbi.

"What the hell are you talking about?" Bobbi said.

Later, Kathy tracked Jen down and explained how she had just caught Bobbi in bed with another woman. To that, Jen responded: "You're lying. I don't believe you."

CHAPTER 33

JEN WAS STIRRING LIKE an agitated parakeet
after she and Bobbi were released from the
downtown Fort Worth Tarrant County Jail on the
morning of May 2, 2004. She'd tried calling her
father, Jerry Jones, to come and get them. According
to Jen, Jerry wasn't home.

Bobbi remembered this moment quite differently, however.

"Her own dad wouldn't come and get her." And
what's more, Bobbi said, Bobbi was released *first*—
that is, *after* Bob Dow bailed her out (but refused
to bail Jennifer out). After that, Bobbi used her
own money to pay Jen's bail. (I asked the MWPD
if they had ever asked for or received a bail receipt
to prove or disprove Bobbi's statement. They answered my question with, "We believe Bob Dow
bailed the girls out." But I never saw a receipt.)

The way Jen explained it in court, she and
Bobbi got out of jail that morning and were hang-

ing around the street near the jail afterward with
no ride back to Mineral Wells (the party house) or
Graford (Bobbi's grandmother's house), the two
places they had been frequenting in those days.

"What are we going to do?" Jen asked. The way
Jen framed this scene, she pushed the notion that
Bobbi had become like a mother to her by this
point. When in doubt, go to Bobbi—she'll know.
There's no doubt Jen liked this aspect of her relationship with Bobbi. Finally there was someone
more mature to take care of her needs and tell her
what to do.

Yet, if this was true, it was all in Jen's head. To
Bobbi, they were party girls. If Jen followed Bobbi,
it was Jen's decision—and hers alone. Bobbi was
upset that she'd been busted for something Jen
had done.

There was a woman they had spent the night
with in the same cell who had also been released.
Jen recalled that Bobbi went to the woman and
asked for a ride. The woman had said something
about her husband coming to pick her up.

"Where you two going?" the woman asked.

"Anywhere you're going," Bobbi said.

It wasn't far. The woman's husband dropped
them off in Fort Worth, near one of those trashy
downtown fantasy shops that sold bongs and
dildos and cheap lingerie.

From there, Bobbi and Jen started walking. Then
Bobbi called Bob. He wasn't answering his cell.

So Bobbi—again, according to Jen's recollection in court—called her mother.

Turned out Bobbi's mother was with Bob Dow.

"Bob has been looking for the two of you all morning," Tamey Hurley told her daughter.

"What?"

"You missed him."

"Missed him?"

"We're going to hop in his truck now and come and get you."

Bobbi explained where they were.

After catching a ride with Bob and Bobbi's mother, Jen and Bobbi headed back to Tamey Hurley's boyfriend's house in Weatherford. Bobbi wanted to see her son, who was at the house with his grandmother.

According to Tamey, as they drove, Bobbi turned to Bob and said, "If it wasn't for you, I wouldn't have nothing. You're my dad. I love you."

"You see, Bob Dow controlled my daughter so many different ways that I had lost reach of her," Tamey recalled for me later. "It was that bond between them of her having a father. . . . Even if it wasn't the 'right way,' Bob was the closest thing she'd *ever* had to a dad."

Bob pulled into the driveway and they all went inside.

Tamey Hurley explained that while Bob, Bobbi, Jen and one of Bobbi Jo's brothers (who was there when they arrived) were inside her boyfriend's house, Tamey's boyfriend pulled her aside.

"Look, I want him out of here," Tamey's boy-friend said, meaning Bob. He said he didn't trust him. "I don't like how he looks."

Sketchy-looking Bob could have that effect on people.

"Bob," Tamey said a moment later, "look, y'all are gonna have to wait outside in your truck. You can't stay in here."

Bob left the house and sat in his truck.

Then Tamey's boyfriend said he didn't want Jen there, either.

"My boyfriend had heard bad things about Jen-nifer and her mother," Tamey later said, "and didn't want any trouble. So he asked me to tell Jennifer to leave, too."

"I'll be out in a minute," Bobbi said to Jen, who then walked outside and waited with Bob inside the truck.

The way Jen recalled this scene in her state-ments to police later on, it went like this: While she sat alone with Bob Dow inside his truck, Bob said, "Y'all cost me my party money for the weekend. You know that?"

Jen looked at him. She knew the tone. She was disgusted enough with herself for getting pinched stealing and spending the night in the clinker. She didn't need Bob and his perverted antics now. And she never went into detail how, but she claimed that Bob Dow was the one who put up the $100 bail money she needed to bond herself out of jail.

"Sorry" wasn't going to cut it with Bob, Jen later testified. By now, Jen knew Bob enough to understand what he wanted. He'd been bugging her to have sex with him, she claimed, since that first time she'd shown up at the party house.

"I know," Jen said. She realized she owed him. She didn't need to be reminded of it.

"You need to pay me back," Jen claimed Bob insisted.

"Yeah, Bob. . . ."

"I need that money back."

"I know . . . I know," Jen said louder. "Look, I'll get a job. I'll ask my dad for the money. I'll do whatever. But I'll *get* you that money back."

"Well, I know a way you can pay me back."

"No, Bob. No way."

"Just have sex with me," Bob suggested.

"No. No way, Bob." Jen opened the door. "No!" she said, slamming it shut.

Exiting the truck, Jen walked back toward the house.

"He tried to rape me," Jen said after walking into the home.

"What?" Bobbi asked.

Tamey shook her head. She couldn't believe it.

Bob sat in his truck, looking on as Bobbi and her mother came outside. He could easily tell that Bobbi and Tamey were furious with him. At this moment, Bobbi and Tamey believed Bob had attacked Jen.

Tamey walked over to Bob as Jen and Bobbi stayed behind.

"You need to get the hell off my boyfriend's property," Tamey shouted. "I don't ever want to see you around my daughter again."

"I'm sorry," Bob said.

"I should have called the cops, right then and there," Tamey told me later. "I wanted to, but Bobbi Jo told me not to."

So Bob left.

Tamey walked back to the house. Bobbi was upset. "She was crying," Tamey said of her daughter's demeanor right then. "And they was both screaming at Bob as he drove away."

Tamey confirmed that this was the impetus for Bobbi to want to get "some of the things Bob had given her" and the rest of her belongings and move out of Bob Dow's party house. It was one thing to ply the girls with booze and dope and then convince them to get in front of the camera or have sex. It was quite another to begin making demands and barter for sexual favors.

Tamey said, "Bob Dow was an evil, evil man."

When Bob first took Bobbi under his wing and started hanging out with her every day, working with her, drinking and drugging with her, Tamey went over to see him.

"Why in the hell are you hangin' around with my daughter?" Tamey asked.

"I'm just helping her and [my stepson]," Bob
said.

This was around the time Bobbi and the father
of her child were living together, and things were
spiraling out of control. When Bobbi moved in
with Bob over at Lila's house after breaking up
with her baby's daddy, Tamey went over to check
on things.

"I went into the room to check on Bob's
mother. Bob wasn't there. And something just
wasn't right. It was—that room and the conditions
she lived under—just horrid," Tamey said.

Tamey cleaned the old woman up and fed her.
Bobbi told Tamey on that day that Bob expected
her to take care of Lila, and Bobbi did the best she
could. Crying, Bobbi added, "I don't know how
to care for an elderly lady." She was flustered. She
felt terrible for the old woman. She'd gotten to
know Lila fairly well over the course of time and
cared deeply for her.

"There was a lot of times that I later found out
that Bob would get Bobbi really drunk, where she
done passed out, and then he would shoot Bobbi
Jo up with drugs and then he would do stuff to
her," Tamey explained through tears. "I don't
know how to explain it, really."

Bobbi, her mother, Bobbi's brother, and Jen
stayed at the house for a while after Bob had

allegedly made that pass (for which only Jen was a witness), and then they all left together. Bobbi didn't seem too upset any longer about Bob demanding sex from Jen. It was over. She'd decided, after some prodding by her mother, to get her things and get out of Bob's. Bobbi could continue living with her grandmother.

"I cannot believe he did that again," Jen claimed Bobbi said as they drove away from Tamey's boyfriend's house.

It had become so routine by then for Bob to ask Jen for sex, or for him to put the moves on her, it didn't seem all that out of place to Bobbi. Bob was just, well, being Bob Dow—a pervert. Bobbi knew his ways. Sure, he'd taken it a step further here, apparently, but Bob was like that: a sex-crazed, creepy dude who thought he could convince any girl to sleep with him.

Apparently, for Jen, though, this was her breaking point. It was time to act on that desire Audrey claimed her sister had had for years: to kill someone.

Jen later said (in one of her five versions) that she and Bobbi decided then and there that they weren't taking it anymore. Bob had to go. "He's never going to leave me alone," Jen told Bobbi. On top of that, he was coming between them. He would never stop.

And here, in the following statement, is the only

available evidence Jennifer Jones later offered as the motivation for Bobbi putting her up to murdering Bob.

"Take us to Bob's so we can pack our stuff and get out of there," Bobbi told her brother. They were on their way to Graford, Bobbi's grandmother's house. Bobbi had stayed there once in a while when she wasn't sleeping at Bob's trailer or at the party house. Jen could stay with her until she found her own place.

Bob owed Bobbi some money for work she'd done. That lifestyle over there was getting old, anyway, Bobbi considered. It was time to end it. Plus, she wanted to start spending more time with her son. Get her act together maybe. Clean up.

Bob wasn't home.

"Wait here," Jen said. She smiled.

Bobbi, Tamey, and Bobbi's brother waited in front of the house.

"I thought she had a key, or something," Tamey recalled. The way Jen had made it sound was that she would have no problem getting into the house.

The house was locked. Bob Dow never allowed Bobbi or Jen to have a key to his mother's house. So Jen walked around to the backyard.

Soon everyone out front heard a loud, crashing sound.

"What the hell?" Bobbi said, shocked by the noise.

Moments later, the front door popped open.

It was Jen. She stood inside the party house, beckoning them to come in.

"What happened?" Tamey asked after walking in. "I heard a loud noise."

Jen explained how she picked up a garden hose and smashed one of the back windowpanes in the door so she could reach in and unlock it.

Bobbi and Jen went around the house and grabbed all of their things.

"I had a backpack full of clothes," Jen recalled in court. "Some pictures . . ."

According to Jen, she went into Bob's bedroom and found Bobbi there. There was a green foot-locker on the floor. Bobbi popped it open and found several guns Bob had stowed away in the chest. Bobbi never said why she was taking the guns, and they never discussed it, according to one of Jen's statements. Bobbi simply walked over and grabbed as many weapons as she could find.

"Maybe three or four," Jen testified.

From there, they locked the house and continued on to Graford.

Bobbi's mother and brother dropped the girls off and left. Jen and Bobbi were the only ones in the house. Her grandmother was gone.

"We should take her truck and go find Bob," Jen claimed Bobbi suggested. Bobbi put the guns away in her room at her grandmother's house. "I want my last paycheck."

Bob Dow owed Bobbi about $150 for some work she had done on an apartment building the previous week.

"You know," Jen said, "I can probably talk my dad into us living at Spanish Trace with him and Audrey."

"That's fine," Bobbi said (according to Jennifer's version).

Yet, Bobbi had a place to stay. "I didn't need to move into that apartment."

As they discussed the best way to approach Bob, Jen first told police, the idea to kill him came up. According to Jen, as they talked at Bobbi's grandmother's house that day, Bobbi supposedly said, "He needs to be killed. We need to kill him."

Jen asked why.

"I'm tired of the abuse. *Tired* of it. I'm tired of him harassing you. This is the only way that we can be together." (Jennifer later said, "It was the sexual abuse of having to pay him to stay there at the house—of him, I guess you could say, borrowing her girlfriends for the night.")

"No, we don't need to kill him," Jen later testified she told Bobbi at the moment Bobbi suggested they kill Bob.

The way Jen told the story (the first time), Bobbi went back into the bedroom she kept at the Graford house, grabbed one of the guns, walked across the hall into her grandfather's bedroom, and started rummaging through his things, in search of bullets.

Jen followed, asking, "What are you doing?"

Bobbi found some ammo.

"You cannot do this," Jen said, believing that Bobbi had made a decision to kill Bob, and there was no turning back. "Bobbi Jo . . . no . . . you *cannot* do this."

It was then and there, Jen claimed (in one version of her story), when Bobbi stopped what she was doing, clicked the chamber of the weapon into place, put a squinted eye on the gun sight, and said, "This is the *only* way we can truly be together."

The way Jen told it, that entire scene sounded as though it came straight out of a film she had just seen.

CHAPTER 34

BOBBI LATER told me, "I was not even *at* Bob's house when Jennifer killed him. I was at the corner store two and a half blocks away. . . ."

The way Bobbi described her version of these events for police, she and Jen got a ride from jail and wound up in Fort Worth on Camp Bowie Avenue, at that head shop, just as Jen had testified. They started walking, same as Jen claimed, toward Weatherford, when Bobbi's mother and Bob Dow showed up. There's some discrepancy here about how they got back to Bobbi's mother's boyfriend's house and who gave them a ride, but they both agreed later that Bob, at some point, made a sexually harassing proposition to Jen, which, in turn, made both girls angry. Not necessarily livid or furious enough for Bobbi to want to go out and grab a weapon and kill the guy, but angry enough, nonetheless, that she felt enough was enough. Bobbi was tired of ripping and running. She needed a break. She wanted to move out of Bob's house, anyway. This was a good reason to push her over the edge and actually do it.

What's important here within this version of the event Bobbi described for me in several letters is the timeline. Jen had the timeline a bit off. In court, Jen didn't account for an entire day. It got lost in her telling of them being bailed out of jail and heading over to Bob's house on the day the murder occurred. The way Bobbi explained it, after they left the jail and made it back to Bob's house, they stayed the night there (in Mineral Wells).

So the next morning, Bobbi wrote, *Bob came and got us—and my mom was with him. He dropped us off at my mom's [boyfriend's house] in Weatherford . . . and Jennifer runs into my mom's house in tears and freaking out. I was puzzled. Bob was leaving. Jennifer claimed he tried to have sex with her. I was in shock. . . . He's a big perv. He'll flirt, but I didn't know what was going on—I wasn't* out *there.*

According to Bobbi, Bob had not been pressuring Jen to sleep with him. Sure, he had asked from time to time, but it wasn't as big a deal as Jen later made it out to be. The idea that Bob was hounding Jen for sex was all part of the ruse, Bobbi explained, the story they made up on the run in order to get Jen out of killing Bob.

From there, Bobbi said, her mother drove them to her grandmother's house. Bobbi had her mom stop at Bob's along the way so Bobbi could pick up her things, including a "set of clothes and my wallet."

Bobbi said the house was open and she went in to get a few things and realized her wallet wasn't there. Bob wasn't home.

Underneath her bed at the party house, Bobbi kept those guns she said (and several others confirmed) had been given to her by Bob. So Bobbi grabbed the weapons, explaining to me: "I was going to have my mother pawn them . . . so I could have some money. She told me, 'Hell no!' The guns were mine, a gift from Bob. . . . After my mom refused, we were dropped at my grandmother's house."

"I wish like hell I had pawned those guns for her," Tamey Hurley explained, confirming this portion of Bobbi's story. "I should have done it." Tamey also said she knew Bob had given her daughter the guns. "Because he told me he did. She needed that money from pawning those guns."

Bobbi and her mother have weathered a fractured, love/hate relationship. ("I don't even know my own mother," Bobbi told me when we first started talking.) Tamey Hurley explained that Bobbi's father ran out on her when she was sixteen and pregnant. She was living in New Mexico at the time. Bobbi's dad? "I think [he] has spoken to her once," Tamey said. "It broke Bobbi's heart," Tamey added, "when Bobbi was old enough to realize that her own father didn't want anything to do with her. And for a good while, after I turned seventeen and had Bobbi Jo, it was just us," Tamey said. "Growing up, Bobbi Jo was quiet, loved sports. . . . She was a tomboy, but then so was I. We were poor."

"I've never known [my father]," Bobbi said. "Never seen his face, except in a photo."

The question people routinely ask, Bobbi said, is one that she cannot answer: Has she always known she was gay?

"No one really knows. I grew up a bit confused. I was attracted to women, but was always told it was wrong. I've never been comfortable with men, because of being molested. My son's father and I were friends, and I began to trust him. But I am not physically attracted to men, like I am to women."

Part of Bobbi's experience as a child centered on spending a lot of time with Tamey's mother and father, Dorothy and Fred Smith. Fred taught Bobbi how to work on cars and take apart motors and put them back together again.

Throughout the years, Tamey had five more kids. "I was young and dumb," Tamey said. "I'm ashamed, really, of how the kids were raised by me. But, you know, you cannot replace the past. You have to deal with it. Bobbi and I were always together when she was young, but then we grew apart because I, well, I had a drug problem. I didn't want to see my daughter around it."

Tamey's problems with drugs, she said, stemmed

from the sexual abuse she sustained as a child by someone close to her.

That dreadful, evil cycle. Bobbi got sucked into its whirlwind.

"When I could, I left," Tamey said. "I guess"—and she paused here, carefully choosing her words through a barrage of tears—"I guess you learn from your mistakes. I cannot ever fix what was done in the past. . . . I thought I was . . . I thought I was . . . doing the right thing for Bobbi [in leaving her] . . . 'cause I loved her so much. I just didn't want her to see me like I was. That was the only way I could heal myself."

In her statement to police (which Bobbi later confessed to me was a mixture of lies and truth to cover the story she and Jen had concocted while on the run), Bobbi recalled going over to Bob's house, Jen breaking in, both taking some of their belongings, and then heading to Graford, where they were dropped off at her grandmother's house. Again, dates line up here with Bobbi's version. She claimed they stayed the night at her grandmother's house, which would have made the date of the confrontation that ended Bob's life May 5.

According to Bobbi, she never stole any weapons while at Bob's (as Jen later claimed). In addition, Bobbi didn't want anything to do with guns at that point, she later insisted. Yes, there are photos of Bobbi squaring off in that traditional gangsta-type pose—the weapon turned sideways, pointed at the camera—along with photos of girls placing the barrels of the guns into their vaginas. Yes, Bobbi wound up with those weapons. But on the day before Bob was murdered, Bobbi and her brother were firing the weapons in the backyard of her grandmother's house and something happened. (Likely, this was the day Jen could have later confused and said she actually saw Bobbi loading the weapon in her grandfather's room.)

"When my brother and I started shooting them [at an old car at the back of my granny's house], they scared my son," Bobbi clarified. Her boy was terrified of the loud, booming noises. His panic, in turn, freaked Bobbi out. She made up her mind that she wanted nothing to do with guns ever again. The reason why she fired them, to begin with, was twofold: for some fun and because her mother had refused to pawn them. Bobbi said she was "checking them so I could sell them to an old-school [gun] dealer, who lived down [the street] from my grandmother's."

Tamey later backed up this claim by Bobbi, adding that Jen had been with them, shooting the guns in the yard on that day, too.

"Jennifer was obsessed with Bobbi Jo," Tamey said. "It was like Jennifer had one leg tied to Bobbi's. . . ."

Why Bobbi changed her story, she said, became a combination of both wanting to defend Jen and stick to the same story Jen was telling at the time, and also being young, stupid, and naïve. Bobbi believed if she and Jen lied about what happened, they would *both* get out of it and face no trouble with the law.

"I never wanted to lie," Bobbi said, referring to her explanations of the week leading up to Bob's murder and what happened inside the party house. She was talking about changing her statement and lying to police about how things went down. "I loved [Bob], but I was (in telling those lies) trying to protect Jennifer by telling the same story that she was—until she changed it, and kept changing it. That's why I've remained silent all these years." (Bobbi Jo has never been interviewed about her case before.) "I admitted to having guns because they were *mine*. Bob had given them to me as gifts. As a matter of fact, I had four of them." But after that incident the day before the murder, when Bobbi's son freaked out, Bobbi said, "I gave Jennifer all my guns (after not being able to sell them). Obviously, she kept them. Where she kept [them] or put [them], I don't know."

The point being: Jen had access to the weapons.

Bobbi said she didn't care "how much [Bob] loved sex and women." That wasn't what mattered to her when she thought back on those years with Bob and what ultimately happened. Not even the abuse she claimed to have suffered under Bob's hand made a difference with regard to how she felt about him.

"It still does *not* justify him to be murdered," Bobbi said.

The reality of the situation was "the only people who know what happened on that day is [Bob] and Jennifer—however, she and I both know the truth . . . ," Bobbi added.

And with that being said, Bobbi concluded, "It's time for it to be told."

CHAPTER 35

BOBBI AND JEN hopped inside Bobbi's grandmother's truck and took off to go find Bob (according to Jen's first statement to police). Bobbi was looking for her last paycheck of $150. As they drove toward Lila's Mineral Wells house on May 5, 2004, Jen claimed, Bobbi suggested Jen kill Bob. (Yet, this revelation from Jen does not come until later, in court, at a hearing, when Jen is facing sentencing for her crime—Jen never gave this information to the police.) They had a gun. It was loaded. As Bobbi drove, Bobbi brandished the weapon, Jen claimed. Made sure no one was around. Then Bobbi fired two shots into the woods from the window of the truck as they sped down the road. Bobbi wanted to be certain, Jen said, the gun was loaded properly. The way Jen framed this part of the murder narrative made it sound as though they were two wild chicks in love, higher than hosanna, on their way to commit the ultimate act of evil.

In a nervous mishmash of words, Jen later spoke to the court deciding her ultimate fate (she had pled guilty already), explaining part of Bobbi's alleged strategy behind having Bob killed: "That I was—that I was going to . . . to give in to the . . . to the sexual favors for him—and that during that time, I was . . . I was going to kill him."

The ruse would be the sex that Bob had asked Jen for earlier inside his truck.

Jen claimed Bobbi outlined the plan in detail as they drove toward Bob's. And while she listened to Bobbi's plan for her to commit murder, Jen supposedly snapped back, "No! It's *not* going to work."

What changed her mind, Jen later said in court, was Bobbi's "continuing of insisting that I *needed* to do it. Just the idea of me and her being apart if . . . if I didn't do this for her."

Here's where Jen's version of a motive falls apart, however. Jen later said under oath that Bobbi never "threatened to leave" her if she *didn't* go through with the murder.

"Not verbally," Jen clarified after being asked to explain how vulnerable she felt while heading toward Bob Dow's on that day. "She [Bobbi] did not say that. But in a sense, she was saying, if I didn't do this for her, then, yes, she would leave me, that there would be no *us*. Because Bob was the one person that was getting in the way of us being together."

One of the problems with this statement is that Jen could not recall Bobbi ever specifically saying, "*You* kill him, or *we're finished*." It was simply a "feeling" Jen got from Bobbi.

Then there's the whole issue of them leaving Bob's with their belongings. They could have easily stayed at Bobbi's grandmother's house. Bobbi had never felt threatened by Bob; and neither had Jen, for that matter. Moreover, did Bobbi really care if she and Jen split up? Bobbi was sleeping with a half-dozen females at the time. There was no ticking clock for them to leave the party house. Bob wanted them to stay, yes. But he never held the tapes over their heads, blackmailing them with releasing them, or giving the girls an ultimatum. Furthermore, whenever Bobbi wanted to get away from Bob in the past, she'd simply head over to her grandmother's and stay a few days. But Bobbi always went back to Bob.

Why?

The drugs.

The booze.

The job.

The girls.

Perhaps Jen was in one of her "reading Bobbi's mind" modes, which she was accustomed to, after getting high? Who knows?

Regardless, what's utterly imperative here became a question Jen could not answer: How

could Bob Dow keep these two girls apart? He
didn't have that much power over them. All they
had to do was leave—which both Jen and Bobbi
agreed later they were in the process of doing on
that day and the day before, anyway. Jen could
always crawl back to her father, Jerry. Killing Bob
for the sake of "being together" made no sense in
the scope of their relationship or their lives.

In any event, Jen and Bobbi later agreed that
when they arrived at the house, Bob was home.
But as they walked up the sidewalk toward the
front door, Jen later said, Bobbi "handed me the
gun and I stuck it in . . . my pants and my back."

(It's important to note here that both Bobbi
and Jen's second statements align with this scene.
They both agreed on this part of the murder narrative at the same time they were asked.)

"Just as we planned to do," Bobbi said. "We had
a story. We were sticking to it."

Throughout that brief period after a decision
had been made to kill Bob, Jen claimed, Bobbi was
"continuing" to say "that he needed to die . . .
just the statements of her saying that that [was]
the *only* way we could be together."

Following Jen's version, Bobbi knocked on the
door.

(Why would Bobbi knock on this door? She
came and went, in and out of the party house, at
will. In Bobbi's second version to police, she

claimed to have waited outside while Jen walked into the house alone.)

Also, according to Jen's version, Bob opened the door. He didn't speak. Instead, he turned and walked back to where he had gotten up from. Bob didn't look so good. A U.S. Navy veteran, having repaired aircraft and aircraft carriers, after being treated recently at the Dallas Veterans Affairs (VA) Medical Center for a reported "leaky" heart valve, Bob had been put on a waiting list for heart surgery. On some days, he looked pasty and moved around lethargically. He didn't have a lot of energy. Add to that all the dope and alcohol the guy consumed, and Bob Dow was probably a good candidate for an early death.

According to Jen, she and Bobbi didn't say much as they walked in.

Bob went back to lying down on the mattress in the living room, saying, "I'm not feeling well."

Jen later claimed Bobbi said, "I need to talk to you, Bob." She stood over the man, looking down at him. Jen stood by her side. All part of a plan they had designed and whipped up before entering the house, Jen claimed.

Bob got up begrudgingly, mumbling something to himself. Then he and Bobbi walked into the back room of the house through the kitchen. Jen stayed behind in the living room.

Then, according to Jen, Bob stopped before exiting the living room, turned around, and addressed Jen directly. "Look, I'm sorry for saying that earlier. I really didn't mean it."

So Bobbi and Bob disappeared for a few moments into the back room and then reappeared in the living room. As part of their plan, Bobbi took the truck, Jen said, and drove down to the corner store at that moment.

Jen said she then sat down on a rocking chair in the living room by the front door and Bob sat across from her on a green chair. At some point, she said, Bob walked over and squeezed her leg.

Jen recalled that Bob said, "I cannot believe you told them."

("I had to push my leg down to get him to let go," Jen told police.)

Jen then got up and walked into Bob's bedroom, she explained, "to get my purse."

Bob followed.

("I picked up my purse, turned around—and Bob shoved me on the bed.")

"If you don't [have sex with] me, I am going to kill you," Bob allegedly uttered between clenched teeth.

Jen took off her clothes.

Bob did the same.

"Now you lay there and don't move!" Bob ordered.

"He got on top of me," Jen explained in her first statement to police. "Then he went down to the end of the bed and started kissing my foot, then he moved up and started kissing my leg, and then he got to my private part and started kissing and licking me."

After that, Bob stood. He said, "I want you to play with yourself."

"He then . . . got some lotion off the nightstand and straddled me and started playing with himself," Jen told police. And, almost as an afterthought, Jen then said in her statement that there was loud music playing in the background. So Bob didn't hear the door open when Bobbi returned from the corner store. But when Bobbi walked in and found them, realizing what was going on, Jen first claimed, in a fit of rage, Bobbi snapped and pulled Bob off Jen. A one-hundred-pound female was, apparently, able to grab hold of a two-hundred-pound male and heave him off the bed.

"He slapped her and they were on the floor fighting," Jen first explained to police. "I covered myself up and was trying to figure out how to get out of the room."

Bobbi and Bob got up on their feet. Bobbi pushed him and he landed on the bed.

"I was getting off the bed as Bob was falling on the bed," Jen claimed.

It was then that Jen said she grabbed the weapon (in fear)—which, she first claimed, was on the dresser next to the bed, but then she later changed this to say it was inside a blanket—as Bobbi and Bob continued to fight on top of the bed. At some point, Bobbi grabbed what Jen described as a "pillow" (it was actually a laundry bag) and placed it over Bob's face.

("I leaned over the bed," Jen told police, "and shot Bob twice.")

Bobbi backed away immediately, Jen said in her first version, and yelled, "I cannot believe that you just *did* that!"

(This is inconsistent with Jen's story of Bobbi insisting during the ride over to the house that Jen kill Bob. If Bobbi had designed this plan and provided Jen with the weapon, why would she utter that statement?)

Jen walked around to the other side of the bed and Bob was shaking, trying to raise his arm in a gesture for help, apparently sensing what was coming next.

("I started shooting again," Jen told police.)

Bobbi then grabbed the gun from Jen and screamed, "What are you doing?"

(Again, this would be an odd choice of words *if* Bobbi had been the mastermind behind this crime.)

Jen said she got dressed while "she [Bobbi] got into his pants and got his wallet out and took his money, checked his other pockets and got a . . . a bag of weed out."

"Hurry up and get dressed 'cause we gotta leave!" Bobbi screamed at Jen right then, according to Jen's version.

Jen said she "dropped the gun on the floor" (a gun, she had said, that Bobbi grabbed from her earlier). But as they were shuffling around the room after the murder, looking for things to take, Bobbi walked over to the second bed in the room and took the blanket.

("Bobbi Jo just got it," Jen recalled for police, "and picked up the gun with the blanket.")

"We need to hurry up and get out of here," Bobbi said. She tossed the keys to her grandmother's truck at Jen. "You drive it back to Graford and I'll follow in Bob's truck."

"I need to stop at my dad's house," Jen said she suggested.

CHAPTER 36

YOU'VE JUST READ what was Jennifer Jones's first version of Bob Dow's murder. Jen's *second* version led up to things in the same manner. But then, as Bobbi and Bob walked back into the living room after going off to have that chat by themselves in the kitchen, Jen claimed Bob looked at her and said, "I need to talk with you."

The way she described this scene (that second time), Jen said she knew what Bob meant by "talking." She claimed Bobbi had cut a deal for them to pay Bob back the bail money: Jen would give the man what he had been asking for since laying his eyes on her. The secret end of that deal Bobbi and Jen had discussed, however, according to Jen, was for Jen to whack the poor bastard while he was having sex with his dream girl—a decision, Jen later insisted, Bobbi had talked her into. (Mind you, this was *after* she pled guilty to murder under a deal, thus setting herself up for a lighter sentence.)

"Let's just get it over with," Jen supposedly told Bob. "I'll do it."

In her second statement to police, Jen talked about how they walked into Bob's bedroom. As Bob undressed, Jen took off her pants, underwear, top, and bra. When Bob went to put his pants on the floor, Jen claimed, she slipped the weapon underneath the comforter on the bed for easy access, and so he wouldn't see it. Then, "I laid down on the bed. And . . . and . . . and he went down on me."

While Bob was performing oral sex, Jen said, Bobbi stealthily opened the door to see if their plan had been initiated. And when Bobbi realized Bob was performing cunnilingus on Jen (the plan had been put into action, in other words), Bobbi shut the door gingerly and waited in the living room.

As Bob got busy, Jen called him off, saying, "I want to get on top. I want to switch positions." (One has to wonder about this story. Jen could have shot him right there, while the guy had his head buried in her vagina. Also, would Bobbi need to look in on what was happening to make sure the plan was going forward? It seemed that if Jen's story was true, the fact that she and Bob walked into the bedroom would have been enough.)

Bob wasn't about to disagree, according to Jen. One fact that cannot be disputed: When an out-of-shape, "disgusting" forty-nine-year-old man—a guy who liked to photograph young, naked girls (some of whom were minors) after plying them with drugs and alcohol—was having sex with a hot eighteen-year-old he'd dreamed of bedding down since seeing her for the first time, he probably would have done anything she asked of him.

After Bob allowed Jen to get up, he lay back on the bed.

Then Jen straddled him and started to ride.

After a few moments, Jen said, "I want you to cover your face. I want to make believe you're someone else." (Jennifer never said she was referring to Bobbi, as others—Audrey and Kathy—would later report.)

Bob grabbed a dirty laundry bag on the floor and placed it over his face.

This gave Jen the opportunity to locate the weapon tucked inside the blanket. As she later testified, "I started shooting."

After hitting Bob in the face with several shots, Jen said, she jumped off and began shooting in a wild fashion (which was likely how Bob sustained that wound to his arm). She wasn't aiming. She had little control over the weapon.

As shots rang out, Jen claimed, Bobbi burst into the room. And when she saw that Jen had gone through with their "plan" and was now standing naked, with a smoking firearm in her hand, Jen claimed Bobbi stood there, smiled, and said: "You look sexy holding that gun."

Jennifer dropped the weapon. She claimed they

both robbed the guy of his wallet and weed; then they took off.

"Wow!" Bobbi commented when I asked her about the scene you've just read. "I cannot believe all of this. . . . It's *not* funny, because I am in prison for *all* of these lies—this 'big joke.' Jennifer thinks it's some sort of movie . . . that she can just tell lie after lie and people will believe her."

Bobbi has spent many a night crying, thinking back to those moments. It's overwhelming and frightening, she explained, that someone could make up so many lies and be believed.

"I'm not innocent. I don't hate Jennifer. I have done bad things. Hurt myself. Hurt others. But can you imagine being in prison, locked up, knowing—*knowing*—you didn't commit this crime, and nobody is listening to you?"

CHAPTER 37

BOBBI'S FACE WAS covered with what appeared to be blood. Her mouth was full of the salty, acidic, bitter bodily fluid. In several of the photographs later seized by the MWPD from Bob Dow's computer, Bobbi's face is buried in Jen's crotch. Bobbi is licking Jen's vagina, performing vigorous oral sex. The photographs are extremely graphic; but, at the same time, they have this almost surreal quality to them. A viewer of the images has to wonder what the person snapping the photos was thinking at the moment. Was it sexually gratifying and/or stimulating for Bob to watch this sort of sexual interplay and document it on film?

Regardless, Bobbi was obviously taking great pleasure in performing cunnilingus on Jen seemingly while Jen was in the bloodiest period of her menstrual cycle. They were having a ball. Both girls enjoyed this moment (with Bob Dow watching).

"Those were the most disgusting photographs I

had seen within the entire bunch," said prosecutor Mike Burns, who seemed to be repulsed by this act more than anything else. "We couldn't believe what we were looking at."

"Chocolate," Bobbi Jo said later. "That is chocolate—not blood!"

The prosecutor was looking at black and white photos and assumed it was blood. But Bobbi had spread chocolate over Jen after being asked to by Bob Dow.

Have you ever looked at [any of] the photos? Bobbi asked me one day in a letter. She was referring to all of them in their entirety—namely, the gangsta-style photographs of her, Jen, and some of the other girls, posing with knives and guns. Bobbi had seen a few photos of herself holding weapons and couldn't believe what she was staring at. For the life of her, she could not recall posing for the photos. She had no recollection of Bob taking them.

"The drugs, the booze . . . ," Bobbi told me.

Blackout.

"Look, you ever seen some of those pictures?" Bobbi's mother, Tamey Hurley, asked me. "There was some photos of the girls having sex with the guns! Weird." Tamey started crying. Then, in a whisper, she added, "That's my baby right there—but that's *not* my daughter. Even though she took those girls to Bob's for those parties, Bobbi Jo gave them a place to hang out, something to eat, a place to sleep if they needed it. She got them off the street."

"I was *very* high," Bobbi explained. "I don't remember a lot of things sometimes because I was so intoxicated on every drug on the streets."

Could Bobbi have not remembered what happened that day Bob was murdered? Could she have been in a blackout?

Bobbi told me she and Jen were as sober as squirrels; they hadn't yet started partying. This fact had never been in dispute.

If an observer happened to take a closer look at that one rather filthy, intimate (a word I hesitate to use in this context) moment of Bobbi and Jen's life together that those bloody photographs documented and then backtracked, an interesting dynamic emerged. Just a few short years before this rather gruesome and graphic sexual act, Jen was a different person, a very young, juvenile. And yet, similarly, there were the rumblings of a teen psyche forming into that murderous, conniving, lying scoundrel Jen would soon become.

At one time, years before meeting Bobbi, Jen was someone who it would be difficult to believe would ever participate in an oral sex act so incredibly adult. Jen's journal, which had become the one true "friend" she counted on to explore her thoughts and feelings, depicted a young, boy-crazy teen—a girl living for and hanging on to every moment of her social life. On the one hand, these were adolescent diary entries, portraying a typical heterosexual teen caught up in the wonder of that world, chasing a good time. Some of the entries seemed entirely innocent and naïve. Yet, on the other hand, as passages were read and examined, a disturbed child with severe psychological problems emerged as her life—without self-realization—spiraled out of control.

For example, Jen would meet boys by the fence near her grandfather's pasture (when she spent time there away from home or her aunt and uncle's) and have a chat or just hang out. She'd go skateboarding and to the movies. She'd play basketball. Or sometimes she would just watch the boy she liked play sports. Her journal proved how vulnerable and characteristically juvenile—and maybe even purely archetypal—Jen's thoughts and behaviors were at one time.

She seemed so, well, *normal.*

[Billy] was flirting with me was a typical entry on any given day.

Jen would write about three other boys she had her eye on and hoped would notice her. Then, in a moment of pure panic, she'd write: *I called my boyfriend's house 3 times. . . . Maybe [he] doesn't want to talk to me?* Then she'd follow that up with a line of self-doubt and blame, noting, *Maybe I said something wrong. . . .*

In one specific entry, Jen went on to say she "hoped" her boyfriend wasn't going to break it off with her because she "had feelings for him."

Jen wrote several times how she felt all that any boy ever wanted was sex—and she wasn't averse to giving it up. All she wanted, in return for that sex, was love. And she was willing to do anything for that comforting feeling of being treasured, cared for, and respected by another human being.

Jen clearly had no trouble going out with one "guy," even though she wanted to be with another. She'd talk about making out with one and "really" liking him, but having on her mind two or three others she wanted to be with. She would plead to the pages of her journal for help in making a decision: *I wish God . . . would tell me who to go with.* This sort of boy-crazy aggressiveness went on during all of the years she kept a journal.

As Jen began to butt heads with her father, Jerry—especially over him trying to discipline her for disappearing all day and staying out all night— she had given up on any chance of a traditional life, which she had yearned for so badly when she first started keeping the journal. It was easier for Jen, she soon realized, to give in to that demon seed she believed her mother had implanted in her rather than fight it. Her own promiscuity became the central focus of her daily life. One of her sisters had been dating a specific boy. Jen was chasing another boy, but she wanted the boy her sister dated, writing, *I'm mad [at her], but I can wait 4 my turn.*

Jerry had tried to track Jen down one night. He wanted his daughter to go home and "wash the dishes," a simple, domestic, daily chore most kids do without much prodding.

Jen told him she'd found a job and couldn't. Then, mocking her father, she wrote how she had lied to Jerry and gotten away with it, bragging, *What a dumb ass!*

After attending church services one day, along with a few friends in a quasi–youth group she hung around, Jen pledged to stay pure until marriage. Then, however, she laughed about it later that night in her journal. She said how she could or could not follow along, but she had broken the covenant already. So what the hell? Why bother even trying anymore?

What also began to emerge near this time was how Jen figured out that she could manipulate people—especially boys—through sex in order to get what she wanted, and there were very little ramifications from it. There was one boy, for instance, she knew to be dating another girl at the same time. She despised him for lying to her face about it. Not saying anything to the boy, she wrote, *But he is cute & got some $$.*

In entry after entry, Jen showed her lack of self-esteem. She did not understand that she was being treated poorly by friends, boys, and even her own siblings—mostly because she allowed it to happen. Yet, Jen didn't have the social or psychological skills to notice or react properly to what was going on around her.

Then tension and bitterness among Jen, her

siblings, and Jerry was evident. She didn't seem to get along with them, unless they were obeying her rules. Audrey became a sister Jen found moody, but she was also someone Jen looked up to in many ways. She'd blast Audrey in one entry, and then write how she "wished" Audrey, who'd visit her from time to time, "would stay forever," ending the entry by stating how much she "loved" her.

Jen would write in passing about a family member hitting her, perhaps feeling she deserved it. Again, her lack of self-esteem was completely honest and pure. It was disheartening to see a girl so mixed up and confused about her feelings and not getting any professional help to deal with what was going on in her life.

We're going to see mommy today, Jen wrote one day, referring to a Sunday visit to the prison.

There was a boy—out of what seemed to be a half-dozen she was seeing at any given time—Jen believed was too good for her. She was over-whelmed by how "cautious" he was when they had sex. Describing how he used *condoms + rubs lotion on it so if the girl didn't doch* [sic] *that it would stink or something* made Jen feel special, as if he actually cared for her. And although she'd go out driving with him and they'd have sex, Jen was a bit skeptical about "going out" with the same kid ex-clusively. She convinced herself that he was *too* good for her. She wrote how she didn't want to get too close to the boy, because he was soon leaving town. Besides that, she added, he made her laugh; which, to her, was a sign that they were actually right for each other and becoming close. And this frightened her.

In the next entry, a day later, Jen talked about how she snuck out of her house late that night to go see this same boy. Another boy had picked her up to give her a ride. And wouldn't you know, while on the way to see the boy she liked, Jen stopped off and had sex with the boy who gave her the ride.

As one spring approached, Jen and her friends from church hung out at a lake. She wrote how one boy, after she and another friend stripped for him and his buddy, whipped out his penis, as if trying to impress them. But, she wrote, how she could "really care less" about the size, "big or not." In the next breath, she talked about how she cared mostly about what was "on the inside." She reconciled that feeling y writing, *That is not what I usually look at.*

Jen believed she found true love one day, but she "didn't know how" to tell the boy. She drew a heart—several, actually—in her journal with her name and his on the inside. She was enamored with this particular boy. She dreamed of him waking her up "every morning." Then, while she was not thinking about her feelings or expressing them to the boy, something happened. He asked her out, but the relationship didn't last more than a few days. Jen sabotaged it by blaming her sisters, saying how they disapproved, and so she was probably better off without him.

One morning, she awoke, terrified, from a "bad dream" of becoming pregnant and having a baby. *I hope that is not a sign,* she wrote. She reckoned that she couldn't be pregnant because *I'm on my period,* but then she questioned that: *At least I hope I'm not.*

Another day and another "crush" on a boy. She wasn't about to tell this one, though, and resigned to keep the crush to herself. There had been too many boys leading Jen on and letting her down: *I'm just a . . . girl with only a broken heart and no one to fix it.* She "wished" she could tell this boy how she felt; but she was terrified of being rejected, so she opted not to.

As she continued to write about her feelings, what became obvious was how Jen longed for attention and open displays of affection. These types of gestures made her feel wanted and loved. It was all she talked about sometimes: that need to be loved (unconditionally) by someone who didn't care what other people thought.

No sooner would Jennifer write about how important love was to her, than she would go out and smoke "3 bowls" and she "could not stop laughing."

Jen figured out quickly that drugs were a way to

forget about what was missing most in her life, along with what she had gone through. She even went so far as to write how proud she was of herself for "going one day and night" without screwing a boy.

She was fifteen years old at the time.

There was a long stretch where all she did was complain to her journal about this boy and that boy, and how—not being able to help herself— she'd cheat on one with the other. That lack of morality broke Jen down and hardened her to be able to commit bigger sins, and she didn't comprehend how it was happening. She understood that she could do more harm to those she loved and those around her without feeling the effects. She became cold and callous and seemed to enjoy not feeling guilt for the things she did. It became easier to be bad—in other words, the more she put it into play. It got to the point where Jen wrote: *Jerry Jones better watch out for me.* It was a clear warning. She felt her strength was in her tenacity to be strong and not have to show or deal with emotion. As this period of her life carried on, Jen became hypermanic, requiring only a few hours' sleep per night. She would often wake up before sunrise, after falling asleep that same day at two or three or four in the morning; and then she would go to school all day without feeling the least bit tired.

All [my current boyfriend] wants is to [screw], she noted a few days before her sixteenth birthday.

Then, as an afterthought, or as a solution to that dilemma, she wrote: *I want to get high tomorrow. . . .*

Hard as it might have been, Jen tried going days without having sex, but she always gave in to temptation. In many cases, she didn't even know the boy's surname, and she didn't care if one of her friends was dating the same boy. To Jen, the need to stuff those painful feelings of being inadequate, unloved, and not good enough by using drugs and sex as a numbing agent was greater than the need to do the right thing. She became hyper-sexualized, a clear symptom of bipolar disorder.

"[Someone in Jen's family] prostituted her to men for drugs when she was thirteen," one law enforcement official told me.

If true, this became a good explanation as to why promiscuous sex was not only a weapon and bartering chip to get what Jennifer Jones wanted, but a way for her to forget about and deal with the stressors of life. It was an emotional release. Without Jennifer even realizing it, the sex became a "getting even" with the abuser type of situation. Moreover, as most studies bear out, poor and low self-esteem and promiscuity go hand in hand. Researchers routinely find one associated with the other.

Sexual abuse leaves many scars, creating feelings of guilt, anger, and fear that haunt survivors throughout their lives, writes Dennis Thompson Jr. in *Everyday Health,* a quote that could be attributed to Jen or Bobbi, really. *Adults who have undergone sexual abuse*

*as children commonly experience depression and insom-
nia. High levels of anxiety in these adults can result in
self-destructive behaviors, such as alcoholism or drug
abuse, anxiety attacks, and situation-specific anxiety
disorders.*

Furthermore, Thompson went on to note,
[that] *damage extends to the sexual abuse survivor's
sense of their own sexuality.*

All true in Jen's case.

Bobbi's too, perhaps.

Jen never talked about it in her journal, but her
behavior lent itself to the idea that sex was something she did for a payment: whether it was love,
affection, drugs, alcohol, or to make (or keep) a
boy happy.

In one journal entry, Jen mentioned how she
had "a guy stay" at the house for a week and her
dad didn't "really care that much." That little bit
of an extended leash gave Jen the notion that she
could get away with more; and if she got caught,
there was rarely going to be a penalty.

As she grew older, crime became a part of Jen's
life. Sex was not filling the void any longer. She
stole a truck and got caught, but she ended up
with only a slap on the wrist (two weeks in the
county jail). She and a friend stole another vehicle
sometime later.

The journal stopped becoming Jen's outlet to
vent as her life became more criminal and difficult

to manage. It was then that a simple piece of paper and pen turned into a way for Jen to list her accomplishments, along with some new goals.

"Messed around with" so-and-so was a popular entry, beside the date of the encounter. Jen became increasingly disenfranchised with her surroundings and lifestyle. Nothing and no one could make her feel complete. She was in desperate need of counseling and probably some medication to relax the anxiety she didn't even know she had.

About a year before she met Bobbi, on January 5, 2003, Jen wrote about coming home from a visit with her mother: *She should get out soon!*

Then she wrote about a boy she was seeing and how she felt the relationship would soon end. The boy didn't trust her, she believed, adding, *I wouldn't trust me either.* She had ruined another relationship that showed a wee bit of promise—all because of her cheating ways and insecurities. She felt "disappointed" and like a "failure." *I am such a bad person,* she wrote.

This was the beginning of the self-hatred Jen had felt most of her teen life manifesting into something much bigger, something much unhealthier than sleeping around and doing drugs. There were longer spans of time now between journal entries. Months would go by without her penning a word.

On June 11, 2003, Jen was feeling especially uncertain about life. Kathy had been paroled and was leaving for Wichita Falls. (She had met a guy, a preacher.) The family had gotten together and Jen was shocked, it seemed, that she "got along with everyone." But for some reason, she had wanted to leave the party the minute she arrived. Being around the entire family was, apparently, too much.

That entry was the last until March 24, 2004, when she turned to her journal to express how bad she had "[screwed] up again." And she realized this latest stumble was part of a succession that revolved around her drug use. Life was spinning in circles: going one way, one moment, another the next. She saw it and felt it, but she did nothing to stop it or tell someone.

Not once in some fifty pages of journal entries (which I reviewed) did Jen ever talk about an attraction to females. It was always boys. And just a week after that final March 24 entry, in which she referred to Bobbi as a "dyke" [sic], Jen never penned another entry—and then, well, she met Bobbi and, in her mind, had found that true love she had been searching for all along.

CHAPTER 38

IN BOBBI'S FIRST VERSION to the police of what happened, she claimed to be at her grandmother's house in Graford with Jennifer on May 5, 2004. She asked if she could use her grandma's truck to go over to Bob's. Bobbi said she needed to pick up her belongings.

"You better hurry, because that's the only vehicle I have," Bobbi's grandmother supposedly said.

Bobbi and Jen left.

When they got there, Bob was moping around. They talked for a while. Bobbi never said what they talked about, exactly, because she couldn't recall. At some point, though, Bobbi noticed a neighbor had blocked her grandmother's truck in Bob's driveway.

"Let me use your truck to go get some cigarettes," Bobbi requested of Bob.

He threw her the keys.

("I went to the E-Z Mart by the Chicken Express,"
Bobbi told police, "and bought some cigarettes and
Jennifer a drink. I drove back to Bob's house.")

Upon returning, Bobbi said she noticed that
her grandmother's truck was not blocked in any
longer, so she parked Bob's truck and moved her
grandmother's vehicle out of the way so nobody
else could block it. All she wanted to do at this
point was get her stuff and leave.

Walking into the house, she heard "loud music
coming from the bedroom," Bobbi claimed. She
looked around, but she didn't see Jen anywhere.
As she was doing this, Bobbi said, she "heard Jennifer screaming." It was not a pleasant noise, as if
Jen was enjoying what was being done to her.

This alarmed Bobbi, she first told police. She
believed Jen needed help.

("So I ran into the bedroom . . . and I saw Bob
on top of Jennifer. Bob was naked and Jennifer
was only wearing a tank top. I ran over to Bob
[and] hit him across the back of the head with my
fist.")

Bob didn't take kindly to that and struck Bobbi,
knocking her to the ground.

Bobbi was now furious. She grabbed the first
thing she saw—a bag of clothes on the floor—and,
stuffing a knee into Bob's chest to hold him down,
hit him repeatedly with the laundry bag. As she
was doing this, "I heard a gun go off. I backed up

and saw Jennifer standing over Bob with a gun," she told police.

Jen had shot Bob once, paused, and then unloaded the remaining rounds of the weapon into him.

Bobbi told a similar story to Jen's, and it's clear that they had conspired to tell this tale to cover for one another.

"That [story] me and Bobbi Jo made up on our way to California," Jen later told police about how this first version of what happened became a pact between them.

The agreement was that since Bob had been attacking Jen and "raping her," they believed the murder would be considered an act of self-defense.

So what did happen that day, according to Bobbi Jo? How did Bob Dow end up dead? Bobbi had told her story to police and then admitted lying about it. She'd never told it again after that admission.

I gave her the opportunity to tell it here for the first time.

It was close to one in the afternoon on May 5, 2004, when Bob called Bobbi at her grandmother's house, she explained.

"He was crying, with his mind games he always played on me," Bobbi said.

"Bob, are you okay?" Bobbi said she asked her substitute father over the phone.

"Yes . . . [but] I want to apologize to you."

Bobbi listened. At one point, Bob said, "I want you to come over so we can sort it all out."

"Okay, Bob." Bobbi thought about being at the party house earlier that day when Bob wasn't home. She had looked for her wallet, but she couldn't find it. "Have you seen my wallet?" she asked him.

"Yeah, I left it in Weatherford. But chill . . . I made a few stops and I have some powder and vodka—we can go get [the wallet] tomorrow. Just get to me now."

"I need to wait until my granny gets back."

They hung up.

Bobbi had her son that day. She was holding him, "kissing his head while he was asleep in my arms," she remembered.

A half hour went by.

Jen looked out and saw that Bobbi's grandparents had returned. "They're here, Bobbi Jo," Jen said.

"Great."

Whether it was the right thing to do or not, Bobbi wanted to get over to Bob's fast. She was feeling the tug of the drugs and booze, gnawing at her, telling her to go out and get her funk on. It had become a daily routine: She would wake up, find out if Bob needed any work done, and then figure out how to get high.

"Gram, if I fill your truck up [with gas], can I use it to run to Mineral Wells?"

Dorothy Smith, however begrudgingly, said yes.

Bobbi kissed her son. Said her good-byes. Then she and Jen took off.

Whenever Bobbi drove, she liked to blast music. As they headed toward Mineral Wells from Graford on the 337, it wasn't that Bobbi didn't want to talk to Jen, "I just didn't want to talk to anyone. My son was on my mind and I was trying to figure out why I was fixin' to go over [to Bob's], knowing I'd end up high and gone from my son. . . ."

It was the juggling act all addicts face: *Today is the last day. Tomorrow I'll stop.*

Bobbi's life had become a pattern she could not deny. She was an addict living in the bubble of her full-blown disease. Bob Dow knew what type of candy to wave in front of Bobbi's face when he wanted her company, or when she got mad at him and left the house. Bobbi would hang out at Bob's and end up either smoking heroin, smoking meth, taking pills, snorting coke, or drinking herself into an oblivion of not knowing what the hell was going on around her. She could not stop herself from doing this. There was not one source I spoke to who could deny this statement. Two things, when I spoke to people about Bobbi Jo, became implicit in the conversations: Bobbi had the heart of an angel, but she loved nothing more than consuming all the dope and booze she could find on any given day.

How bad had it gotten?

"I know that Bobbi Jo had even tried shooting tequila and vodka" into her veins "at one time. I saw it!" said one woman who frequented Bob's party house.

Bob's house was Bobbi's escape from the reality of everyday life and the pain of her past and present. She understood that walking through Bob's door meant she'd soon become numb to the emotional mayhem of her life. In doing this, she'd be away from her son "for weeks at a time," Bobbi recalled, and it bothered her immensely. However, the pull of the drugs and booze was stronger than that maternal instinct.

"I was lost and desperately trying to get away from everything that was around [me]. I was on a one-way street to hell—and my addictions were killing me slowly."

A devout Christian, having grown up in the church, Bobbi said she couldn't understand "why God never answered my prayers." She was "very depressed after having" her son, "and his father and I split on very bad terms."

Talk of being involved in the Wiccan culture and black magic, which Jen later recalled while speaking to *Texas Monthly* and then under oath in court, was a baffling concept to Bobbi. When Jen claimed she and Bobbi were reading minds and found a notebook inside Bobbi's grandmother's house written by their other friend, Bobbi could not recall any of it. One particular day at Bobbi's grandmother's house, Jen and Bobbi had a friend over. They thought the friend had cast a spell on them, Jen told reporter Katy Vine. So they burned anything she had touched, including all of the pieces of that notebook they found ripped up and inside drawers. Bobbi did not recall it ever happening.

"I don't know anything about a notebook and I *never* brought anyone but Jennifer to my granny's house. I know better. There was never anyone with us but my son, or my baby brother . . . so I don't know *anything* about *any* notebook story."

The Wiccan connection was something Bobbi had no recollection of whatsoever.

"I've never been involved with any kind of Wiccan. I've been a Christian. My grandmother raised me with 'religion.'"

Moreover, Bobbi maintained, "I don't know anything about voodoo." She was confused and asked me, "Jennifer told you this?"

"Yes."

"I believe it's more of [Jen's] fictitious lies. She don't even know how many stories she's told."

Jen's aunt Melanie Brownrigg seemed to confirm what Bobbi was saying, telling me, "She lied all the time. Jennifer was a really good liar. . . ."

Driving and listening to music, puffing on a cigarette, with thoughts running through her head about missing her son and all that dope and booze she was about to devour, Bobbi almost drove off the road at one point, she said. "Tears filled my eyes." What got Bobbi was thinking about what she was doing to her son by darting off to Bob's to get drunk and high—again. Bobbi was disappointed in herself. She had let her son down by leaving him.

Jen was staring at Bobbi, wondering what was going on. *Why are you crying?* But Jen didn't say anything, Bobbi remembered. "Jennifer never spoke. . . . [She] just grabbed and held my hand."

This relationship with Jen, as Bobbi remembered it, was one more in a long line of women Bobbi was seeing at the time. According to Bobbi, Jen was not her girl. Jen was there, in front of Bobbi at the time. Jen might have been head over heels for Bobbi, but all Bobbi wanted was the sex and a partying partner. Furthermore, with all the dope and booze she was consuming daily, Bobbi was in no position to love anyone.

Bob Dow—at least the way Bobbi Jo later explained it to me—was waiting at the door for them when they arrived. As they approached, Bobbi noticed Bob had been crying. When Bobbi walked past him, into the house, Bob reached out and grabbed her in a loving way. He pulled Bobbi in close and kissed her on the forehead, as if she had been a long-lost daughter, now returning.

"I love you," Bob said. "I don't mean to act the way I do."

"It's okay, Bob."

They stood in the living room for a few minutes. Bobbi could tell Bob had been partying; he was loopy and seemed out of it (something his autopsy report confirmed). He had called, she now figured, because he was lonely and wanted someone to hang out with.

"Are we going to work in the morning?" Bobbi asked.

"Yeah," Bob said. He pulled out $100. "Hey, go down and get me three cigars and a pack of menthol smokes—get whatever you want, too."

The cigars, Bobbi understood, were for the drugs. "We'd cut them open," Bobbi recalled, "and pull all the tobacco out and filled it with weed—sometimes coke and heroin."

Blunts.

And this is where the story of what happened to Bob Dow becomes a bit more complicated. Bobbi went to the corner store without Jen, she told me, which was something Bobbi did all the time.

When she returned and got out of the truck to go back inside the house, Bobbi said, she "heard one gunshot go off."

Bobbi didn't think too much of this sound at first. After all, they were in Texas. There was a "young couple," Bobbi explained, "living nearby." They liked to party a lot and do crazy things. Not to mention that some people in Texas feel it is their right to fire a weapon off in the private confines of their own property, whether allowed by the law or not.

While Bobbi walked toward the front door as she heard that gunshot, she looked up and saw Jen running out of the house.

Jen appeared alarmed, scared, in shock. Totally out of it. All she had on, Bobbi told me, was "a spaghetti-string shirt and no panties. . . ."

When Bobbi took one look at her, confusion set in. Bobbi knew something terrible had occurred. Not only was it written all over Jen's face, but that blood on Jen's body, which Bobbi soon noticed, meant that some kind of violent incident had occurred inside the house.

CHAPTER 39

BOBBI WAS "puzzled" when she saw Jen outside in front of Bob's party house on that afternoon, moments after hearing "one gunshot" from somewhere near the house.

"Take me to my mom's apartment," Bobbi said Jen demanded after she walked out of the party house and approached her. She must have meant Jerry's Spanish Trace apartment, Bobbi knew, because Kathy Jones did not have a home in town.

"What's wrong?" Bobbi asked.

Jen "never spoke," Bobbi later told me.

As Bobbi got closer, she saw "blood all over the side of [Jen's] face and her hand."

"I shot Bob," Jen finally said.

"You *what*?" Bobbi asked. ("I was in shock," Bobbi told me. "And I didn't know what to do or think.")

Bobbi's version then skips over the next few

moments and picks up at "these trashy apartments," after Bobbi and Jen pulled up to Spanish Trace.

No sooner did they walk into the apartment than Audrey and Kathy took Jennifer "in the back room and left me standing there," Bobbi explained. "They already had two little bags full of clothes packed."

According to Bobbi, Kathy and Audrey were ready to leave.

After a few tense moments alone in the kitchen, Bobbi heard Audrey, Kathy, and Jen walk out of the back room and then enter the kitchen.

"Help us," Bobbi recalled Kathy and Audrey pleading with her.

"I was looking at all three of them . . . ," Bobbi said. "I felt stupid because I didn't know what to . . . feel."

Bobbi never mentioned Krystal, Audrey's girlfriend, being at the apartment that day. The next moment, Bobbi recalled, involved all of them taking off in both vehicles, traveling away from Spanish Trace speedily. The entire focus of any conversation they had was on protecting Jen from what she had just done. Kathy and Bobbi were together inside one vehicle with Audrey. Jen followed with Krystal (who was definitely with them, whether Bobbi remembered or not).

Bobbi recalled Kathy and Audrey laying into her.

"It's all your fault. It's all your fault. It's all your fault," Kathy kept repeating, according to Bobbi. Kathy was saying that "over and over" as they raced away from the apartment. What Bobbi took from Kathy's rant was that Bobbi should be the one to take the rap for Jen and the murder because it was Bobbi who got Jen involved with Bob Dow, to begin with. Kathy said Bobbi was supposed to be the smarter and more mature of the two. It was clear to Bobbi that Audrey and Kathy wanted to shield Jen any way they could from what was about to happen next.

"You'll love prison because you love women," Kathy, a veteran of years behind bars herself, pled with Bobbi. "Jennifer's in love with you. It's *all* your fault."

This seems to be a believable scenario. Bobbi never came out and said it to me, but the idea was (and the known facts seem to support this) that Jen, in all of her madness and irrational thinking, believed that killing Bob was what Bobbi *wanted* her to do. Jen could have taken Bobbi's complaining of Bob as an indication that Bobbi wanted him out of the picture—without Bobbi actually coming out and saying it. And when Bob made that pass at Jen inside his truck, an idea was born. Then when he did it again inside the house after Bobbi went off to the store, well, Jen lost it. Her entire life of pain and suffering and disappointment had come to a head. Someone had to pay.

Audrey piped in at one point, Bobbi recalled, also blaming her.

"You don't say a word, bitch," Bobbi snapped back at Audrey. There was still some animosity there between them, Bobbi said, because they had just broken up.

Bobbi said Kathy began bugging out, thinking back to the times she had been over to Bob's house and had stripped for him in front of the camera. There were even things Kathy had done that she did not remember.

"I want all of his computers. . . . Drive back to the house," Kathy demanded to Bobbi. "I want anything else he has, too."

"You'll have to kill me first, before I go back there," Bobbi said. "You're not taking anything from [Bob]."

"Just turn yourself in, Bobbi," Kathy suggested, settling down. "Turn yourself in. You'll love prison."

Bobbi remembered driving straight from Spanish Trace to Bob's Weatherford trailer. She did not recall stopping at Krystal's house first. Bobbi had some money (in her wallet) at the trailer, along with her engagement ring. She knew she needed that money if they were going to take off. The entire situation, from Bobbi's outlook, was fluid— all happening in the moment. The way Bobbi told it later, she was trying to go with the flow and figure things out as they went along. After all, Jen had just murdered a man Bobbi loved, a man Bobbi had known since she was a kid. Life had become suddenly serious, much more than drinking and drugging every day. All she had done was wake up, had a conversation with Bob, and then decided to go over and party with him.

And now Bob was dead.

In Weatherford, at what Bobbi referred to in all her letters to me as "Bob's and my place," she showed Kathy and Krystal (whom she brought into the narrative for the first time here) the keys to the trailer. Krystal "punched the glass out" before Bobbi even had a chance to open the door with the key.

The feel I got from Bobbi's version was that the girls—Audrey, Kathy, and Krystal—were acting as though this was some sort of a free-for-all road trip—maybe just another day in the life of partying and taking things to the limit. The idea that Bob was dead never really came into focus for them at first. It was as if they didn't believe it. And Jen became like a shadow: She was there in the background, but for the most part forgotten.

"What are you doing?" Bobbi yelled at Krystal. "Come on . . . stop that!" Bobbi shoved her. By Bobbi's guesstimate, Krystal weighed about "325 pounds," as opposed to Bobbi's one hundred. However, Bobbi had grown up with six brothers.

"I used to fight my old man," Bobbi said, "so I was used to physical abuse."

Bobbi ran straight toward what she called "my bed" inside the trailer. "And my wallet was on my lil stand." (Just as Bob Dow had promised on the phone.)

She grabbed it and then ran back into the main

room of the trailer, where the rest of the women were now, Bobbi realized, rummaging through Bob's possessions.

"Kathy, Audrey, Krystal, and Jennifer were taking Bob's TV, and all kinds of shit," Bobbi told me. "I was angry and confused."

After they left the trailer, Kathy "made" Bobbi stop and pawn the TV.

From there, Bobbi's story resembled what the girls later told police about the road trip, save for a few minor, inconsequential details. The way Bobbi portrayed her role in all of this was that she had never gone into Bob's house after Jen killed him. She also didn't know Jen "had sex with Bob, till she said it."

One of the major discrepancies within the road trip narrative became what happened in Arizona. According to Bobbi, "When we arrived in Arizona, I put Kathy and Jennifer's sister [Audrey] out. I tried to leave Jennifer, but she refused to get out of the truck." When they got to Blythe, California, Bobbi claimed, "I called my mom, told her what happened. . . . I was petrified and afraid. My mamma then called police for me and told me to stay there, right where I was. When the California police surrounded us, Kathy [had already] told them I murdered [Bob] and kidnapped her daughter. It felt like they had over twenty guns to my head. They were not even going to arrest Jennifer."

PART FOUR

MIND READERS

CHAPTER 40

ON MAY 9, 2004, AFTER Audrey Sawyer returned from Arizona and was able to have a quick sleep in her own bed for the first time in nearly a week, she and Kathy were summoned to the MWPD. They weren't under arrest or in trouble (which seemed strange in the scope of this crime, seeing that both women could have been charged as accessories, or aiding and abetting fugitives). Sure, they could have been given life sentences for bad judgment; but the MWPD considered Kathy and Audrey to have gone along for the ride and guilty of nothing more than being stupid. At least that's what Kathy and Audrey said—and, apparently, without yet speaking to Bobbi or Jen, the MWPD was not questioning any of it.

Captain Mike McAllester asked the women—after they had both given their statements—to help him find the weapon that, according to

Krystal, had been tossed out the window of the truck as they drove down the road out of Mineral Wells.

"I know where it is," Kathy said. She explained.

"No," Audrey interrupted. "You're wrong, Ma. It's not there. *I* know where it is."

McAllester led them to his cruiser.

Finding a weapon tossed out of a moving vehicle window was probably a long shot, McAllester knew. The gun could be anywhere. On top of that, a couple of kids or someone collecting cans and bottles could have stumbled upon it and taken it home.

They pulled over to where Audrey remembered— "Between a mailbox and a fence post"—and McAllester parked his vehicle.

"Across the street," Audrey explained.

The grass had just been cut. McAllester found his way over to the side of the road and—wouldn't you know it—there was what had been described to him as "the murder weapon" staring back up at him.

CHAPTER 41

BRIAN BOETZ NEEDED to head out to Blythe, California, to pick up his two murder suspects, separate them, and get each to lock down a statement of what happened in Mineral Wells. Bobbi and Jen were being held at the Riverside County Jail in Riverside, California. The girls' arrest took place at 3:45 A.M. behind a pool hall in Blythe, after Bobbi called home and gave them up. According to a report filed by the Blythe Police Department, the girls had not been surrounded by a SWAT team of cops, armed with cocked and loaded weapons pointed at their heads. Sergeant Angel Ramirez's brief four-paragraph report was straightforward, as those clerical types of law enforcement things go. The Blythe PD had received information that Smith and Jones were in the Blythe area and "were wanted for homicide out of Texas." Ramirez was given a description of the girls and the vehicle and, along with one other officer,

went out to "supervise and assist with the arrest."
There was no showdown at the O.K. Corral, no
foot chase through the desert, no firefight. The
girls were actually sleeping (or half asleep) when
the cops arrived. They put up no fight. In his
report, Ramirez never mentioned how many officers were involved in the arrest.

Ramirez and another officer searched the area
around Bob's vehicle, as well as inside, to see what
they could come up with.

"I ripped the pawn ticket up and tossed it in the
parking lot," Bobbi told one of the officers after
being asked if they had any weapons.

Sure enough, after a quick search, all the pieces
were scattered about the parking lot where the
truck was parked.

I collected the torn pieces of paper, Ramirez reported.

The pieces of paper were not that pawn ticket,
however. They were pieces of paper that were actually part of a handwritten letter and a Western
Union receipt.

Jen and Bobbi were locked up, Bobbi said, in a
"restroom for men" that night. Bobbi was told by
the Blythe PD that "they had nowhere to take us,
so we stayed in that nasty restroom."

The following morning, a bus headed out to the
local jail.

"They put us in the front cage," Bobbi explained.

The bus was full of men (on the other side of
the cage, in the back of the bus) heading out to
various local prisons.

Bobbi was handcuffed to the fence and behind her back, her feet shackled to the floor. Jen wasn't handcuffed at all, Bobbi recalled. The men in the back were whistling and calling to Jen with sexually aggressive remarks.

"She thought it was cute," Bobbi remembered. "I was in total shock."

As they stopped at the prison and the men were led out, as each passed by Bobbi and Jen, Bobbi was the target of a slur of some sort, she felt, because of the way she looked.

"Pussy sucker," said one man, who then spit on Bobbi.

"Dyke bitch," said another.

Several more men walked by and said nothing, but they spit on Bobbi.

This was all new to Bobbi. She was terrified. She had never been in a situation so humiliating and seemingly barbaric.

"I had spit all over my hair, in my ear, on the side of my face by the end of it," Bobbi said. "Jennifer didn't even wipe it off for me—she turned her back, like she didn't know what was going on."

Brian Boetz took his colleague, Detective Penny Judd, and headed out to Blythe, a twelve-hundred-mile, eighteen-hour drive (without stops) from Mineral Wells. They left at 6:00 P.M. on May 8, knowing that the girls would eventually be arrested. By ten-thirty the next morning, May 9, they

were at the Buckeye, Arizona, PD, picking up that
pair of videotaped interviews that Buckeye authorities had recorded with Kathy and Audrey.

When they reached Riverside, California, Boetz
and Judd were told the paperwork to release
Bobbi and Jen was going to take a few days. So the
detectives decided to go see the girls and conduct
interviews with each while they waited. Why waste
the time, moping around, waiting on paperwork?
Boetz told me. After a good solid rest, Boetz and
Judd headed in to see the girls on the morning of
May 10.

Bobbi and Jen had decided on a story they were
going to stick to. According to what Jen told the
Texas Monthly, this conspired tale of what happened emerged as Jen and Bobbi were holed up
together inside a cell in Riverside. They talked
while locked up and decided to see if they could
get Jen out of it all. They decided to tell lies to
make it seem as though Bob had been raping Jen.
If they stuck to it, perhaps the authorities would
believe them and feel the crime was committed in
self-defense.

Jen walked up to Bobbi, who was sitting on the
floor, her back to the cell wall. Jen said, "I have an
idea" (according to what Jennifer told *Texas
Monthly*). Jen explained to Bobbi how "no one
really knew what happened inside Bob's bedroom."
Because of that, she and Bobbi could concoct any
story they wanted, as long as they stuck to it. Jen
even mentioned Bobbi's son and how he would be

without his mother if Bobbi went to prison. It just wasn't fair. They had to do this.

"I'm going to take the blame for you," Jen said she told Bobbi as they waited inside that jail cell.

After they chitchatted a bit more, Bobbi said (according to Jen's version in *Texas Monthly*), "You know I'm going to be with you forever if you do that."

This is the first time (and it's important to note that the *Texas Monthly* story would publish merely weeks before Bobbi's trial) that Jen ever gave the impression that Bobbi had had something to do with the murder. Before this, it was entirely on Jen.

Neither of the girls asked for a lawyer. Boetz and Judd interviewed Bobbi first. According to Boetz, Bobbi Jo was wired, wispy, and gaunt. (Note that I called and e-mailed Penny Judd numerous times, but she never returned my calls or e-mails. This occurred after Brian Boetz had told me he had spoken to her and she had agreed to an interview.) It was clear Bobbi Jo had been beaten down by her days on the road. And yet, the one characteristic Bobbi (and Jen) showed more than any other, Boetz told me, was the notion that they hadn't really done a bad thing. From what Brian Boetz felt, the girls were under the impression that this was some sort of misunderstanding that was going to go away as soon as they returned to

Mineral Wells and were given the opportunity to explain themselves.

Boetz recalled upon first meeting Jen that she was "hysterical, crying, nervous, tired, hungover . . . and it sounds kind of funny, but she was every one of them" at the same time.

There were moments during the course of Jen's first interview when she even appeared to be laughing.

The main story line both girls got across during their initial interviews in Blythe, California, with the MWPD was that Bob had been coming on to Jen for weeks and made one last aggressive advance toward her, which forced Jen into protecting herself by killing him.

Jen and Bobbi told a tale of Bob bailing them out of jail and then wanting sex from Jen as payment. When he came at Jen demanding payment, she shot him.

Boetz listened. He had problems with the girls' statements, knowing what the crime scene looked like. (The girls had spoken of a struggle inside Bob's bedroom—which Boetz could not reconcile with the scene after being inside the room.) Boetz let them talk through their stories without interrupting them, or playing any of his cards.

After each girl signed her statement, Penny Judd and Brian Boetz convinced the girls to waive extradition and allow the MWPD to transport them back to Mineral Wells.

Each agreed without even asking what it actually meant in the scope of their cases.

On May 11, 2004, early in the morning, Judd and Boetz picked Bobbi and Jen up at Riverside County Jail.

"Look, this ride back home is not going to be the time or place to talk about what happened," Boetz explained as they got into the car. "We just talked about it all here. We'll have more chances in the future to talk. You both understand?"

Bobbi and Jen said they did.

"And listen . . . there's not going to be any touching each other or any affection going on, okay?" Boetz explained a bit sheepishly.

Both agreed.

The plan was to drive straight back to Texas.

Brian Boetz said watching the two girls along the way became like "looking at two people in love, to be honest. They'd stare at each other, laugh, joke around, talk of things that I had no clue about whatsoever. Then they'd turn around and be crying. . . ."

This didn't sound so much like love—but perhaps adolescent fixation, coupled with the physical and emotional difficulties and complexities of coming off a monthlong bender of using hard-core drugs and booze daily. Both girls had to be suffering from some form of withdrawal. That giddiness and mixture of emotions were their addictions draining from their pores. Their emotions were riding on that clichéd roller coaster.

"They were scared and nervous," Boetz said. "I think, during that twenty-four-hour period of driving back, we got to see a lot of different emotions from them at different times. It told me that they really didn't understand the severity of what happened and what they'd done."

Boetz listened as best he could. "As I heard them, I believe they thought that when they got back to Texas that they'd be set free. There really were times when I thought that they thought they'd be set free because [Bob Dow] was a bad guy himself."

They arrived in Mineral Wells on May 12, 2004, at 1:45 P.M. Jen and Bobbi were held at Palo Pinto County Jail, a local facility with an old-fashioned holding tank and shoe box–sized cells with white-washed walls, a metal plate sticking out of the wall that a thin mattress sat on, a corner shelf for belongings, a library about the size of a walk-in closet, an entirely closed-in basketball court with one hoop, and a jail administrator donning a ten-gallon hat, big ol' gun clipped to his belt, and a no-holds-barred attitude. This was where Bobbi and Jen would be held until their cases were adjudicated.

Most important to Brian Boetz was the crime scene photographs compared to Bob Dow's room. Jen and Bobbi had each spoke in their first statements of a fight going on with Bob inside that room and Jen's inability to protect herself— hence the need for the weapon and killing Bob.

However, when Boetz placed the crime scene into that context the girls had described, the problem Boetz had was how Bob had been found.

"Because of the way he's lying there, and the way the bag is covering his head and the blanket is covering . . . part of his body," Boetz later said.

All of this seemed inconsistent with a struggle: Bob was lying on his back. The laundry bag was over his head.

"Right," Boetz added. "He's lying on his back— to me, as if he was just lying there, not struggling or fighting with anyone."

Boetz then read through the statements the MWPD had taken up to that point from Bobbi, Jen, Audrey, Kathy, Krystal, Dorothy Smith, and the Cruzes. And that was when something became clear: "I decided that they weren't being truthful."

Boetz went to see the girls. He didn't reveal his hand; instead, he asked, "Would you mind taking a polygraph?"

Both girls said they didn't have an issue with taking a lie detector test.

Still, neither asked for an attorney.

CHAPTER 42

BOBBI AND JEN WERE able to stay in touch
while held inside the jail at the Palo Pinto
County Sheriff's Office (PPCSO). Jen later said in
court that this was when she and Bobbi "[came]
up with a different story." Why they decided to
change the story again, Jen never mentioned.
Perhaps it was because the MWPD had ratcheted
up pressure by asking them to take a polygraph.

At first, when asked why she decided to come
forward and give a second statement (which was
ultimately the second time she lied about what happened), Jen responded, "I thought if I told a lie,
then I wouldn't be convicted of a crime. . . . That
if I lied, and I made it look like I was the person
that was—that was getting in trouble—I was, you
know, I was the person that did it and everything,
then I wouldn't be in that much trouble." Jen
stopped and collected her thoughts. Then she
added: "If I was the person that . . . he attacked . . .

and everything, then I wouldn't get that much time."

She was also trying to protect Bobbi. In coming up with this second story, Jen explained, she was hoping to spring Bobbi from jail. She said Bobbi wouldn't leave her alone while they were locked up in Palo Pinto—that Bobbi kept complaining about not being present for her family.

"I need to get out of here," Bobbi allegedly told Jen one night. "My whole family is falling apart. . . ."

On May 14, 2004, first thing in the morning, the girls were driven from the Palo Pinto County Jail in Palo Pinto, Texas, to the Behavioral Measures & Forensic Services, in Dallas. Detectives Brian Boetz and Penny Judd were convinced the problems within the stories they'd heard from both girls had been the result of lies. They wanted the truth.

"We had held them overnight in Mineral Wells at our holding facility," Boetz later recalled, "and there was one reason why we did that. Based on the stories that they gave us in California and the evidence . . . we thought they weren't telling us the complete truth."

Boetz and Judd asked the girls to wait inside a conference room while they met with the polygraphist in the hallway. After looking over the case report Boetz handed him, the polygraphist clarified how the test would work. "One girl at a time," he explained. "There's a television monitor in that room over there, where you can watch and listen."

Bobbi went into a room with the polygraphist, while Jen was escorted into a separate room to wait. (There was some confusion later about this simple fact, and that the girls might have been polygraphed at the same time, but it's clear that each was polygraphed separately.) Bobbi had rested since being back in town. She looked somewhat adjusted but also scared, nervous, and in great need of what her body craved most: drugs and alcohol. Not the ideal conditions with which to walk into a polygraph, but the examiner had seen worse.

As he explained to Bobbi how the test worked, giving her a chance to review all of the questions he was going to ask beforehand, Bobbi "broke down and started crying," Brian Boetz, watching from a video monitor, later said.

"You all right, ma'am?" the polygraphist asked.

Bobbi Jo continued to cry.

From the other room, Boetz looked on. He'd seen this before. Suspects are brought to a breaking point and they crack. Boetz felt Bobbi was ready.

"Miss Smith?"

"I lied to the cops," Bobbi told the polygraphist. "I lied. But I want to tell the truth now."

The test was over before it started.

* * *

I asked Bobbi Jo about the polygraph and this second story, which she and Jen supposedly invented. Why would she break down like that during the polygraph?

I don't have anything to say about it, she wrote back. *I mean, they wanted me. And I was no fool to that test. It was all set up to try and break Jennifer and I.*

Bobbi was right about that. Boetz told me he didn't believe them, so he set the polygraph up to see what would happen, to see how they'd react.

As for the second statement Bobbi was about to give the MWPD, she said, "I tried to stick to the story Jennifer and I had talked about [in the jail]."

The problem was that when a person told the truth, she didn't have to remember details. The facts came easy. When a person lied, she got caught up in her own stories and began to back-pedal. And with a young girl who'd never been arrested, going up against an experienced cop holding her freedom in his hands, the cop would win every time. Bobbi also believed then that she and Jen were a team; they had designed a new strategy and were going to stick to it

Detective Brian Boetz escorted Bobbi into a room in the same building where the polygraph had been held. He asked her to sit down.

"You want to give us another statement?" Boetz
asked.

"Yes," Bobbi answered, following along with the
plan she and Jen had discussed.

Boetz had Bobbi wait for him. He needed to call
the MWPD and have someone fax a blank statement and new Miranda warning document for her
signature.

Meanwhile, Penny Judd walked Jen into the examination and sat her down.

"I'll be in the next room," Judd told Jen.

Jen nodded, indicating she understood.

Judd watched on the monitor.

The polygraphist explained how the test was
going to work, where the connectors would be
placed on her body, and how the questioning
would progress. Yet, just as the test was about to
start, Jen turned on the tears.

Right on cue.

"You all right, Miss Jones?"

"I'm sorry . . . I want to tell the truth now."

The polygraphist unhooked Jen from the
wiring and walked her out of the room. Penny
Judd was waiting in the hallway by the door.

"Talk in there," the polygraphist said, pointing
to an open room.

"Come on. . . ."

After sitting down, Judd asked Jen what was
going on.

"Penny, I'm sorry for lying to you. Don't be mad
at me."

"Mad? No, Jennifer. I'm not mad. What's going on?"

"I want to tell you the truth."

Penny Judd felt Jen was referring to that first statement she had given back in California.

"I want to give you another statement," Jen said.

Bobbi and Jen sat separately with Boetz and Judd and talked through what became their second statements regarding what had happened.

Why?

Because the MWPD did not believe the first statements. It was as if those two statements the girls gave back in Blythe, California, were tossed aside in lieu of what was now, the girls were saying, the real truth.

The road trip and the lead up to the murder came out about the same this second time around. In that regard, not much had changed from the first time they told it. What was different here became the murder itself and how it occurred. According to Jen now, she and Bobbi walked into the house together. Bob apologized for the comments about wanting sex in trade for the bail money he had apparently put up. After Bob's apology, the following action transpired. Jen explained the events to Penny Judd in her statement:

I walked in the bedroom, Bob's room, got the gun out of the green lockbox [the chest] that was under the bed in the bedroom. I checked to see if the gun was loaded and it was. I placed it between the

*nightstand and Bob's bed between a stack of clothes
and a striped pillow. I walked into the living room,
Bobbi Jo had just received $20 from Bob and they
were still arguing about her paycheck. She then bor-
rowed the keys to Bob's truck to go to the store and
buy me and [her] something to drink. Bobbi Jo left
and Bob kept telling me he was sorry. I kept telling
him that it was okay and I insisted that I repay
him. Bob kept on saying no, and I kept on saying,
"It's okay, I don't mind."*

*Bob and I walked into the bedroom where I took
off my clothes and laid down on the bed. Bob did
the same thing. Bob took the lotion off the nightstand and used it to try to make his penis hard. Bob
then went down on me. While Bob was doing that,
I took the gun that was between the pillow and
placed it beside my hip. I told Bob I wanted to be on
top. . . .*

*Then I pulled the gun out from underneath the
covers, then I shot Bob twice. Then I got off him and
I saw that he was still alive, [and] then I shot him
three more times. Bobbi Jo walked in screaming,
"Oh, my God . . . I cannot believe you actually
did it."*

Two important factors emerged from this
second statement. One, that Jen took full responsibility for the murder. Two, "The reason Bobbi Jo
said that"—the "I cannot believe you actually did
it" statement—"is because when we were between

Graford and Bob's house," Jen said, "I had told
Bobbi Jo that I was going to kill Bob. Then I said,
no, I wasn't."

From there, Jen's second statement was fairly
consistent with her first. It was clear Jen was taking
the onus off Bobbi and putting it on herself.
Bobbi, in turn, later claimed she never once asked
Jen to take the blame for her, simply because she
didn't need her to. Jen had committed the
murder and Bobbi had had nothing to do with
planning or executing it. All she had done was lie
about what actually happened with the hope of
protecting Jen.

Bobbi sat with Boetz and gave her second statement. She acknowledged that a good portion of
her first statement would be consistent with what
she now wanted to say. So, as strange as this
sounds, they actually skipped over some details
and got right to what Boetz wanted to discuss.

This second narrative of the crime, which Bobbi
told, began with Bobbi's mother being with her
and Jen during those days before Bob was murdered. Bobbi explained how Tamey drove her and
Jen over to Bob's, and Jen broke the back window
and they all went in. Bobbi mentioned how she
wanted to take a .22 long-range revolver out of
Bob's green chest so she could pawn it because
he owed her money.

"After work [the day before the murder], Bob Dow asked me if he could have sex with my girlfriend, Jennifer Jones," Bobbi told Boetz in her second statement. "We both said, 'No.'"

Bobbi then discussed that drive over to Bob's on the day he was murdered, telling Boetz, "I gave Jennifer the gun. She placed it in the back of her pants and then covered it with her shirt. She told me to wait outside. I came back in one time and Bob Dow was in between her legs. . . ." Bobbi left the room. When she went back "three to five minutes later," she noticed Bob "was shaking really bad."

"Is he dead?" Bobbi asked Jen, according to Bobbi's recollection.

"Yes."

"Make sure," Bobbi told Jen.

"I grabbed his hand," Bobbi explained to Boetz. "I was so scared. So was Jennifer. She was also shaking. So I grabbed the gun and her clothes and told her to get out of the house. I grabbed Bob's wallet and took one hundred and fifty dollars out of it. . . ."

The remainder of the statement was nearly the same as Bobbi's first.

Clearly, as Boetz and Judd looked at these second statements, studying them, matching them up against the girls' first statements, something did not coalesce.

"In my mind, I was thinking that there was

probably still some truth not there," Boetz recalled. "But they were getting a little closer."

Regardless of what Bobbi had told them—much of which the MWPD still seemed to think was mostly untruthful, according to my interview with Brian Boetz—it was enough to charge Bobbi with first-degree murder. Apparently, five words within the statement Bobbi Jo had just given—" I gave Jennifer the gun"—were enough to warrant her arrest on conspiring and convincing Jennifer Jones to murder Bob Dow.

I asked the MWPD if they recorded either of the two statements on video or audio.

"No, sir. We were not able to record them, sorry."

"Why?" I pressed.

"When we talked to them in California," Brian Boetz explained, "we were under the mercy of that department. We asked for a room that would record. We were told that they were all being used, so they put us in a room in intake, which had no recording. Their second statement was when we were in Dallas, Texas, for the polygraph. The girls broke during the preinterview with the polygraph operator. They placed us in a room with no recording, so the only option we had in both cases [was] to write or type out their statements. I hope that clears it up for you. Sorry."

CHAPTER 43

IN LATE MAY, AS Jen wandered around the jail one afternoon looking for someone to talk to, she sat down with a gal named Betty Gardner (pseudonym), an older convict doing a short bid on a drug possession felony. Gardner was slated to be released in a matter of weeks.

What struck Betty was that as Jen explained why she was locked up, she "laughed" about Bob's murder. It was as if the crime she had committed was funny. Listening, Betty felt Jen showed zero "remorse" for what had happened to Bob and was even "happy" about killing him.

Some days later, Jen spoke to another inmate about Bob's murder. Here she expressed a somewhat similar demeanor, the woman later said. "She just seemed indifferent, I guess. Just 'nothing' would be my best word for it."

No emotion—as if Jen did not care that she had taken a life.

This side of Jennifer Jones falls more in line with the woman I contacted and spoke briefly to in early 2012. By the time I reached out to her, Jen had told five different versions of her story. She'd lied about details she didn't need to. And when she sat down with reporter Katy Vine for the *Texas Monthly* article I've quoted throughout this book, she altered the story once again. It was as if Jennifer Jones had been describing someone else's life, or telling a story, a tale. For Jen, she had told so many different versions of Bob Dow's murder and the days leading up to it and after, she couldn't keep track any longer. This was one of the reasons I wanted so badly to interview her.

Bobbi wrote me an angry letter laced with raw emotion and an exhausted frustration at me repeatedly asking her tough questions that had to do with timelines, things people said, and those discrepancies in Jen's different stories. I'd ask the same question different ways. There were times when Bobbi didn't know what I was talking about. It was clear to me she had no idea where the information had come from.

Look, all those [girls: Audrey, Kathy, Jennifer] you keep talking to used to come over and [give Bob oral sex]. There's photos of it. I used to tape it! . . . Jennifer and Audrey and Kathy, and all those chicks, were sexing Bob 24/7 for a high, Bobbi wrote.

The bottom line here was: Don't trust anything they say. Half of what they do remember is probably clouded with an agenda to protect themselves.

"No," Detective Brian Boetz said after I asked him if he had ever seen any photographs of Jen either having intercourse with Bob or performing oral sex on him. "It was other girls who we could not identify."

Bobbi called Jen, Kathy, and Audrey "hos." To that, Bobbi said there was one thing she was proud of from that entire time they were all together that she could take to her grave: "I never sold *my* pussy."

Jen had always come across as an innocent, effeminate girly-girl, and it helped her cause later when she was busted. Bobbi was the polar opposite, if we're judging books by their covers. Bobbi was rough around the edges, had tattoos, a butch-style haircut, carried a chain wallet, etc. It's easy to point a finger at Bobbi and assume she was the mastermind behind this murder, pulling Jen's strings, telling her what to do. Even Jen played off this dynamic with Katy Vine when she told an incredibly bizarre story about Blythe, California, "authorities" pulling her aside on the day she and Bobbi were arrested in California to tell her something: "We know you didn't do it. That tattooed girl did it. Don't you dare take the rap for her."

That is simply preposterous. Those cops had no idea who Jen was, and very little detail about the crime the girls were being suspected of. They showed up to arrest the girls and to hand them over to the MWPD.

"I slept with other chicks I knew and met," Bobbi admitted to me, speaking of those days when she hung out with Jen. "I knew Jennifer twenty-seven days! We were not even in a relationship. I don't know. It was more like she knew I would be there for her. I had much love and care for Jennifer, but 'in love' is different. . . ."

Within many of the photographs left behind by Bob Dow, this statement of Bobbi's rings true. In several, which police found inside Bob's computer, Bobbi appears frog-eyed and wasted, with droopy shoulders, a sad look on her face, as if her body is caving in on her. There's almost an aura in some of the photos indicating that Bobbi is forcing herself to snuggle up to Jen. Jen is the aggressor, with her arm around Bobbi, sometimes kissing her. It's a testament to Bobbi's declaration that she was in it for the sex and a good time. The idea that Bobbi—after knowing Bob Dow since she was an adolescent, him being the (step)grandfather to her child, the master puppeteer of her life, arguably her surrogate father and provider of drugs and alcohol and employment—would decide to kill him with Jen—someone she had known for twenty-seven days at the time—does not fit. Moreover, it makes little sense in the scope of the lives the three of them led.

"I lied to the cops," Bobbi told me time and again. "I did. I lied. I thought I was going along with Jennifer so we could both get out of it all."

* * *

In her response to a second letter I sent (after not hearing from her after an extended period of time), Jen finally spoke. She came across extremely bitter, apprehensive, and even unsure of what she was writing. In an odd choice of words, she said she was "unhappy to inform" me of her "lack of interest" in talking about her life, "then or now." Continuing, she explained how "sure" she was that I would have "plenty of false facts to complete" my project, once I started talking to other people. Of course, she mocked, I would get the "ever-needy" Bobbi Jo's "side of things," along with Jen's "infamous sister, Audrey," and her mother, who would surely "help paint a picture" of Jen.

Besides a few more pokes at Audrey, and some sarcasm tossed in for good measure, Jen ended the pithy letter by asking me not to write back.

And so I never did.

CHAPTER 44

ON THURSDAY, JUNE 24, 2004, Bobbi and Jen were indicted by a Palo Pinto County, Texas, grand jury for the murder of Bob Dow and arraigned on first-degree murder charges by Judge Bobby Hart. Both bonds had been set at $700,000. This was surely not a joke anymore as the girls stood and listened to the court speak of how they could each receive terms of five to ninety-nine years, or even life, if found guilty. Jen looked quite grown-up by now: that light-skinned glow of a young teenager (although she was only nineteen, same as Bobbi) was long gone and re-placed by a convict look, which Jen had entirely embraced. The change was complete. Jen had set a path for herself to turn out like her mother and here she was, filling those shoes perfectly. What's more, there had been about thirty days when Jen had actually seen her life—and that "path" she be-lieved she had taken long ago—come full circle when she found herself serving time in the same jail as her mother.

"We laughed, cried, hugged, told stories, forgave each other, and just bonded," Kathy Jones later told me of that time in prison she spent with her daughter.

Bonded?

It had taken this sort of forced sobriety for both to realize there *was* some love within an unhealthy, dysfunctional relationship they had come to grasp throughout their lives.

District Attorney Tim Ford had to recuse himself from the case because he was kin to Jerry Jones. Both girls were appointed attorneys—Kenneth Tarlton for Jen, Bob Watson for Bobbi.

No trial date had been set during the short hearing.

CHAPTER 45

BOBBI WAS FEELING THE full weight of prison life while waiting for her case to churn through the American justice system. Via a phone call back home, Bobbi was given some grave news.

"A man just wanted to see what it was like to kill somebody," Tamey Hurley later explained, "and [my son] was there at the wrong time."

Someone had shot and killed Bobbi's twenty-four-year-old stepbrother. He had been shot multiple times in the chest.

"So Bobbi was put in jail, and several months later, her brother was shot and killed," Tamey added. "It was horrible. Absolutely horrible."

Bobbi was devastated. Her life—a life that didn't seem to be able to fall any deeper into the abyss—was continuing to crash and burn on the way down. Light and hope were gone. Bobbi was not adjusting to prison life.

CHAPTER 46

OVER THE COURSE OF the next year, the girls were held at Palo Pinto County Jail, although separated in different sections of the prison, not allowed to see each other. But according to Jen, this did not stop them from communicating.

During the day they yelled through the bars . . ., Katy Vine wrote in her *Texas Monthly* article, and were able to hold conversations.

At night, when the lights dimmed, the mice came out and inmates read, watched television and played with themselves. Bobbi and Jen—if we are to believe what Jen later told a magazine—were also able to communicate through the air ducts in the jail. And, as Jen told it, what an interesting series of conversations they had! It became a time when their relationship and loyalty to each other was put to the test, Jen explained.

Jen would remind Bobbi that Bob was scum and had it coming, and he was "going to get busted," anyway. So they were going to get out of jail soon enough and people would "thank" them for ridding the earth of such a pathetic piece of garbage.

Bobbi would respond, Jen said, by saying she believed that, too. They'd always end their conversations with an "I love you," Jen told *Texas Monthly*.

"That never happened," Bobbi told me. "Never. Just more lies told by Jennifer after the fact. She was making things up as she went along."

CHAPTER 47

MIKE BURNS GREW up in Mineral Wells.
Before becoming a prosecutor in 2001,
Burns spent the bulk of his time in law enforcement in Corpus Christi, working as a police officer
and special investigator, climbing the professional
ladder all the way up to captain, and even the chief
of police, in Mesquite, Texas, a suburb of Dallas. It
was then, in the early 1980s, when Burns decided
law school was his future. It was 1994 when Mike
Burns passed the bar and became a licensed attorney in the state of Texas. His first gig was as a
defense attorney. By 2001, after moving back to
Mineral Wells, when a vacancy in the local district
attorney's office opened, the governor appointed
Burns to the job.

Burns had gotten the call about the murder of
Bob Dow about a week after the girls were brought
in from Blythe.

"Look, I'm going to have recuse myself from

this thing," the county prosecutor Tim Ford said.
"Would you be willing to take it on as a special
prosecutor, Mike?"

"Sure," Burns responded.

For Burns, when he looked at this case, the one
word that came to mind was "bizarre." After re-
viewing the police reports, interviews, and other
documents, Burns came to this determination:
"The more that I looked at it, I couldn't believe
that this sort of thing was going on in Mineral
Wells for some length of time, under the radar of
most people (especially law enforcement)."

What the prosecutor meant by that was the amateur pornography filmmaking sessions and drug
binges taking place at Bob Dow's party house.

When Burns looked at the relationship between
Bob Dow and the girls, in addition to how Bobbi
had paraded women and young girls in and out
of the house for Bob, all of the drugs they had
consumed, and the fact that nobody knew a darn
thing about it, he could only shake his head in disgust and disbelief. It was incredibly appalling to
Burns. He was sickened by it all, he told me.

"We tried to track down every girl in those
photos," Burns said, "and weren't lucky enough to
find them all. Some of them certainly appeared to
be underage."

Still, Burns had a murder victim to represent in
court, regardless what he felt about the crimes the
victim might have committed. And when he looked
at the case, the most powerful, critical evidence

Burns felt he had to run with became the girls'
turning on each other.

"Of course, you have evidence of them fleeing,
taking the truck, pawning the dead guy's property"—
actually, it was Kathy Jones who pawned the items,
not Jen or Bobbi—"the statements of Audrey,
Kathy . . . and it all fell into place as far as the
timeline as to what happened. Once Bobbi Jo and
Jennifer gave it up, it all matched the forensic evidence. But each of the girls was the most damning
evidence against the other."

When Burns put it that way, the case sounded
like an episode of *CSI:* Cut, paste, print! Juries,
jaded by all the true crime on television today, certainly liked to see a well-rounded forensic case
presented by the prosecution. Juries wanted flair
and flash. They wanted to witness a slam-the-book-
on-the-table piece of science that brought it all
home. Prosecutor Burns seemed to have just that.

The fact that Burns didn't have a sympathetic
victim, however, somewhat nagged at the special
prosecutor as he prepared his case.

"You see, down here in Texas, there's the
unspoken [law of] 'He needed killin','" Burns
commented. "Even though that's not a legal
defense, it comes up from time to time in murder
cases—especially when your victim is perceived as
somebody viewed as not all that likeable. So, sure,
I worried about that. He was not—and I don't
mean to speak ill of the dead—but he was not a
candidate for Citizen of the Year."

To say the least.

The fact remained, and Burns knew it, if law enforcement had caught up to Bob and figured out what was going on inside that house before he was murdered, he might have wound up in jail doing time on several serious, felonious charges. And yet—most will agree—no matter what someone does, nothing excuses another person from taking the law into his or her own hands and murdering him.

CHAPTER 48

ON **APRIL 19, 2005,** a few weeks shy of the year anniversary of Bob Dow's murder, Special Prosecutor Mike Burns addressed the jury deciding the ultimate punishment Jen would receive for her role in Bob Dow's homicide. Lo and behold, Jen had cut a deal. The guilt or innocence portion of Jen's case would never take place. Jen had admitted (pled) to her crimes. It appeared that since Jen was arrested, she had ditched Bobbi and found a new love behind bars: Jesus Christ.

"I got baptized on September 17, [2004], and . . . it's just so much easier to live with God and just to know that the burden is lifted and that I'm forgiven for what I've done, even though it's not right that I took someone's life with my own hands," Jen told the court. "And God gives me—lets me know that His love is good enough. I don't have to seek someone else's."

Jen walked into a Joyce Meyer/Beth Moore

prison ministry program one Tuesday night, and as it happened, a light shone on her. She was immediately saved.

New relationship with the Lord aside, it was time for Jen to face jurors deciding how long she'd have to pay for her crimes. Lest everyone forget: Jen had admitted to murdering a man. In Texas, and a handful of other states, a jury decides a defendant's sentence; but there must be a hearing under the "punishment phase" term first, in which a defendant is allowed to essentially plead her case for leniency. What's important to note here in this situation is, because Jen pled to murder, the hearing was her chance to shirk the blame, essentially, and place it on the shoulders of someone else, thus arguing for a lighter sentence. The opportunity presented itself for Jen to do that because she (and Bobbi) had lied several times to police. There was no one narrative set in stone. Jen could effectively invent *another* version (which would be the third at this point) of what had happened.

One of Jen's biggest obstacles in doing that, however, was that she *had* changed her story so many times. By now, it was hard to keep track of how many lies she had told. And then the question had to become: If she had lied so often and easily to law enforcement, why believe her story now? Jen wasn't challenging guilt, after all. As Burns put it, her argument was for the "appropriate punishment." The responsibility on Burns was to help the jury decide what that fitting penalty should be. Did Jen deserve a second chance at some point in her life? Because she was admitting guilt and was supposedly willing now to "tell the truth," did this teenager deserve a break?

Mike Burns explained to the jury: "On May 4, 2004 . . . the evidence is going to show that . . . Jennifer, Bobbi Jo, and Bob went over to the Ridgmar Mall . . . ," and this was when the entire plot to murder Bob was initiated, in Burns's opinion. Call it fate or something less pious, but when Bobbi and Jen were caught stealing, the stars aligned for that final straw to be drawn in Bob's life.

Burns said Bob made a pass at Jen inside the truck, she got pissed, told Bobbi, and they hatched a murder plot. Burns summed it up that succinctly. Most interesting, Burns placed the first official words of a murder plan in Jen's mouth, stating to jurors: "On the way back to Bob's house, Jennifer tells Bobbi Jo, 'I'm going to kill him. I'm going to kill him.' And as they drive a little bit farther, she tells her, 'No, I'm not going to kill him.' Nonetheless, they arrive at Bob's house and Bob is now home. So they walk in and Bobbi Jo starts talking to Bob. . . . And while Bobbi Jo is talking to him . . . Jennifer goes in the bedroom. . . ."

Burns said Jen checked the gun inside the bedroom, to make sure it was loaded, while Bobbi spoke to Bob (keeping him busy) in the living room. He told jurors Jen hid the weapon. Then, certain she had a loaded gun ready and waiting, Jen demanded that she and Bob sleep together for repayment of the bail money, quoting Jen as saying, "No, no, come on, [Bob], we need to have sex."

Then the oral sex.

Then the "I want to get on top" scenario.

And then, Burns quipped, "She straddles over the top of Bob and they begin having sex. . . . And after he does that (puts the laundry bag over his face), Jennifer pulls the pistol out and she shoots him twice through the laundry bag. . . . [She] gets off him and stands to the edge of the bed and Bob is still moving. So she stands at the edge . . . and she shoots him three more times."

Mike Burns told jurors Jen acted alone in killing Bob Dow.

"Bobbi Jo runs in," Burns continued, "and says, 'Oh, my God! Oh, my God, what have you done?'"

This was where Burns placed Bobbi as, he said, she whipped into action, directing Jen, telling her what to do next, so they could get out of there quickly.

Then Burns explained how they drove to Spanish Trace and the first words out of *Jen's* mouth were "I killed Bob."

Burns said Jen immediately took the rap for the murder while at Spanish Trace, before Bobbi finally piped in and told Kathy and the others, "No, I killed Bob."

The scene, as Burns described it here, came across panicked, lots of "statements going back and forth."

Nowhere in Burns's comments to the jury did he implicate Bobbi in the murder of Bob Dow in *any* form or fashion. His entire argument centered on Jennifer, one would guess, so she was certain to be given the harshest sentence the jury could administer.

The condensed case Mike Burns presented over the next day bolstered his opening argument that Jen was a cold-blooded murderer, acting alone, killing a man after his repeated requests and even attempts to have sex with her failed. And that one final demand for sex as payment pushed Jen into taking a gun and killing him.

If one listened closely, and put Burns's argument into the context of Jen's promiscuous life of growing up addicted to sex, it would certainly bolster an opinion that Jen had snapped. Bob had pushed the wrong button one too many times; Jen responded by allowing all of that repressed anger—a volcanic rage, which she had harbored and built up over the years—to explode in one violent, fatal moment.

Closing out his case, Burns stated the obvious: "Murder is the most heinous crime on the books. It holds one of the highest penalties. And this is a case that is of the utmost seriousness because of the nature in which it was committed and because of the future dangerousness of this defendant."

When speaking of Jen's "future," an argument could be made for less time in prison. Prison might harden this girl. If anything was clear by this point in Jen's penalty phase, it was that she was probably more of a danger to herself than to anyone else.

Concerned about covering all bases, Burns then keyed in on a defense tactic he believed Jen's attorney would soon implement: the strategy of blaming the victim.

"I suspect when counsel for the defense gets up, you're going to hear a litany of crimes, bad acts, and otherwise about the deceased. Do not chase that rabbit trail, because the victim in this case is *not* Jennifer Lynn Jones. The victim in this case, no matter what you think of him, is Robert Clair Dow Jr."

Burns encouraged the jury to think about a few things while Jen's attorney inevitably attacked Bob's character and likely bantered that Jen "should be spared for ridding our community of this bad man. . . . How can you save the living by defiling the deceased? It don't work that way."

Then, concluding, Burns said, "I'll talk to you in a few minutes about what we think is an appropriate punishment. . . ."

CHAPTER 49

FIFTY-EIGHT-YEAR-OLD Kenneth Tarlton lived up to the reputation Mike Burns had set up for him. After approaching the jury and arguing on Jen's behalf, quite emphatically, Tarlton stated that the issue at hand was not whether Jen deserved punishment, but what the appropriate punishment should be considering her "involvement" in Bob's murder.

Burns leaned back in his chair, took a deep breath, and placed his pen down on a yellow legal pad in front of him. This was going to be worth his undivided attention.

"You can only consider facts and circumstances as evidence," Tarlton said smartly. It was an important declaration. Jurors literally held Jen's freedom in their hands, Tarlton knew. They could give her a minimum—a slap—of five years' probation, or a maximum of—overly aggressive, perhaps—

ninety-nine years to life. Burns knew shooting for something in the middle was probably reality, but Tarlton could go for the moon and stars if he chose to.

Tarlton respectfully went about detailing what evidence law enforcement witnesses had found inside Bob's house when they first arrived. He bypassed—conveniently, of course—the reason why they were there to begin with: Bob Dow's murdered corpse. He described how the responding officer found Bob's mother's room in "disarray" and "dirty," adding how the woman had "been there a long time," lying in her own filth. Then he talked about how Detective Brian Boetz "reacted" understandably shocked by what he uncovered inside Dow's computer.

"Robert Clair Dow Jr. was providing alcohol, pills, and drugs to young, underage girls in exchange for sex," Tarlton said.

The indication was clear: Was there a more reviled human being on the planet than a man who did such a thing?

Maybe a pedophile, sure. But guys like Bob Dow came in a close second.

"He determined that there was voyeurism going on," Tarlton said, describing one of the conclusions Boetz had drawn while studying the crime scene and searching the house. "That simply means you like to watch people doing things. Everybody was using drugs, alcohol, pills, marijuana."

Tarlton repeated one of the questions he had once posed to Detective Boetz: "'Were you able to identify all the young girls in the photos and video-tapes?'" Then he answered his own question, saying, "'Some, but not all of them.'" Out of more than six hundred photos, Detective Boetz agreed with the attorney that a "majority of them were very graphic-type photos . . . that they were *under-age* girls in them and that it was obvious that the girls had been paid."

Burns called it right. Tarlton was doing his best to smear Bob's character, which wasn't so hard to do. Most jurors probably agreed the guy was a criminal and morally repugnant; he preyed on young girls, molested a few of them, and treated most women as sex slaves.

But was that the matter at hand? Burns had made a point to say earlier.

No. The issue was murder.

Did that behavior, as vile as it was, give Jennifer Jones a license to kill?

Tarlton was smart enough to know it didn't matter. If a lawyer can get a jury to hate the victim for what he did to underage girls who hardly knew any better—one of them being the defendant—and they'd sleep better at night, knowing they'd taken it easy on his killer.

Tarlton explained what a witness had testified to earlier that day, saying, "Think about what she said. . . . She did tell you that he didn't care about his mother. He was neglecting her. . . . She saw a lot of drug use. She could identify painkillers, Xanax." Tarlton allowed that comment to hang for a moment before delivering the punch line: "She even saw heroin being used. She said there were young girls being brought in for sexual purposes." He repeated what the witness had said: "'I seen it!'"

He next focused on how Bobbi became Bob's "chick magnet." How Bob could "have any young girl he wanted, as long as he kept [Bobbi] happy."

He talked about how Kathy Jones told law enforcement and the court that she didn't give her daughter "any guidance except with alcohol and drugs."

Reminding the jury of the brief testimony it heard was a good strategy. It could work. There was a fine line, though, that a defense attorney didn't want to cross. An attorney never wanted to beat a subject down the throats of jurors; they'd come out of it feeling patronized, and probably would turn on the lawyer.

Using one witness's account, Tarlton then told a hideous, evil, criminal story about Bob. He talked about "the scariest" thing was how "[Bob] came up with this big, grand scheme to make some money, to scam his employer." What was it? Tossing "his then-wife down the stairs so she would miscarry." Then Bob could "sue somebody." So his wife left him. "And how did he react to that? . . .

He followed her around. Found her in . . . a woman's shelter! Drove around, threatened her with a shotgun or a rifle, until she gave in and she had to go back with him."

Tarlton implied Bob was planning to make a snuff film with Jen, adding, "Then he . . . at various times, he had threatened violence toward the little girl. . . . Y'all are entitled to take these pictures back. . . . This is Bob Dow," he stated loudly, making reference to the actual photos. "This is the Bob Dow we know right *here*. I didn't make these pictures up. . . ."

Spinning his case back to Jen, Tarlton said, "She didn't dodge the question—*she* didn't make up some grand scheme. She had told you what she had done here." He mentioned Jen's mother and how Jen was raised, concluding with a nurture argument, blabbering on about Jen never having a chance in life. "She was," he said, "raised by wolves." Then, some moments later, he said, "Her mother came back into her life in her mid-to-late teens and you heard her mother say that they started doing things in common. Drinking and doping, drinking and doping." He talked about how just over one year ago was when Jennifer "finally met Bobbi Jo Smith. She loved her."

This got Tarlton going. Continuing what had turned into a rant, he blamed Bobbi for corrupting Jen with the help of Bob Dow, asking: "Anybody—*anybody*—lower than Bob Dow? Virtually no redeeming social qualities—and that's *not* counting the way he treated his poor mother."

From Tarlton's tone in the way he portrayed Bob, Jen had done the world a favor by killing him.

"Nineteen-year-old girl steps up here in front of twelve strangers and half a courtroom full of people and admits that she committed a crime— admits that she committed a *horrible* crime! . . ."

Always end with a rhetorical question seems to be the winning flavor among defense attorneys. Allow the jury members to take that question back and, internally, ask it to themselves. Make it a moral issue on the grounds of good versus evil; or, as Tarlton did elegantly, justice versus mercy: "You know, everybody is familiar with the statute of Lady Justice," Tarlton concluded, walking slowly toward jurors, his head down, staring at the floor. He was lost in this moment. "She's the lady standing there with the scales and with the blindfold on." He looked up, scanning the faces of jurors. "We know that Lady Justice may be blind, but she's not without mercy, not at all." Then he posed this: "What would you do if you found out that a middle-aged man had given drugs and alcohol to your teenage daughter, filmed her having sex when she was under the influence, and then *paid* her money for sex?"

He strategically paused and waited a few beats.

"May peace be with you in your verdict. Thank you."

CHAPTER 50

MIKE BURNS HAD somewhat of a cocky smirk on his face, not to mention a slight note of sarcasm in his voice, as he stepped up to deliver his final words. For Burns, he needed to bring the case back to, well, reality. It was fine to blame the victim. Hell, what other chance did Jen really have? But this case wasn't about Jen's poor upbringing, her mother's drug use, the fact that Bob did some really horrible things to young girls.

For Mike Burns, it was about one relatively simple fact: murder.

"Ladies and gentlemen," Burns said during his rebuttal, "I know, and certainly hope, that you're a lot smarter than I am because, my goodness, I got confused there for a minute. I forgot who the victim was and who the defendant was when I was listening to Mr. Tarlton tell you about his case. Bob Dow is the . . . um . . . yeah . . . no! Bob Dow is the *victim*."

In the totality of the case, Burns had said the right thing. The impact the statement would ultimately have on jurors was another story, of course. But still, the prosecutor needed to say it, knowing that the human heart is a strange apparatus. Justice doesn't always mean that the truth and the law is served. There is so-called street justice abounding in courtrooms throughout the world. This jury could punish Bob Dow by allowing his killer to walk out of the courtroom. Mike Burns knew that.

Yet, even in the scope of that, Burns might have taken it a bit too far, however, when he said next: "The . . . man [is] lying on his back, having the most intimate relationship with a woman, and gets three bullets shot up into his brain—and that's the victim in this case."

If there was one certainty within a fog of lies, it was that Jen and Bob did not have an intimate relationship. Not by any means. Burns might have served his purpose better had he focused on the lure factor—how Jen, using Bob Dow's own affection for her, tricked him into that bedroom so she could kill him. Put that way, her crime sounded more diabolical and sinister. Entirely premeditated, in fact.

"And regardless of what a low-down skunk he might have been," Burns continued, "whether he was or not, I don't know." (Another miscue.) "Regardless if he didn't have any redeeming social values, I don't know, but I tell you what. . . . She don't get to make that decision."

Smartly, Burns dug a bit deeper into the Robin Hood aspect of Tarlton's previous argument—telling the jury, rightly so, how Jen had the chance to turn Bob Dow over to the police, to report his vulgar and criminal activity. He explained how she had "every opportunity" to "call these officers right there and say, 'This man is doing these things. He's giving young kids drugs. He's giving me drugs. He's making us do this.'" But that's not what Jen did, Burns added. Then he pointed at her, hammering his claims home. "*She* doesn't get to take the law into her own hands and take a human life."

That one statement ignited a firestorm of facts out of Burns's mouth. He went on, letting jurors know Jen was an *adult* woman when she made the decision to kill Bob Dow. And as an adult, she also made the choice to star in Bob Dow's motion pictures and take drugs and partake in sex with him and the other girls. Life was one big party for this woman, whose days and nights revolved around drugs, booze, and sex. It was an evil path, sure. But it was one that Jennifer Jones *chose*.

"She knew what was right. She knew what was wrong," Burns said. "And when the day came to shoot three bullets into Bob Dow's brain, she *chose* to do it." He mentioned how "thousands of young people have bad lives" and how thousands more grow up without parents. And still, thousands more "live on the street." Yet, "I submit to you, ladies and gentlemen, that thousands of kids do not sit on top of a person, have sex with them, and shoot bullets into their brain. . . ." He called what Jen did "depravity that defies justification," before fixing that by stating: "That is depravity that defies mercy." He finally concluded by saying, "Depravity that defies civilization. . . ."

Burns might have taken things too far, but his point was well taken. The jury seemed interested.

After a little soapbox proclaiming, Burns went back through the crime, noting how Jen planned and executed it in a sinister manner, suggesting that Jen and Bobbi got off on planning the crime and carrying it out. The point was: At no time was murdering another human being a hard decision for Jen to make. She didn't think, *Oh, I'm ridding the earth of a scumbag.*

No, in Burns's view, Jen planned this crime for a thrill, robbed Bob Dow afterward, and took off on a trip through New Mexico and Arizona and California because she wanted to have a good time. This wasn't some sort of Robin Hood and her merry women fantasy of stealing the life of a monster for the sake of righteousness, and protecting the village during the process. Don't be fooled, Burns warned, by Jen's baby face and ploy of "poor me, poor, poor me."

"And the other thing . . . we all know what a sociopath is, right?" Burns asked near the end of a rant that surely shot up his blood pressure. "A sociopath is a person who has no conscience, and that's basically the definition. A person who is unable to feel remorse, unable to feel—"

Kenneth Tarlton had heard enough. He stood. "Your Honor, I'm going to object. This is introducing new matters before the jury."

"This is common knowledge that people know, Your Honor," Burns defended.

The judge considered both statements. Then: "All right, ladies and gentlemen, you'll be guided by your recollection of what the *evidence* is." Then he asked Burns to continue.

Burns traveled back down that road of Jen being an unremorseful, unconscionable killer, who had total disregard for the law and for her fellow man. At one point, Burns turned it around and put the jury's decision on the backs of each as if he or she was speaking for the community as a whole. Regardless of how one feels about the crimes committed by a man, Burns articulated rather well, the ultimate crime of murder can never be justified by taking that life.

"We don't do that in this county," Burns said. "We don't do that in this part of Texas. Don't cheat these young officers sitting here. Don't cheat the state of Texas. And let's don't cheat our community. Let's send a message, no matter what the situation is, when you take matters into your own hands as callously and unfeelingly—if that's a word—as you did and kill somebody, take a human life . . ."

And again, Burns would have been better off wrapping things up here. However, he went on and on, sounding more like a prosecutor not so much begging for the ultimate punishments, but a man who felt his case might be slipping away.

The wide range of sentencing options was a bit confusing, Burns explained.

"I got a recommendation. I think what you ought to do is start your deliberations at the very top of the scale, life or ninety-nine years. All right. And then consider what facts that you've heard that tend to mitigate this crime. And if it starts coming down, then that's your duty to come to a consensus to see what it is. But I wouldn't start at five years' probation and say, 'What makes it bad?' and say, 'Oh, well, maybe it ought to be seven years. . . .' We don't tolerate murder in this community, and I ask you to give this young woman a substantial sentence to where that message is sent to the community. Thank you."

CHAPTER 51

THE JURY DIDN'T take long deciding Jen's punishment for taking Bob Dow's life. That same day, April 20, 2005, word came back that a decision on her sentence had been made.

As Burns thought, the jury split the difference. Jen was sentenced to forty-eight years. Her projected release date was set for May 8, 2053. Jen would be a sixty-seven-year-old woman if she served all those years. Her first parole eligibility date was scheduled for May 5, 2028. She'd be forty-two.

Either way, Jen was going to spend decades behind bars.

As Jen was waiting to be transferred to Gatesville, Texas, the women's prison, she spent a few more nights at Palo Pinto County Jail. And according to her, she and Bobbi had one more conversation shortly before that transfer to her new home came through.

During the penalty phase of Jen's plea, there had been an exchange between Jen and Mike Burns (during Jen's testimony) that implicated Bobbi as the driving force behind the murder. Jen had told the court that Bobbi was in on the entire plan and convinced her to "finish him off." The conversation between Jen and Mike Burns centered on that "you look sexy standing there with that gun in your hand" scenario, which Jen had described in her second statement.

Bobbi had heard what Jen testified to in court. She wasn't happy about it. It was upsetting to Bobbi that Jen was continuing the lie. And now, Bobbi considered, Jen was lying simply to take revenge on Bobbi.

According to the *Texas Monthly, Bobbi Jo . . . yelled to Jennifer through the air ducts one last time. "I'm getting out," [Bobbi] said. "You can't be there for me no more. . . . I've found somebody new."*

This was the story Jen told Katy Vine.

When I asked Bobbi about this alleged conversation, she did not recall that it had ever taken place. Yes, she said, she was pissed off at Jen for lying on the witness stand; but she had no idea what, exactly, Jen had said, and she never spoke to her through the bars that night.

"I have no idea where she got that stuff from," Bobbi said.

CHAPTER 52

ONE OF THE OBSTACLES facing Bobbi and her fight for freedom came when her court-appointed attorney, Bob Watson, decided he wasn't the man for the job. But instead of going to the judge first, according to Bobbi and several additional sources, Watson called a colleague.

"I think this is a case you might be interested in," Watson explained over the phone to that colleague. "I really don't want to keep trying the case."

"To [Bob's] credit, he called me and told me that I should take on Bobbi's case," Jim Matthews, a well-known attorney in Palo Pinto County at the time, told me.

Only problem was, Bobbi had no money.

That was okay with Matthews, he later said. He wanted to help.

The judge, however, wasn't all that crazy with the change. He allowed it, sure—as long as it did not affect the timeline of Bobbi's scheduled fall trial. Strangely enough, the judge was firm: He was not going to grant a continuance (even with this bombshell of a move: the handing over of a murder case from one lawyer to the other). What's more, it was public knowledge that the interview Jen had given to *Texas Monthly* was going to be part of a story about the case published in the weeks before Bobbi was slated to face jurors. For some reason that nobody wanted to admit, it was as if Bobbi's case was being fast-tracked. She had a new lawyer, and there was that lengthy article based on Jen's point of view published by one of Texas's most prestigious journals set to debut just weeks before one of its main subjects was going to face a jury. (Bobbi, under her former attorney's orders, had refused to speak to the magazine.)

At least on paper, it appeared that this case was a perfect example for one of the reasons why a trial should be postponed.

The judge, however, remained steadfast: No way. This trial was going on, as scheduled. No more discussion about it.

I also heard, in fact, from two independent, credible sources that when Jim Matthews received Bobbi's case file, one crucially vital piece of the case was missing from it—some of the more graphically explicit videos that Bob had filmed of the girls having sex.

Jim Matthews faced a mountain of difficulties and preparation.

"We burned the midnight oil," Matthews told me. What else could he do?

CHAPTER 53

MIKE BURNS'S THEORY OF what happened to Bob Dow—which he aimed to prove during Bobbi's trial—was now different from what it had been during Jen's sentencing hearing. The plot to take Bob out began, Burns explained, when the girls were caught shoplifting. The aftermath of that arrest—Bob Dow bailing the girls out, a fact nobody I spoke to could present any type of documented proof of—put into play a situation where Bobbi had supposedly initiated a plot to have her lover, Burns argued, murder Bob for her. To convict Bobbi, this was the situation Burns set out to prove.

"And Bob," Burns told me, "who had that fixation with Jennifer and really wanted to have sex with her and had been for a long time . . . [he] bonds them out of jail. And then Bob gives them that ultimatum. 'I bailed y'all out of jail, so I want me some of Jennifer as my payback.' I think the plot is hatched at that point."

Except, from all accounts, Bob didn't present his "ultimatum" to *them*, as Mike Burns had explained it to me. Instead, Bob Dow allegedly had propositioned Jen alone in the truck.

Burns believed that was the magic moment when, he believed, Jen and Bobbi said to each other, "We got to get rid of this son of a bitch." Because when Burns looked at their actions from that point forward, he explained further, it was clear to him that every step the girls took from that moment forward was "a premeditated plan to kill Bob." Burns believed Bobbi told Jen to seduce Bob in the bedroom so Jen would have an opportunity to whack him. Bobbi's motive, Burns was now certain, turned out to be as unpretentious as most murder plots. He theorized Bobbi said: "We'll be free of this guy and we can go on with our lives. Move to California. Live in the sand and surf." And Jennifer agreed with it, Burns alleged.

The glue holding this theory together turned dry and brittle, once it was applied to the evidence. For one, Bobbi could have walked away from Bob Dow whenever she wanted, same as Jen. Bob Dow was in no condition or position to stop Bobbi from doing anything she didn't want to. Look at the evidence of Bobbi telling Kathy and Audrey that she wanted to go to Mexico. Bobbi was fleeing a bad situation of her friend having just murdered someone, not pursuing a pipe dream, as Burns put it, of moving to California with Jen and starting some white-picket-fence life together. In addition, Bobbi had left Bob before this moment, several times. More than any of that, though: Bobbi had a strong motive to keep Bob alive. He was her source of everything she desired most in life (even more than her own child): sex, drugs, and alcohol.

From where Burns decided to prosecute his case, he believed Bobbi was "inside the house in the living room" when Jen capped Bob in the bedroom. "When [Bobbi] heard the shot, she runs into the bedroom. Jennifer climbs off the guy. He's still moving and kind of groaning. So Bobbi Jo says, 'He's still moving, so finish him off.' And Jennifer stands at the edge of the bed and unloads the pistol into his head and one in the arm."

Burns got this entire scenario from Bobbi's second statement. It all fit into the design Burns had constructed; and it even sounded good on paper. The question remained, though, could Burns prove his theory to twelve jurors? Bobbi refused to plead guilty. Bobbi couldn't believe what was happening. She was innocent. Nobody would fall for this nonsense Burns was spinning.

Here it was, November 29, 2005; Jen was locked up in Gatesville Prison, already serving her time, and Bobbi, alone, seated in a courtroom with a new lawyer, was facing the rest of her life for a crime she claimed to have had nothing to do with. And as Bobbi sat in court, listening to Burns lay out the state's case against her, she couldn't have scripted the tale this guy was putting out there.

Mike Burns boiled his thoughts down into one basic argument, beginning the state's opening with: "This is a case about relationships between two young women . . . and it's about murder. And I believe the evidence will show in this case the following—Bobbi Jo Smith, the defendant, and a young woman by the name of Jennifer Jones were lovers, and they lived together under the roof and in the house of a man named Bob Dow. . . ."

From that moment forward, Burns did his best to sell his theory of an extreme (maybe even obsessive) love affair between Bobbi Jo and Jennifer that turned into a need to rid themselves of what Burns projected to be the one obstacle standing in the way of their happy ever after.

"And the evidence is going to show that this defendant took advantage of the dependence that Jennifer had on her. . . . The evidence will show that the plan was to *kill* Bob Dow—and the evidence will show that it was Bobbi Jo's idea."

A bold offering from an experienced attorney—after all, proving an *idea* was about as hard as proving how much in love the two girls were.

Nearly impossible.

Next, Burns put words in Bobbi's mouth, explaining to jurors how Bobbi once told Jen: "We need to kill Bob. . . . We have to. We have to kill

Bob because that is the only way that we can be together and be free of this man. He's not going to molest me again—anymore. He's not going to molest you anymore. We're going to kill Bob."

All very audacious statements Mike Burns attributed to Bobbi Jo Smith, but he did not say where each word had come from.

As he continued, Burns painted Bobbi as the mastermind/puppeteer to Jen's more naïve, willing, and weaker character, placing the entire onus of the crime on Bobbi.

He spoke of how Jen lured Bob and how they walked into Jerry Jones's Spanish Trace apartment after the murder. Meanwhile, entirely changing his theory from his opening statement during Jen's penalty hearing, Burns said: "This defendant, Bobbi Jo, told the girls, 'We just killed Bob.'"

In his opening statement that past April, Mike Burns said Jen first announced, "I killed Bob." But now, during Bobbi's trial, he put those words into Bobbi's mouth.

And nobody challenged this.

Then Burns moved onto that now infamous road trip, focusing on how Bobbi tossed the weapon out the window as they drove out of town.

How Bobbi called the shots as they made their way across Texas.

How Krystal decided she wanted out.

How, Burns said, "they"—Bobbi and Jen—worked "on their story" during the entire road trip.

How Bobbi and Jen ditched Audrey and Kathy

in Arizona because Bobbi believed they were talking to the police.

How they "cooked up" their first statements—admission documents Mike Burns himself referred to as "hogwash"—to "protect themselves." And how a second statement Bobbi gave to police was not gibberish at all (like her first), but what law enforcement believed to be the truth: Bobbi gave Jen the gun after loading it and then sent her into that bedroom to murder Bob. And yet, Burns left out (either knowingly or unknowingly), nowhere in that second statement did Bobbi ever admit to convincing, asking, or manipulating Jen into killing Bob Dow.

Still, the question—rhetorical or otherwise—that no one seemed interested in asking hung in the hot air of Mike Burns's opening: Why believe the *second* statement of a defendant's if you are not going to believe the first? And what about that one line Jen had said to her mother during the road trip? After Kathy had asked Jen how it felt to kill someone, Jen allegedly replied, "Pretty fucking good." Did that sound like a young woman being *forced* into murder?

Lastly, Burns promised the jury that they'd hear from Jen herself, now a born-again Christian, who was ready to tell the true story of what happened, clear her conscience, and send Bobbi to prison. He failed to say, though, that this would be Jen's fifth version of the events in question: first and second statement (one and two), her testimony from the penalty phase of her sentencing hearing (three), her bizarre tale of clear, outright lies in *Texas Monthly* (four), and now this, Jen's imminent testimony in Bobbi's trial.

"And when all of the evidence comes in . . . ," Burns concluded, "we're going to come back to you, and we're going to ask you to find this defendant guilty of murder."

CHAPTER 54

BOBBI'S ATTORNEY, Jim Matthews, later claimed he had been paid only $50 for taking Bobbi's case. "That," he told me, "and a night in a hotel room." Essentially, Matthews had taken the case pro bono.

With his sharp and noticeable Texas drawl, Jim Matthews approached jurors and said there was "quite a different story" to tell from what Mr. Burns had just whipped up. Matthews called it "the rest of the story," quoting famous radio personality Paul Harvey.

"Bobbi Jo just didn't do it. She just didn't do it. And the evidence is going to show that Jennifer Jones, *not* Bobbi Jo, murdered Bob Dow in cold blood—*not* in self-defense."

Important point.

Bobbi needed jurors to accept this scenario in order to walk. Not that she didn't have anything to do with killing Bob; that wasn't at issue here.

But Jen, after a cumulative life of emotional ups and downs, sexual abuse and promiscuity and chronic drug use, snapped, taking a shitty life of letdowns and emotional pain (baggage) all out on Bob Dow, who had made one too many passes at her after treating the woman Jen loved so horribly. Effectively, Jen became obsessed with Bobbi. That obsession and the fact that Bob was treating Bobbi like his personal sex slave, and Jen sat back and watched, had manifested into an evil plot within Jen's fragile psyche. She couldn't take it anymore. She wanted Bobbi all to herself, so she murdered the guy.

Matthews began with a play on what Burns had said earlier, noting how "the first *two* statements were hogwash."

Bobbi's attorney then walked over to a projector his legal aide had set up.

Mike Burns took notice.

"Is that focused?" Matthews asked his aide.

A photograph of Bobbi, as a baby, was projected onto the screen for jurors. Matthews began, "She was—like anybody else—brought up into this world the natural way."

Burns could not believe what he was seeing and hearing. *You've got to be kidding me!* The prosecutor nearly came out of his skin. He stood. "Your Honor . . . I object. This is improper for an opening statement. This is *evidence*."

"Sustained. You may give verbal without the—"

Matthews interrupted, finishing for the judge: "Photograph?"

"Photo*graphs*!" the judge snapped. "*Unless* they're submitted into evidence."

Then Ninth Judicial District judge Jerry Ray said something interesting. He explained to Matthews that the use of photos and videos in his courtroom during Bobbi's trial was going to be limited and watched carefully, adding, "I don't want to see that trash in my courtroom."

Judge Ray said it "very sternly," Matthews recalled.

"It (those sexually explicit photos of Bob Dow and the girls) was here during that first trial (Jen's penalty hearing)," Judge Ray continued, "and if you want to present it again, you had *better* have a *damn* good reason for it."

Strange thing to say about actual evidence that was, in many respects, a focal point of this case: the fact that the girls were starring and participating in these films.

Nonetheless, Matthews took the hint, telling me later: "They needed those photos and videos during Jennifer's penalty phase because it helped *them* say that Mr. Dow was a slime bag and deserved it and here's all this proof. . . . It was fine with me that Judge Ray didn't want it. My argument wasn't that Bobbi did it and Mr. Dow deserved it. My argument was that she *didn't* do it."

Still, those photographs tell a story. A court watcher would think that they'd be crucial to

Bobbi's case. There are plenty of films that display Bobbi's and Jen's chronic drug use. They also show how Bobbi and Jen had sex in front of spectators, and that the sex wasn't some sort of intimate moment between two females in love, but more or less another day in the life of Bobbi, who was bouncing through all of it with the sole intention of getting high.

Without showing the photographs, Matthews fell back into Bobbi's history. He spoke of her early life as the only girl in a family of boys and how, as a child, Bobbi took pleasure in taking the blame for things her siblings often did. Bobbi's life was actually going well, according to Matthews, until she met her son's father and fell in love and had a child. When Bobbi and her son's father split up, Matthews added, "Bob Dow welcomed Bobbi Jo into his home and really became a close friend of hers. She looked at him as a father, a friend, and even sometimes a lover . . . and you're going to hear that even at one point [Bob Dow] proposed marriage to her."

Marriage?

As Bobbi sat and listened, she considered that Matthews did not give the jury a complete picture of the relationship she'd had with Bob. But what could she say? She trusted Matthews and placed her freedom in his hands.

"She turned him down," Matthews continued. "But not because she was mad at him. He was just a lot older than her. . . . She just couldn't see him being her husband for the rest of her life."

Matthews, knowing full well that conservative Texas courts liked to keep things clean, walked jurors slowly into what he obviously viewed as a taboo subject to approach inside Judge Ray's court-room: Bobbi Jo's sexuality.

"[You] may or may not agree with what you hear about Bobbi Jo and some sexual things. But that doesn't make her a murderer. She and Bob Dow . . . they liked each other. He cared about her. She cared about him."

The idea with this opening was to paint a complete picture of the Bob Dow/Bobbi Jo Smith relationship. Matthews did a fair job of it. He spoke of how Bob taught Bobbi the construction trade, took her on as an apprentice, and even ex-plained how the business side of things worked.

"She was kind of a tomboy," Matthews explained, adding how Bobbi "enjoyed being outdoors" and "working with her hands and . . . she could begin to try to feel self-supported and maybe someday raise [her son] on her own."

The way Matthews portrayed the relationship, a listener would be hard-pressed not to believe that Bob Dow and Bobbi Smith, at one time, had a loving bond—same as maybe a father and his daughter.

But then Matthews digressed, delivering the ugly punch line to his father-daughter bombast: "You're going to learn that Jennifer was jealous . . .

of the relationship between Bobbi Jo and Bob
Dow. She didn't like Bob Dow. Bob Dow didn't
necessarily like her. He kind of wanted to have sex
with her, but he was kind of like that. And that's
one of the reasons that you'll hear that Jennifer
killed him. She *wanted* him out of the way." Then
Matthews raised his voice, shouting: "She didn't
like the triangle. Two is company and three is a
crowd. And she wanted to end that. . . ."

If one was to look at the case objectively—and
neither lawyer could do that, of course—one
would draw the conclusion that Jim Matthews, on
the basis of the law, had a solid argument here. If
he was to take Jen's journal and build on all of the
self-hatred she'd harbored, her promiscuity and
disobedience, her criminal record, on top of the
low self-esteem she brought into the relationship
with Bobbi, he'd have one hell of a case to present
for a girl gone bad—a girl gone terribly wrong,
who was in no position to enter into a relationship
with a woman for the first time. And when Jen testified, Matthews could easily impeach her testimony with her own words from that journal. Jen
had been let down again and again by her lovers.
Here, she met Bobbi and—there can be no doubt—
became immediately infatuated and arguably
obsessed as soon as Bobbi showed affection and
cared for her. She followed Bobbi everywhere. She
would not allow Bobbi out of her sight. Even when

faced with the notion that Bobbi was not exclusive to her, Jen continued the relationship.

"The photos of Jen and I having sex was all at once," Bobbi told me. "Our 'sex life' was not what you think. All of those photos were taken with several other women. . . . I remember having sex with Jennifer . . . [but] she had a boyfriend. She'd leave and go with him all the time. [Our affair] wasn't a 'relationship'—it was drugs."

Part of the problem Bobbi had (and she didn't even realize it) in proving how desperate, despondent, codependent, and abandoned by love Jen was when she walked into Bobbi's life turned out to be that Jen's journal (which would have told jurors a lot about Jen's character) was sitting in a box inside her aunt's house collecting dust. It would never be entered into the record as evidence. Nobody had interviewed Jen's aunt and found out about the journal. Bobbi's legal team of Jim Matthews did not have the resources to hire a private investigator to conduct its own investigation (which might have produced the journal and more), or located other witnesses to back up the idea that Jen had a history of violence and her life was spiraling out of control when she met Bobbi.

Bobbi also believed—and Matthews backed up her claim—that part of the reason she was so vigorously prosecuted (and perhaps grossly *over-*prosecuted) fell into a well-choreographed plot to punish her because she was a lesbian.

"In reality," Bobbi explained, "they all could not

stand me. The county jail (where Bobbi was being held) threw me in a cell with no water and not even a toilet. I had my skin break out and they refused to treat me. They did me wrong . . . just because they knew I was gay. They wanted to ridicule me and put me alone so [as I was told over and over] I'd 'stop screwing women.' They called me names for being gay. . . . They lashed out over my sexual preference and tried me in a court, where I had no chance!"

Matthews became somewhat grandiose at one point during his opening, asserting, "And, you know, Bobbi Jo is many things . . . and it's so important what you're doing as a jury. This country is the greatest country on the face of the earth. We have the most powerful military. We have the most powerful political system—"

But Burns had heard enough. "I object. This is argument, *not* opening statement, Your Honor."

"Sustained. . . ."

"Anyway," Matthews continued, "I hope that you keep your hearts and your minds open to hear the rest of the story, because there is another side. It is very important to hear the other side of the story and to know everything before you begin to make up your mind about it." He paused. "Thank you."

For Jim Matthews at this stage, there were just a few words about Bobbi and Bob, and no promises of groundbreaking evidence or a surprise witness who would persuade the jury. It was as if

Matthews was confident on the merit of his case alone, and he didn't need to carry on with rhetoric or conjecture. He wanted to get on with the trial.

The judge took a fifteen-minute recess.

CHAPTER 55

AFTER THE BREAK, MIKE Burns introduced his star witness. Jennifer Jones had changed. She was nineteen and had packed on some prison weight, about thirty pounds by several estimates. She had that hard, weathered look of a woman who had become part of the penal system. She was a number now. No longer that light-skinned, smiling teen, effeminate and girly, out in the world looking for a good time. Here was a woman, by all accounts, who clearly was comfortable in her new role as a convict.

Jen admitted she had been convicted of murder in this case. Burns eased into her life and had Jen explain where she was from, where she lived, and how she met Bobbi. Throughout this biographical portion of her testimony, Jen did not tell the story she had recently given in detail to *Texas Monthly*, wherein she had met Bobbi beneath a tree in front of the town library after

Bobbi called; and that when Bobbi planted one on her, Jen was immediately swept off her feet in some sort of fairy-tale love affair. Nope. She never said any of it. According to what Jen now claimed (her fifth version), she met Bobbi over the course of a few weeks while Bobbi was dating Audrey; and then, at a party one night at Bob's, Jen and Bobbi "hooked up" (a story that Bobbi later agreed with).

Jen talked about how difficult a life she'd had: dropping out of school, doing drugs, having sex with any boy who wanted it, moving around a lot, her mother in prison, a father unavailable to her the way she wanted. What became most interesting about this exchange was how Jen explained that she had never really felt loved or had ever gotten that parental approval, which all kids crave. She was marrying that thread of her testimony with meeting Bobbi and, for the first time in her life, feeling all those things from Bobbi.

For Jen, it was about the attention she got. Bobbi made her feel wanted and whole—and she lapped it up.

"Was it a good feeling?" Burns asked.

"Yes, it was."

"Did there come a time when you fell *in* love with Bobbi Jo?"

"Yes, there was."

A few questions later, after Burns introduced Bob Dow into the dynamic of Bobbi and Jen's love affair, he asked, "All right, did Bobbi Jo and Bob have an intimate or a sexual relationship?"

"Yes, they did," Jen said without expanding beyond how Bobbi was forced to "sexually give herself to him in order to get something in return . . . [and she would] have to sometimes give up her girlfriend and sleep with Bob to get what she wanted. . . ."

Jen said she and Bobbi had a name for this: "paying the rent."

Bobbi sat, listening, shaking her head in confusion. She was deeply hurt by this explanation of her life with Bob. This was not the truth Bobbi had remembered living.

What in the world is Jennifer trying to prove? Bobbi asked herself as she listened.

Here was Jen lying under oath and nobody was challenging her. Bobbi was beside herself.

How could Jennifer tell one story after another and not be held accountable? What is Mr. Matthews thinking?

"How did you feel about her having to do that?" Burns asked, referring to Bobbi allegedly selling herself to Bob.

"I didn't think it was right."

"Did it make you jealous of the relationship between Bobbi Jo and Bob?"

"No, it didn't make me jealous."

"Why not?"

"Because it made me more disgusted. . . ."

In one breath, Jen had said she fell in love with Bobbi; in another, she claimed not to feel any jealousy when a man she hated was having sex with the woman she loved.

Jen said she felt Bobbi did not want to talk about the sex she was having with Bob whenever she brought it up, adding, "It had been going on before I came."

Burns asked next: "Now, were there situations in which you felt pressured that you would have to do that (have sex with Bob) as well?"

Quite contradictory to what Jen had said on several other occasions, nearly blowing the state's motive to bits, she answered, "Yes."

"Did anyone protect you . . . from that happening?"

"Whenever that came about, Bob asked Bobbi Jo for permission. And she had asked me if I wanted to, and I had said, 'No.'"

The way Jen talked through it, that offer of sex seemed like it was casual and consensual, as though Bob had made the suggestion and the girls simply said no and moved on. Furthermore, when I later pressed her about this, Bobbi insisted, "Jennifer, Audrey, and Kathy *all* had sex with Robert. All the chicks that came over got high and sexed him. . . ."

Right or wrong aside, the indication was that none of the girls—and the tapes left behind seem to back this up—were ever forced into having sex on camera or having sex with Bob.

"So Bob would ask Bobbi Jo for permission to approach you?" Burns asked.

"Yes," Jen said.

Burns made his move to place Bobbi in the driver's seat of the relationship after that, asking Jen several leading questions relating to which one of the two controlled the relationship.

Jen talked about how they practiced Wicca together.

How they cut their fingers and exchanged a blood bond.

How Bobbi, acting as director, told Jen what she needed her to do as Bob filmed them making love and taking off their clothes.

How they'd sit down and get high, watch the films, and laugh.

How they took pleasure in creating the videos and photographs.

How they had parties at the house just about every night.

How they went to the mall that day and got busted shoplifting, which led to Jen's version of that conversation in the truck she'd had with Bob—the motivation for Bob's murder.

One of the problems with all of this was that there had been no buildup to Bob's proposition being anything other than another day in the life of these three. Yes, Jen claimed, this was a "final straw" moment for *them*. Yes, Jen said, Bobbi had "had it" with Bob making advances toward her. Yes, Bobbi was upset about this particular remark and paying him off with sex. But there had been no precedent set by Jen's testimony. In fact, if I were to argue precedent, it would be the opposite—that this proposition by Bob was no different than any other time. Besides, Jen admitted, they went from Graford to Mineral Wells to "pick up our things" at Bob's "because me and Bobbi decided that we didn't want to stay there anymore."

"Was his proposition kind of the driving force behind that decision?" Burns asked.

"Yes, it was."

Jen spoke of how she broke the window to get them inside, a fact forensic science later proved. And after they collected most of their belongings, Jen testified, "That's when Bobbi Jo got inside the chest or whatever, and she got some guns out and took them also."

"And was there any discussion between the two of you of why she was taking those guns?" Burns asked.

"No."

"But you saw her do it?"

"Yes, sir."

Jen never said Bobbi Jo rushed to that chest to "steal" the guns. Instead, she testified, *"She got some guns out and took them also. . . ."* (Emphasis is the author's.)

Bobbi later claimed she grabbed the guns to pawn because Bob owed her money. If they were moving out, she wanted her money. She also claimed Bob had given her the weapons as gifts. Jen's testimony did not disprove this—actually, her testimony bolstered it. In addition, there were plenty of nights when Bobbi and Jen went into that same chest to get those guns and have fun with them, placing the barrels in their vaginas and taking photographs.

Leaving Bob's, according to Jen's new version of the events, they went to Graford. While at Dorothy Smith's house, Jen claimed, she and Bobbi discussed going back to Bob's to "ask him for Bobbi Jo's check." Along the way, Jen testified, "the idea of getting rid of Bob came up. Bobbi Jo said that he just needed to be killed, that he needed to . . . that we needed to kill him."

"And why?"

Stumbling through her words, Jen exclaimed, "Because she was . . . she was tired of . . . tired of the abuse that . . . that she was getting." Then she stopped. And, almost as an afterthought, added, "And she was tired of him harassing me, and she said that *that* was the only way that me and her could be together."

Jen claimed Bobbi "brought it up first."

She said she saw Bobbi load the gun.

She said she tried to talk Bobbi out of it, but Bobbi insisted, telling her, "This is the only way that we can truly be together."

She said Bobbi fired the gun (to test it) on the way back to Bob's. And that was when Jen decided to do it herself—this, after trying to talk Bobbi out of it. If it had to be done, Jen explained, she wanted to be the one to do it.

Why?

"Just the continuing of her saying that he needed to die—just the statements of her saying that that's the only way we could be together."

"Did you believe that?"

"Yes, I did."

"Did you want to lose her?"

"No, I didn't."

All Bobbi could do was cringe in her seat while listening to this.

But we were *together. . . . Bob wasn't splitting us up. . . . Why isn't anyone questioning these lies?*

What Bobbi went on to explain was that she and Jen had been spending lots of time together, and nobody was coming between their friendship. If anyone was making a stink about Jen living at Bob's, it had been Kathy and Audrey. It was not Bob. Jen and Bobbi could do whatever they wanted.

Jen then told the story of Bob and Bobbi heading to the back room to talk. And how Bobbi came back and told her Bob needed to "talk to her" in the bedroom.

Then Jen admitted shooting Bob in the face as she straddled him during intercourse. "I kept shooting at him," Jennifer explained, breaking down in an uncontrollable crying fit.

Burns asked if she needed a break.

Jen said she could manage.

Continuing, she talked about how Bobbi "came into the room" after Jen had unloaded the weapon.

"And what did she say to you when she saw you standing there?"

"She said that I 'looked sexy holding that gun.'"

Bobbi dropped her head. *My goodness, she's back to the lie we both agreed to tell.*

Jen told the story of them heading over to Spanish Trace and saying "we" killed Bob. Not "I killed Bob" and then Bobbi saying, "We killed Bob." But now she was *certain,* absolutely clear, that they barged into the apartment saying in unison, together, "*We* killed Bob."

Jen's new version of the road trip was condensed.

Then she explained how she had lied in her first statement to Brian Boetz and Penny Judd and also lied in her second statement; but that the only parts of both statements she had lied about—you guessed it!—were the narratives of the actual shooting and what had happened leading up to the murder.

The only time Jen said she told the absolute truth was when it mattered most: in court, during the penalty phase of her case several months ago, and here on this day.

After a few more questions underscoring Jen's newfound religious experience of being saved and now having a clear conscience, Mike Burns concluded his questioning: "But for Bobbi Jo, would Bob Dow still be alive today?"

Jen said, "I think he would."

If Jen's testimony was a boat, picture the slats of its sides coming apart, water spilling in, its one passenger trying desperately to bucket the water out, but the boat half in the water, on its way toward the bottom of the ocean. A solid defense attorney, worth his weight, would be able to bury Jen and her lies, sending her back to prison with her tail between her legs, begging for a chance at redemption.

CHAPTER 56

THE ART OF cross-examining a witness lies within the technique of trying to poke holes in her story, thus catching her bolstering a certain version of the events to support an agenda. There is a science to cross-examination. F. Lee Bailey, one of the most experienced and certainly most notorious cross-examiners from the past fifty years, a man who literally wrote the book on how to do it right, stressed the importance of eye contact with a witness, and pacing with his questions.

"*The greatest challenge most cross-examiners will face is the intelligent, but deliberately mendacious, witness,*" Bailey said.

He described this type of witness as having the "*agility to state facts, which do not actually reside in his memory, but are in whole or in part fabricated.*" And once an attorney picks up on what's going on, it becomes imperative for him or her to "*gain control*" of such a witness "*as early as possible.*"

Jen was not that smart. For an experienced criminal defense attorney, ripping her testimony apart would be as easy as having her restate most of what she had said. It was clear from all of the stories Jen had told that she had trouble lying. Some people can lie with a straight face and recall those lies at will.

Not Jennifer. She was a seasoned liar, yes; but she had trouble keeping track of all of the lies simply because there had been so many.

Cross-examining Jen was the cusp of Jim Matthews's case. According to the rules of the game (jury instructions), if he could prove Jen to be the liar she was, Bobbi would walk out of the courtroom a free woman.

Slam dunk.

Matthews started with Jen's motive for coming forward to help the prosecution. After a bit of banter back and forth, a crackling, feistier Jen agreed that *she* had contacted the prosecution with her willingness to testify against Bobbi. It was not the other way around.

"Okay. And that was *after* you were convicted?" Matthews wanted clarified.

"Yes, sir, it was."

It was a solid beginning. The reason why she had contacted the prosecution after her conviction would come up again. Matthews was versed in defense courtroom rhetoric to know that he needed to leave the jury with that information at the end. Not here. Not now.

After that, Bobbi's attorney established how the first time Jen told *anybody* but her lawyer that Bobbi Jo was involved in pushing her to murder Bob was "in front of a jury" during the penalty phase of her case, the previous April. The idea of Bobbi being the driving force behind the murder hadn't been part of Jen's narrative before then.

"Yes, sir," she agreed.

Matthews brought up the point of Bob raping Jen and how it was a complete fabrication.

Jen agreed it was.

Over the course of several minutes, Matthews and Jen traded barbs, and the testimony was confusing as Matthews referred to "the first statement" Jen gave police and asked, point by point, what was true and what was false.

One needed a flowchart to keep track.

The risk in this was that jurors would toss out both statements, simply because it was too hard to follow the truth, and perhaps rely solely on Jen's courtroom testimony—which Matthews did not want.

Matthews agreed with Jen about all the consistencies in her first and second statements: "One of them was that you said Bobbi Jo was *surprised* that you actually killed Bob?"

"Yes."

"Another consistency . . . is that *you* are the one who actually *did* kill Bob. The first one was, it was self-defense, but the second one is just a cold-blooded murder, right?"

"Yes."

"And . . . another consistency . . . is that Bobbi Jo *wasn't*—not only *wasn't* present in the bedroom—she *wasn't* even in the house in either version, right?"

"Yes."

(And yet, what never came up here was how Jen had just testified during questioning by Mike Burns that Bobbi had walked into the bedroom after Jen killed Bob and laid that sexy line on her. No one, however, pointed out this enormous contradiction in fact.)

A few questions later, Matthews brought up something Mike Burns had said in both courtroom cases, asking, "And in both statements, you said that you told your mother, Kathy, that *you* killed Bob?"

"Yes, sir."

"And in both, you didn't say anything about . . . Bobbi Jo giving you a gun or planning it or helping you in any way, did you?"

"No, I did not."

"So the third time that you [talked about] killing Bob to officials *under oath,* you were testifying to it in front of a jury that was going to decide *your* sentence, correct?"

"Yes."

Matthews was on a roll. He had Jen against the ropes. She told jurors how she had lied and lied and lied; but only when it served her purpose, did she ever say she told the truth.

"In your earlier testimony," Matthews continued, "in *your* [court case], you testified that you and Bobbi Jo were *not* fantasizing about killing anybody?"

"No, we weren't."

"And . . . you testified that Bobbi Jo never did take the gun and shoot Bob," Matthews said a few questions later.

"Yes."

"And, in your trial, you admitted that after having several hours to reflect on everything, your mother asked you how it felt to kill somebody and you said, quote"—Matthews stopped here and went back to his paperwork to make certain he got it right, allowing for a little pause to build up tension—"'Pretty fucking good.' Right?"

"Yes."

He then got Jen to admit that "it was not Bobbi Jo's fault that [I] killed [Bob]."

One would have to wonder, was there anything left for Jen to say at this point? She had just admitted, in no certain terms, that *she* killed Bob Dow on her own, without any direction or pressure from Bobbi. Amazing. The more she talked, the more it seemed that Jen had murdered Bob Dow without Bobbi knowing anything.

"Okay," Matthews asked, "I know you shed some tears today, but you did not feel any remorse about killing Bob, did you?"

"Yes! I did!" Jen snapped. This question ignited a rise out of her.

"You *did*?"

"Yes. I did."

"Did you feel like that after having . . . sitting on top of a guy having the most intimate relations that a man and woman could have, you have him cover his face up, and just, in cold blood, you shoot him in the head? And then later, when your mother asks you about that, asks you how it felt, you said, 'Oh, pretty fucking good.' Is that your *definition* of showing *remorse*?"

"Objection!" Mike Burns stood, shouting. "Compound question!"

"Sustained," Judge Ray said. "Rephrase."

Jen agreed that her actions and words did not project remorse. It was now, after having her revelation and reintroduction to Christ, that she was feeling remorseful. She had repented and confessed her sins.

Matthews had Jen answer questions regarding how she met Bobbi and moved into the party house. How she willingly took part in all the gunplay and taking photos and having sex and drinking and drugging. How all of it was by her own volition, and that nobody had made her do any of it. And, to be clear, a lot of the time, her own mother and sister had taken part in what went on at the party house with her, Bob Dow, and Bobbi, as well as scores of other girls.

Jen's response: "Yes, sir."

She agreed she had participated and had never been forced to do any of it.

Matthews even caught Jen in a lie when he asked, "Now, you introduced yourself to Bobbi Jo, correct, when y'all first met?"

And she responded, "Yes, sir, I did."

He established that Bobbi and Audrey were dating then, asking, "So you kind of took her away from Audrey?"

"Yes, I did."

As the questioning leaned more toward her view of the relationship between Bobbi and Bob, and how it progressed, Matthews asked, "You said you guys are—that, you know, you got into witchcraft?"

"Yes," Jen said.

"So do you *believe* you're a witch?"

"No, sir, I do not."

"Did you at the time?"

"No, sir."

"Do you believe that Bobbi Jo is a witch?"

"Not exactly a witch, sir. She's just—she was *into* that stuff."

"Well, do you believe that she has some kind of supernatural powers?"

"Could you explain 'supernatural powers'?" Jen wanted clarified, demanding a more clear description of the phrase. She seemed fascinated in talking about this. It was obvious the subject had piqued Jen's interest.

Matthews smiled out of the corner of his mouth. He thought for a moment. Then: "Well, do you *think* she can put a spell on people?"

"Yes, I do."

He allowed that bizarre response to hang in the silence of the courtroom for a moment.

"Do you think she still has that capability?"

Bobbi sat and listened carefully, entirely bowled over by the conversation taking place in front of her. She could not recall sharing with Jen a desire to partake in witchcraft or put spells on people. It seemed so foreign to Bobbi's Baptist upbringing. So entirely opposite to what she and Jen did after meeting near April 6, 2004, in what amounted to just twenty-seven days they spent together. It must have been all the dope, Bobbi surmised. Jen had bugged out and believed that Bobbi had some sort of supernatural power, when it was Bob Dow who had collected all those Wiccan books at the house. Even Audrey later admitted that she was into Wicca, but she had never, ever heard Bobbi mention it.

Had Jen dreamed up the idea that Bobbi was a witch by connecting her to Bob and Audrey while she had been messed up on dope? Was this Jen's reality? Was she confusing that world of being high with the natural order of things in her life at the time?

("She must have been," Bobbi told me. "I have no idea where she got that.")

"Yes, sir," Jen explained to Matthews, admitting (with a straight face) that she felt Bobbi Jo Smith, her codefendant, could cast spells on people.

"Do you believe that *you* can read people's minds?" Matthews asked. Jim Matthews couldn't

believe the state's star witness was talking about
witchcraft and saying the defendant was capable of
casting spells. It was not only laughable but incredibly demeaning to listen to Jen speak as if such
highly arguable nonsense was fact.

"Not now, no," Jen answered.

"Do you believe that you ever had that capability?"

"Yes."

"Do you believe that Bobbi Jo can read people's
minds?"

"Yes, sir."

"Can she just read somebody's mind anytime
or—"

Jen interrupted: "If she chooses to, *yes.*"

Matthews did not know where to take this
line of questioning. He was overwhelmed by Jen's
ability to place herself in the realm of fantasy and
claim Bobbi was a mind reader and witch who
could cast spells.

Could a jury believe anything Jen had said then,
during her court case, in *Texas Monthly,* or in any
of her statements to police after hearing such
mythical, fairy-tale nonsense?

Jen then explained that she had since given up
reading minds. It was a power, she told jurors, she
could take or leave. And she had chosen not to do
it anymore. She mentioned Bobbi's birthday as the
last time she had chosen to read a mind—a day
that had started with meth and booze, and had
ended with cocaine and more booze and more

meth. And it was clear in her statement to the court here that she was confusing reality with being high, saying, "Some weird stuff was going on at the house. We had just stayed up, like, a week or so doing drugs. . . ."

This was the same witness who jurors were now supposed to believe was telling the truth about what happened and, based on that testimony, send a woman to prison for what could turn into a life sentence.

CHAPTER 57

JENNIFER JONES AND JIM Matthews continued to take pokes at each other. They talked about the green trunk, Bob Dow's life in general, how Bobbi and Bob had known each other for a longer period than Jen originally thought. Then Matthews asked an important, pivotal question: "Your claim today and your claim at your [court case] in front of your jury was that it was all Bobbi Jo's idea to kill Bob, right?"

"Yes, sir."

"Even though that Bob is the guy that's meeting most of your . . . needs, right?"

"Yes, sir."

"Even though . . . she's getting an income from Bob, right?"

"Yes, sir."

This "yes, sir"/"no, sir" went on, back and forth, as Matthews directed Jen through a litany of questions, before establishing that Bobbi had had

several girlfriends before Jen had come into the
picture.

"Yes, sir, she did."

"In fact, she was a girlfriend with *your* sister?"

"Yes, sir, she was."

"Okay. So making that transition from Audrey
to you, she didn't murder Audrey, did she?"

"No, sir."

"She didn't try to talk *you* into murdering Audrey,
did she?"

"No, sir."

"She didn't try to cast a *spell* on anybody to
murder Audrey that you know of, did she?"

"No."

"She didn't cast a spell on *you* to murder Audrey,
did she?"

"No, sir."

Over the next ten minutes, Matthews was able to
trip Jen up on several occasions, showing jurors
how she had continually contradicted her prior
testimony and those two statements she gave to
police. In the scope of the murder narrative and
what happened before and after she killed Bob, all
of it was extremely hard to follow.

One of the questions Jen stumbled on was that
she had known Bobbi for merely weeks and there
she was supposedly killing for her. On merit, it
didn't make much sense. Matthews qualified Jen's
description of the affair as a "deep, loving relationship," making the implication that he saw the relationship differently and Jen, perhaps, was *so*

"afraid" of Bobbi leaving her, that she went so far as
to commit murder for her? Sort of a "kill him or
else" ultimatum was the hypothetical situation that
Matthews posed with his line of questioning. A girl
who had never before been in a lesbian relationship had met and hooked up with her sister's girlfriend (whom she referred to as a "dyke" just twelve
days before they began dating). After a mere three-
plus weeks of being with her, she had committed
the ultimate act of evil under her direction. How
were jurors supposed to believe such a thing?

"Yes," Jen answered. "Because she had already
shown me that she could leave."

Matthews sarcastically said, "Right—and she had
cast a spell on you?"

"By cheating on me," Jen swatted back. "She
had already showed me that I was not the only
person in her life."

"You knew that going into the relationship that
you were not the only person in Bobbi Jo's life,
right?"

Matthews expected an argument, but Jen said,
"Yes."

This was where a solid investigation into Jen's
background—had Matthews done it—would have
come in handy. According to Bobbi, Jen was sleeping with some guy at the same time she was ripping
and running with Bobbi.

Matthews continued with a question the jury
should have taken note of and, honestly, relied on
to immediately toss out everything this woman had

ever said about this case. During the penalty phase of her case, *after* she pled guilty to murder, Jen had already testified under oath and given an account of what had happened. Her testimony was public record. So, Matthews asked, why volunteer after *that* to testify at Bobbi's trial? There had to be a reason. Here, Matthews was completing the cycle: ending where he had begun.

"Because at that time I had gotten a large sentence and it scared me," Jen admitted. "And I didn't want to go to prison."

"And you were looking for a deal from the prosecutor?"

"Yes, I was."

Matthews asked one more question and passed the witness. It was a solid point to end his cross-examination on. It was clear to jurors that Jen had pled her case and then, after thinking about it, went hunting for a deal to get her sentence reduced. Again, how could a juror believe anything this witness said after that?

Sitting and staring at her former close friend and lover, Bobbi was stunned. She felt entirely betrayed and blindsided. It was almost as if Jen was purposely lying to spite her. Complete revenge. Bobbi couldn't help but think of how, while they were in California after being busted and Blythe police officers had Bobbi handcuffed behind her back, sitting on a chair, Bobbi felt this different side of Jen emerge for the first time. Jen had stood in the same room, not wearing handcuffs. When the cops left the room for a moment, Jen walked over and, for no reason, choked her, Bobbi revealed.

"And I couldn't do anything to stop her," Bobbi told me. "They caught her and stopped her. And when they asked her about it [later], she said she was 'playing.'"

As she sat in the courtroom, listening to her case unfold in front of jurors, Bobbi felt as though Jen once again had her hands around her neck.

"Look, I lied," Bobbi admitted. "I was trying to have the same story as Jennifer. I said what she told me to say. What we agreed on. But after that second time (second statement to police after the lie detector), I've kept my mouth shut. Now she, on her own, has changed her story. . . . What, six or seven times? In the *Texas Monthly*, it changed three times alone! And then [during] my trial, it changed *again*. After the second time (that second statement), I never opened my mouth because I didn't know what she was going to say."

Part of what Bobbi felt riled Jen the most—the impetus for Jen's revenge-fueled attack—was what happened when they were locked up. Bobbi confessed to me, "Yes, after Jen pled guilty . . . I told her I didn't want to talk to her anymore because I was involved with someone else." It was after that, Bobbi said, when Jen "flipped." She was determined to see Bobbi pay for betraying her.

Regarding the statements, Bobbi said, "Jennifer and I were never separated. We talked twenty-four/seven, and in California they kept us together. I tried to have the same story she did. She told me we'd come out of it if we kept the same story. I was very confused. . . ." Bobbi couldn't understand what was going on when, after calling her grandmother, and knowing that Dorothy was going to call the police, Bobbi became "the main suspect." She was especially perplexed by this, for there was never any question that Jen had taken the gun, seduced Bob into the bedroom, and pulled the trigger.

CHAPTER 58

MIKE BURNS BROUGHT IN Audrey Sawyer to describe some of what took place during the road trip. Audrey answered questions from the prosecution and Jim Matthews, but she added very little to the ultimate question of whether Bobbi coerced or convinced Jen to kill Bob Dow.

Then Krystal Bailey (who would die tragically in a horrible motorcycle accident sometime after Bobbi's trial) came in and also talked about the road trip. When Matthews got hold of her, he began by having Krystal reveal that Bobbi was a typical type A personality who liked to have the attention cast upon her. And yet, although she craved being the center of attention at the parties, Bobbi had never rubbed Krystal as being sinister or evil or a person who could kill anyone—let alone Bob Dow.

Matthews raised the topic of Wicca and that mind-reading business Jen had been so certain of, asking Krystal, "Do you believe that Bobbi Jo can cast spells on people?"

"Yes, I do," she said.

"Do you believe that Bobbi Jo can read people's minds?"

"Yes."

"Okay. And I think you also said that Bobbi Jo's scatterbrained?"

"Yes."

"Okay."

"Fickle," Krystal said out of the blue.

"You weren't in the room when Jennifer murdered Bob Dow, were you?"

"No, I was not."

"You weren't in the house?"

"No, I was not."

"Weren't outside?"

"No, I was not."

"Weren't peeking in the window?"

"No."

"So you don't have any personal knowledge of what happened exactly? You just know what people said?"

"Just what Jennifer and Bobbi Jo said."

"And that story has been changed around, right?"

"That's right."

While sitting at his table in front of the witness stand, Matthews took a moment. Then: "Pass the witness."

The judge explained a few legal matters to Krystal Bailey and released her from the stand.

Kathy Jones was up next.

CHAPTER 59

KATHY JONES HAD lived a hard life. There was no way for Mike Burns to put a shine on what had been decades of drugs, jail, and personal problems. Kathy had done time on a litany of charges and had been sentenced to what could be termed as nothing less than perpetual parole. Kathy had a street-smart Texas toughness about her. It was, at times, hard to follow her speech because she bounced around so much when talking. She spoke fast, and she spoke with a significant Texas brogue.

Because Kathy had been busted for everything under the sun, Burns had her admit it all to the jury. In addition, there was also no hiding the fact that Kathy was, at the time her testimony was being given, residing in the Hobby Unit, in Marlin, part of the Texas State Prison. She was under lock and key for violating her parole as part of an eight-year sentence, which she had received for robbery. She was slated to be released in just a few days, however, on December 1, 2005.

The most important part of Kathy's testimony came when Burns asked her what happened on the day the girls came bursting into the apartment.

Kathy explained.

"Okay, well," Burns said in a strange choice of words, "what did you hear who say what?"

"Well, I don't know," Kathy answered. "I can't recall who said what first. But 'We killed Bob.' And . . . and Jennifer was saying that she was pretty upset."

In her only statement to the MWPD, Kathy had stated the following: "Jennifer and Bobbi Jo came to the apartment. . . . They both ran into the apartment and said that they had killed Bob. Jennifer said that she had killed him, and Bobbi said 'they' killed him."

To the jury, Kathy described Jennifer's demeanor on that day as "uncontrollable . . . shaking, crying. . . ." Whereas, Kathy said, "Bobbi Jo didn't . . . She was just kind of, like, it was just . . . like, excited, adrenaline rush, I guess. I don't know how to—not showing, you know, no emotion."

"No emotion" could be easily confused with disbelief or shock. Bobbi wondered why no one was challenging all these women coming in and saying she didn't care about what Jen had done to a man she arguably loved like a father. Or that she was in total disbelief and astonishment that Jen had actually murdered Bob.

She had just killed [Bob]. . . . I couldn't believe what was happening.

Mike Burns had Kathy explain the road trip, beginning with robbing Bob Dow's trailer, and ending with how they went their separate ways in Arizona. What became clear in Kathy's version of what the girls had said about the actual murder while on the road was how fluid and ever-changing their stories became over time. Jen and Bobbi had told several different versions of what had happened; each time they talked about it, a new alteration was inserted. Kathy, Audrey, and Krystal were never certain of what happened to Bob, or who actually pulled the trigger.

What might have hurt Bobbi was an exchange Kathy and Burns had near the end of Kathy's direct testimony. Burns asked about any statements Bobbi had made during the trip. Out of the blue, Kathy said something she had never told the police or anyone else: "What I recall Bobbi Jo saying while we was in the truck, she let me know, she said, 'I brainwashed your daughter.' And she said, 'She'll do anything.' You know, it's *anything*—Bobbi Jo knew that anything she told Jennifer to do, Jennifer would do, or just asked."

Bobbi dropped her head. *What the hell?* She couldn't believe it. It was something, as she recalled, she had never said. Why should a jury believe Kathy, a career criminal—the mother of the woman who had murdered Bob? She had partied with

Bob, right beside two of her own daughters! She'd even had sex with Bob . . . on camera. There were several photographs and films left behind to prove it. But maybe most important, this was the first time Kathy Jones had ever recalled this conversation (which she said was between her and Bobbi, with no one else around).

Jim Matthews went right for Kathy Jones's jugular. He tried to prove that, despite how sure she was of herself now, she had a hard time in the past—much like her daughter—keeping her stories straight.

"Okay, Miss Jones," Matthews began. "Let's talk about y'all . . . when y'all were riding in the truck and the gun got tossed out the window. Do you recall making a statement to the Arizona Police [Department] about that incident?"

"Yes, I believe I did."

Matthews and Kathy talked about the statement being videotaped.

"Do you recall that you told the Arizona police that it was *Jennifer* that wiped off the fingerprints [from] the gun?"

"No."

"You didn't tell them that?"

"I don't recall that."

On the videotape, Kathy told the Arizona Police Department that Jen explained to her how she had wiped off the weapon; and while Jen said it, Kathy thought, *Oh, good—at least they won't get Jennifer's fingerprints off it.*

"You don't remember telling the Arizona police that?" Matthews asked.

Kathy thought about it. "I might have said something like that."

The point was that Kathy Jones couldn't recall a lot of what she had said. Thus, based on that and her criminal history, her testimony shouldn't be taken at all seriously. How could jurors be expected to believe one statement and not the other? Here, clearly, Kathy had thought she said one thing, but she had said something entirely different.

There was some discussion about the videotape and authenticating it, but Matthews's point had been made.

The day ended with Kathy on the stand.

On the following morning, November 30, 2005, Kathy Jones came in for a few brief moments, answered several inconsequential questions, and was shipped back to her prison cell.

Detective Brian Boetz was next. Boetz walked jurors through the crime scene and how the MWPD came up with Bobbi as a suspect based on that interview with Dorothy Smith. For anyone seated in the courtroom, it might have seemed that Mike Burns skipped over the entire investigation portion of the case—and for good reason. There were no phone records to discuss. There were only a handful of interviews conducted with the main players. And there was no ticking-clock chase to track Jen and Bobbi down, although they had been branded "armed and dangerous" in every APB that had gone out. It was as if the MWPD found a body, felt they had their killer, and then sat back and waited for the girls to emerge. In the scope of murder investigations, it was a rather open-and-shut case. To the MWPD, there were no other suspects beyond Bobbi at first—and then Jen, after Krystal Bailey returned to Mineral Wells and gave her statement.

Quite shockingly, Burns had Boetz read Bobbi's first statement, which the state, the MWPD, and Bobbi had rejected—all of whom had admitted at one time or another that it was inaccurate and blanketed with lies. Burns himself had called the document "hogwash" during Jen's court case.

At one point, Burns asked Boetz what he did after they got back from Blythe and he decided Jen and Bobbi's first statements did not mesh with the crime scene.

"We made an appointment with a polygraph examiner in Fort Worth."

"So, did you take the defendant to Fort Worth?" Burns asked.

"Yes, sir."

"So what happened when you got to Fort Worth?" Boetz explained how the girls "broke down" and "started crying" and claimed they had been lying, but now they wanted to tell the truth.

The Behavioral Measures & Forensic Services institute, where the polygraphs had been scheduled, is located in Dallas, not Fort Worth. (Boetz made a point to correct this later when I asked him about it. And yet, in a court of law, on the stand, Boetz or Burns could not get this simple fact right.)

Then Burns had Boetz read Bobbi's second statement. In that statement, Bobbi told a story of her mother going into the house with her and Jen after they went back to Bob's on the day of the murder. She also said Jen admitted killing Bob after they arrived at the Spanish Trace Apartments. And when Kathy Jones stood in the kitchen and asked why, Jen responded, "Because I'm tired of what he is doing to Bobbi and the rest of these little girls."

Motive.

Implicating herself in Bob's murder, essentially the only evidence this second statement produced, came when Bobbi said she had asked Jen, "Is he dead?" And Jen responded, "Yes." To which, Bobbi said in that second statement, "Make sure."

"So the defendant told you in that [second] statement that she broke into the green trunk?" Burns asked Boetz.

"That's correct."

"And that she broke into it and obtained a twenty-two pistol out of that trunk?"

"Yes, sir."

After taking those second statements from the girls, Boetz said, the MWPD believed they had a solid case of murder against not only Jen, but now Bobbi, based on those few lines in Bobbi's and Jen's second statements.

"Aside from a few other things, did that pretty much complete your investigation?" Burns concluded.

"Yes, sir."

"What did you do when your investigation was completed?"

"I submitted the case to the DA's office."

CHAPTER 60

JIM MATTHEWS FOCUSED HIS cross-examination of Brian Boetz on the trunk, asking, "So you have no idea who pried [the trunk] open?"

"That's correct," Boetz admitted (contradicting his prior testimony).

Matthews established how there was no forensic evidence pointing to anyone in particular as the person responsible for prying open the trunk.

"Okay, so it's possible then," Matthews pondered, "that it could have been pried open by someone *other* than Bobbi Jo?"

"It's possible," Boetz answered. "But Bobbi Jo said in her second statement that she pried it open."

(Actually, Bobbi said in that statement that she "broke into [it].")

Matthews had Boetz explain how Bobbi became a suspect in the actual shooting based on the statements from the Cruzes and Dorothy Smith, adding,

"And in looking at that information now, that absolutely is *not* the truth, is it?"

"No, sir."

Boetz said he did not believe Bobbi's or Jen's first statements, but he did believe their second statements.

Matthews asked, "Seems like in Bobbi Jo's statement, you read where Jennifer Jones and Mr. Dow apparently was engaged in—he was performing oral sex on her, Bobbi Jo walked in the room, and Jennifer turned to Bobbi Jo and said, 'Get the [heck] out of here'?"

"Yes, sir," Boetz said.

"So that sounded like Jennifer was telling Bobbi Jo what to do?" Matthews suggested.

"I suppose."

An interesting exchange between Matthews and Boetz came at one point when Matthews asked Boetz about his interview with Dorothy Smith, Bobbi's grandmother, and the Cruzes. Without perhaps realizing it, Boetz brought out an important piece of exculpatory evidence, proving how Bobbi had lied in her statements to police, perhaps revealing why Mike Burns had not called Dorothy Smith to the witness stand.

"Okay, and Bobbi Jo told them [the Cruzes and Dorothy], apparently according to your conversation with [them], 'I shot Bob . . . ,'" Matthews said.

"Yes," Boetz responded.

"And looking at that information now, that absolutely is not the truth, is it?"

"No, sir."

* * *

Mike Burns called Captain Mike McAllester and Dr. Joni McClain (who was not the ME who conducted the autopsy on Bob Dow, but managed the person who did), and both explained their roles. Jim Matthews, then, did not question them at any length or with any obvious agenda, and the state rested.

In total, Mike Burns had called seven witnesses, none of whom gave him that thunderous, slam-the-book-on-the-table piece of devastating evidence to bury Bobbi and prove she had masterminded what Burns projected to the jury as a diabolical plot to murder Bob Dow so Bobbi and Jen could ride off into the sunset together.

After hearing the state's case, jurors had to wonder where the rest of it was. If Dorothy Smith's and Richard and Kathy Cruz's original statements to police had been so revealing and incriminating, why hadn't Burns called them? Likewise, if Bobbi's mother could verify parts of the girls' second statements (because she had been there for most of that day, save for the murder), why hadn't the state called *her*?

During Matthews's cross-examinations of Brian Boetz and Mike McAllester, it became clear there was zero forensic evidence linking Bobbi to Bob Dow's murder. And even the green trunk, which Bobbi, in her second statement, admitted breaking into to retrieve a gun, did not produce any fingerprint evidence that Bobbi had ever touched it. All of the forensic evidence the prosecution had was Jen's, which included blood on the back windowpane, blood in Bob's room, and the bodily fluids found on Bob Dow.

The bottom line for Matthews was that as soon as the MWPD and the prosecutor's office got hold of Bobbi's second statement, their investigation—about five days old at that point—ceased. There was no reason for them to go any further. They took one line from Bobbi (during her second statement) and believed it was enough to bring it to a grand jury and get a conviction if the case went to trial. In fact, Matthews was able to draw out of his cross-examination with Boetz and then McAllester that no investigatory body working on Bob Dow's murder did anything *after* those second statements from the girls had been taken. No investigator went out and backed up (or checked out) with corroborating witnesses, interviews, or evidence what Bobbi or Jen had said.

From where the MWPD had seen the case, they had gotten confessions and the case was closed. There was no need to follow up.

CHAPTER 61

JIM MATTHEWS BELIEVED his client was innocent. At best, Bobbi could be brought up on a lesser charge. But, for crying out loud, *murder*? All because she said in a second statement to police (in which several things she admitted to in that same statement could be proven false), "I gave Jennifer the gun"?

Looking at all of the evidence (or lack thereof), one had to wonder how this case had even gotten to this point? There's that old cliché that a prosecutor could indict a ham sandwich the way in which the system is set up, but this case proved that perhaps indicting a lesbian in the conservative state of Texas was a hell of lot easier than even that.

Interesting enough, in the second statement Bobbi gave after that failed polygraph, the phrases "I gave Jennifer the gun" and a few other lines (including, "I said, make sure") were underlined in blue pen by someone. It was as if that person thought: *That's it. We got her. There it is!*

In Jen's second statement, she had said: "I walked into the bedroom, got the gun out of a green lockbox that was under another bed. I checked to see if the gun was loaded and it was loaded. . . . When we were between Graford and Bob's house, I told Bobbi Jo that I was going to kill Bob. . . ."

Jen doesn't even claim Bobbi gave her the gun and loaded it; and her statement contradicts what Bobbi said in hers.

Matthews wondered, *Is that not the basis for reasonable doubt, or in disbelieving and tossing out all those statements entirely?*

Matthews had a track record of wins behind him. A lot of those came, he said, "because I chose to put my client on the stand. Juries *want* to hear a defendant say she didn't do it."

Everyone wondered if Matthews would take that same approach here.

I asked Bobbi about the alleged marriage proposal Jim Matthews had referred to in his opening statement. To me, this was an interesting development. It showed, in part, how close Bobbi Jo Smith and Bob Dow were.

"Bob did ask me to marry him," Bobbi clarified. "He said stupid shit all of the time when he was high. I'd always laugh at him. . . ."

This sparked an important point Bobbi later made—one that becomes imperative to insert here in her case as the defense portion of her trial was set to begin. As Bobbi explained to me, "And as for [Bob] wanting to marry me, Mr. Phelps, when people are strung out on drugs, they are not themselves. It's something I can't explain to you. You have to just be in the situation. . . ."

Opening Bobbi's case, Jim Matthews called a woman, old enough to be a grandmother, who had come forward to say Jen had been bragging about killing Bob Dow while in jail. The woman had been on parole for four years, and she had done two and a half years for a drug-related felony. She was currently on parole for a charge of driving under the influence (DUI).

She admitted to drug and alcohol dependency. Yet, she added, "I'll always have a problem, but I am in rehab. I attend AA meetings, and I go to Aftercare. And it's . . . a disease, and I'll always have it."

"You know some things about the case, and you felt driven by your conscience and by the 'do the right thing' that you needed to contact me?" Matthews asked.

"Yes."

"Was there a time that you ever met Jennifer Jones?"

"Yes, sir."

Further along, after talking through dates and times and places, Matthews asked, "Did you ever have conversations with Jennifer . . . about the murder of Bob Dow?"

"Yes."

"In those conversations, did Jennifer Jones ever make a statement to you that indicated what her motive may have been for killing him?"

Mike Burns objected. There was a fine line surrounding the hearsay rule. This witness could not testify as to what Jen *might* have meant, only what she had said directly.

After a rather heated discussion between the lawyers after approaching the bench, the judge listening closely, it was decided that Matthews could continue, but under certain conditions and restraints.

Matthews asked another round of questions and Burns objected, saying it was "leading." Judge Ray kicked the jury out of the room so the lawyers could discuss the matter further.

When the jury was allowed back, Matthews was able to get his witness to admit that Jen did not only display zero remorse for killing Bob, but she had also laughed about the murder. It sort of fell in line with Kathy Jones saying earlier that Jen admitted feeling "pretty fucking good" after unloading that weapon into Bob's head.

It's called corroborating evidentiary testimony. And here it was.

Burns had no cross-examination questions for the witness.

Since Burns hadn't, Matthews decided to call Richard Cruz and get his narrative of what happened.

Jim Matthews quickly had Rick Cruz describe how the information he gave to police was second-hand, from Dorothy Smith, and he had no "personal knowledge" of what Bobbi actually had said that day when she returned from Spanish Trace with all of the girls.

Burns asked Cruz a series of questions that spoke to Bobbi's behavior outside the confines of the family. He even brought up Bobbi's sexuality, asking, "Are you aware that she engaged in homosexual conduct with other women?"

"I did," Cruz said.

Bob Dow's first wife was called. She spoke quite pointedly about Bob's infatuation with witchcraft and how he collected books on the subject.

Matthews brought in another witness who had come to him and said she had information about Jen. This witness had been in trouble with the law on drug-related charges, too. And she was now clean and sober, too. What was compelling about this witness and the first woman Matthews had called—both of whom had spent time with Jen in prison—was that neither of the women knew Bobbi. They'd had no contact with her.

Under the constraints of the court, this second woman could add nothing other than telling jurors that Jen was happy while the two of them spent time in jail together. The idea for Matthews was to have the witness, even in an indirect way, clarify that Jen was a cold-blooded killer, who did not care about taking another life.

Matthews paced a bit. It was clear he had other things to discuss with the witness, but he worried again about walking that fine line of hearsay.

The judge dismissed the jury so they could hammer it out.

The woman stayed on the witness stand. And without the jury present, Matthews continued asking questions.

She had spent about two and a half weeks with Jen in Palo Pinto County Jail. During that time, she had gotten to know her fairly well. As they talked, Jen said she had murdered Bob solely because "she was tired of being abused" by him.

"Anything else?" Matthews asked outside the presence of the jury.

"All the abuse."

As Jen talked to her about the murder, the witness testified, she was unemotional. "The tone of her voice and the look in her eyes—she just, there was *nothing*."

Not one time during that period they talked about the murder did Jen ever say Bobbi had had anything to do with the crime. In fact, the witness said she had not even heard of Bobbi's name until much later on.

Mike Burns objected to the testimony being offered in front of the jury.

The judge agreed.

And so the witness was released—and Bobbi watched sadly as a potential lifesaver walked out of the courtroom without being able to tell her complete story to the jury.

CHAPTER 62

JIM MATTHEWS THOUGHT about having his client testify. It was a gamble every time. Those throws of the dice had paid off for Matthews in the past. But here, with Bobbi, there just weren't any guarantees that the jury would sympathize with her. What's more, Bobbi would have to sit on the stand and admit she had lied repeatedly to police. How could she convince the jury she was telling the truth now?

Then there was the question of her sexuality: What if she alienated one juror?

She was done.

"I would just like to ask . . . just to put it on record," Matthews told the judge as he stood and addressed the court, "that Bobbi Jo Smith and I have had numerous conversations about the pros and cons of her testifying. And as our final decision, she has indicated to me that she does not want to testify. She wants to exercise her right to remain silent."

This decision would become a contentious issue for Bobbi as we discussed it at length. Bobbi told me she wanted to testify, but Jim Matthews talked her out of it. Matthews told me he wanted her to testify, but Bobbi repeatedly said she was scared and couldn't do it. It was a dilemma many defendants face afterward, and one I hear as a journalist all the time.

Hindsight.

"Miss Smith," the judge said. "Stand up."

Bobbi pushed out her chair with the back of her legs and stood, staring stoically at the court's keeper.

"Miss Smith, you have thoroughly discussed with your legal counsel the rights that you have, as well as the opportunities that you have, regarding testifying in front of the jury?"

"Yes, sir, I have," Bobbi answered.

"Have you had ample time to consider the pros and cons, the ups and downs, the goods and bads, the risks and rewards, of doing that?"

This was Bobbi's chance to speak her mind.

"Yes, sir," Bobbi said.

"All right. And it is your decision to exercise your right to remain silent and not give testimony in the presence of the jury?"

"Yes, sir."

"Do you have any doubts or hesitations or questions?"

"No, sir."

The judge then began a long explanation, pointing out something courts and counselors and judges run into all the time. Judge Ray said the "reason" he was asking Bobbi about this was because it was not uncommon at this stage of a trial to make "tough decisions"—decisions that would affect a defendant's life. He said how "difficult" a choice it must have been for Bobbi to come to this conclusion and wanted her to be absolutely certain it was what she wanted.

Why?

"Many, many, many, many, many times down the road—six months or a year or something like that—we have people say, 'Well, my lawyer didn't do me a good job. If he or she would have allowed me to get up there, I could have had testimony that would have been important or maybe helped me,'" the judge outlined. "So that's the reason I'm taking this opportunity to give you plenty of time to think about it and to make up your decision."

Bobbi explained she had indeed been given all of the time she needed to decide. She also agreed she had no questions about the advice her attorney had given her. She said she understood it completely.

"All right," Judge Ray said, "when we call the jury back in, is it the intent of the defendant to rest at that time?"

Matthews said, "Yes, Your Honor."

The testimony portion of Bobbi's murder trial

had lasted all of one and a half days. It was finished. Now it was time for both attorneys to wield their best magic at closing, convincing jurors of their truth.

The judge acknowledged how little time the trial had taken when Matthews asked for an hour to give his closing so as not to be forced or rushed through it.

"I'm not likely to give you an hour," the judge said sternly.

"Okay," Matthews said disappointedly.

"I was going to ask for thirty minutes," Burns said, almost as if sucking up to the judge and smacking Matthews's request down.

"Well, I think that's certainly reasonable. The testimony only took a day and a half. I've tried cases that took a heck of a lot longer than this one and not had an hour to close."

"Can I compromise at forty-five?" Matthews pressed.

The judge said thirty minutes, but it would be okay to "run over" a bit.

CHAPTER 63

THE RIGHT WORD can sometimes make all the difference. Mike Burns's colleague gave the state's closing argument, beginning by thanking everyone. And as the assistant prosecutor (AP), Soria Joslin, continued, little time was wasted getting to the crux of the state's final argument, as Joslin referred to Bobbi's second statement as a "confession"—a word that implied guilt right out of the box.

Confession . . .

Ah, that's right: She confessed.

Once the AP got going, it was clear why Burns had chosen to allow his assistant to put the bow on the state's package. The AP talked about the state not having to prove "why" one person—or, in this case, two persons—committed murder. "There are a whole host of reasons why it's possible. Power trip. He was a disgusting human being and they wanted to get rid of him. It was something to do. . . . These were two teenagers, young and irresponsible, strung out, in love, and not thinking. But we don't have to prove to you the 'why.'"

Then the AP focused on the "murder in general," and how, in aiding and assisting another person in the act of a homicide, makes a defendant in Bobbi's position "just as guilty of that crime." Putting the law into the context of the case, the AP detailed, "If you bring a shooter the weapon, you hand that weapon to the shooter, see that shooter go into a room, and that person kills somebody, you are guilty as a party to the murder."

And this was the state's contention: Bobbi Jo Smith took a pistol, loaded it, gave it to Jen, and sent her under the ruse of sexual intercourse into Bob's room to kill him.

From there, the AP broke down the case of Bobbi being a "party to murder." The focus here was on the state's "most telling" piece of evidence, "Bobbi Jo's own statement."

That *confession.*

The AP never said it outright, but often referred to that second statement. "And that statement alone—that statement!—she tells you she gave the murder weapon to Jennifer. You can look at that statement and see what she said. That statement hangs her on the law of parties as part of this murder."

The remainder of the prosecutor's brief closing was built around Bobbi's second statement and Jen's testimony. The state concluded after only a few minutes by saying, "Bottom line is this—Bobbi Jo got the gun. This defendant loaded the gun. This defendant talked about killing Bob. This defendant drove Jennifer over there. This defendant handed her the gun. This defendant saw her put it in her pants. This defendant saw Jennifer walk in that room. This defendant waited." Then, after pausing briefly, "What you are looking at right here"—and the AP pointed to Bobbi, who looked like a student being scolded by her principal—"is a murderer."

What wasn't mentioned, however, was that the state's closing consisted of elements from *both* of Bobbi's and Jen's statements. And the only corroborating evidence the state had was an admitted pathological liar who told five versions of this tale of murder.

Jim Matthews rose. His job was to take the state's closing and pick it apart, pointing out for jurors how, within those remarks, there were several instances where the prosecution had combined one statement with the next to bumpily slap its case together. Not to mention using a liar to back it all up.

The state's case, if one was to look at it in context and entirety, was based not on what a thorough law enforcement investigation had yielded, but rather how each step the MWPD took led to a conclusion it had developed from the start.

Matthews needed to get jurors to understand that
Bobbi was a lot of things, had committed crimes
herself, and had not been the most law-abiding,
upstanding citizen. Indeed, all of that was true.
But she was no murderer or mastermind behind a
cold-blooded, evil act. Bobbi had lied to police once
and then, same as Jen, lied again. But since that
second statement, Bobbi's story had not changed.

"Jennifer Jones," Matthews began, "murdered
Bob Dow, and she did it by herself. She did it without the help of Bobbi Jo. She murdered a friend
of Bobbi Jo's, all on her own. Jennifer Jones murdered Bob Dow all by herself."

Matthews talked about the instructions the
judge had given jurors at the end of the testimony
portion of the case—a very important point of
law. Each juror would have a copy of the charges,
Matthews explained. He asked that each take the
time to read through the *second* page. Then he
quoted from it, stating emphatically, "'You are further instructed that a conviction cannot be had
solely upon the testimony of an accomplice unless
the jury first believes that accomplice's evidence
is true.'"

The state's case, in the scope of the law, hung
on those instructions. Bobbi, therefore, should
have been allowed to get up and walk out of the
courtroom at that moment. Because it was clear
when you looked at Jen's various versions of the
case that she had repeatedly lied. And even if you

take Bobbi's supposed *confession* into it all, you'd still have to come out of any decision with reasonable doubt because of the lies.

Matthews was correct in saying that despite Bobbi's own statements, despite anything anyone else had said during the trial, the first hurdle in convicting Bobbi was to believe Jennifer Jones. If a juror did not believe Jen, there was plenty of reason to doubt that Bobbi had conspired to commit this crime.

"Remember," Matthews stated, "you have to find that the credibility of her testimony—someone who believes in witchcraft, someone who believes that other people can cast spells, someone who believes that other people can read peoples' minds, someone who believes that somehow Bobbi Jo is this powerful, supernatural-powered person who can cast spells on people and make them commit murder and who can read minds . . ."

The way Matthews packaged the state's argument, it sounded fanatical and fantastical. Jen had admitted on the stand, after all, that she believed Bobbi still had the power to control her thoughts. It seemed ridiculous, as if Bobbi was some sort of puppet master. And if she was, why wouldn't she make Jen tell jurors that Bobbi was innocent?

It was as preposterous as it sounded.

The facts spoke for themselves. Jen—along with Audrey and Kathy—later made the claim that Bobbi turned Jen into a doper. But Jen's own journal told that story, as did Jen, when she admitted on the stand that at the age of fourteen she had started using drugs and sleeping with boys.

The point Matthews tried to get through to the jury—quite alarming but valid—was that Jennifer Jones did what Jennifer Jones wanted to do from the time she was a young teenager, and nobody ever stopped her.

He talked about how from the time Jen was fourteen, "she began to get into drugs." He said it was "long before she ever met Bobbi Jo. At the age of fourteen, she told us that she lost her virginity. That's long before she ever met Bobbi Jo. Jennifer wanted . . . Jennifer took!" He continued beating this drum, saying how when she was fourteen, Jen "wanted to have sex" and so "she had sex." When Jen "wanted to get into drugs," she "got into drugs." And when Jennifer Jones, he added, "wanted to move into Bob Dow's house to continue that lifestyle unencumbered by her dad," well, lo and behold, Jen did that, too.

Unaltered facts.

Jen and Audrey admitted Jen had left the apartment at Spanish Trace because she couldn't do what she wanted, when she wanted to do it, while living under the rule of Jerry Jones.

Matthews discussed how Jen talked about an endless love she claimed to have for Bobbi, and how Bobbi was "meeting all of [her] needs." It became clear that Bobbi was "finally the one person in all the relationships [Jen ever had] . . . meeting all [her] needs." In fact, as Jen had testified herself, "she felt so strongly about that, that even the unsupported fear that Bobbi Jo might leave her drove her to commit a cold-blooded, perverted murder." Then Matthews offered a solid point, adding how Jen refused to tell the court "that Bobbi Jo was having sex with Bob Dow. That didn't bother her! That's *not* consistent. That's *not* human."

In other words, how could Jen be so committed to Bobbi, be so in love with Bobbi, and not feel jealous about Bob and Bobbi having sex? It went against human nature.

"You just love them, and they are everything to you," Matthews said. "I don't care if they have sex with other people." He paused. "That's just not reasonable."

Matthews got into Bobbi's "unconventional lifestyle" and how she shouldn't be punished for the way in which she chose to live her life. It was a way of life, Matthews contended, that Bobbi "chose, nevertheless, long before Jennifer was on the scene. And you know what, it never led Bobbi Jo ever getting into trouble with the police until Jennifer Jones came on the scene."

Bobbi had never been arrested. Jen was the one who stole cars and broke windows and got caught breaking and entering before she was old enough to drive a car. And this led Matthews to make a great point: "We heard zero testimony that Bobbi Jo ever said a thing about, 'I want that watch. I'll leave you if you don't give me that watch.' Jennifer made that decision. Jennifer decided [to steal], *not* Bobbi Jo."

Another fact Matthews pointed to was that Bobbi Jo Smith and Bob Dow shared sexual partners. It was Jen, jealous and controlling, who wanted Bobbi all to herself, Matthews insisted.

It was Jen who became jealous of Bob Dow. . . .

Jen who decided to move out of Bob Dow's party house . . .

Jen who decided to go back over there *after* they left . . .

Jen who decided to smash the back window and break in (without Bobbi or the others knowing what she was doing) . . .

Jen who let Bobbi and her mother into the house . . .

Jen who told Bob to meet her in the bedroom . . .

Jen who had sex with Bob . . .

And it was Jen who shot Bob Dow in the face during intercourse.

Bob Dow literally had locked his mother in her bedroom. But as far as Jen, Matthews said, she was never "locked in a closet." There were "no chains."

"No ropes. No force."

Matthews broke down all of the stories Jen told. The first was "that Jennifer Jones murdered Bob Dow . . . in self-defense." The second was that Jen "broke down and cried and said, 'Boy, I'm tired of the lie. I'm just going to tell the truth this time.' Maybe she did. Maybe she actually had a moment of conscience because, you know, even Detective

Brian Boetz said that's the story *he* believed." He finished that thought by talking about how "a professional with training" like Boetz, a cop with "experience in interviewing witnesses, in taking statements," would pick up on that sort of thing.

The third story, Matthews said, "surprised everybody—even the prosecutor when he was asking her. . . . The third story was self-serving. How? She was sitting in front of a jury. . . . But that jury, she'd *already* pled guilty."

Jen had admitted guilt and fought for a lesser sentence.

The fourth story, Matthews said, was the one Jen told during Bobbi's trial. It was the "witchcraft" story and how all of the mind games became part of Jen's new life narrative.

Oddly, Matthews never mentioned the *Texas Monthly* article, or how the timing of publication might have hurt Bobbi and soured jurors on her.

Matthews was interrupted at one point by the judge, breaking any momentum Matthews might have accrued. The judge let him know he had five minutes left. And perhaps Matthews did go on far longer than he should have, but the guy's passion for his client's innocence took control.

Matthews concluded after a long rant about Jen trying to take two lives: Bob Dow's, of course, and now Bobbi's. "Remember, [Jen] admitted [she was] trying to get a good deal with the prosecution's office. She called [the prosecutor]. Why? She was looking for a good deal. . . ." He then said how Jen had wanted to look "good on her parole papers when" the time came for her to face the board. Then he concluded with one final thought: "Please stop the train. Thank you."

Mike Burns stood. The state had twenty-three minutes left on its allotted time; Burns chose to close out the state's case himself.

He talked about a tangled web of deception, bordering on taking things over the top by quoting a Sir Walter Scott poem in what seemed like a terribly unwarranted, forced analogy, warning jurors not to "fall into that trap." Then he asked jurors to come along with him on a "road trip." Not down the highway leading the girls into Arizona and California, where one might reckon with the truth being in that "pretty fucking good" statement Jen told her mother, but the "highway of deliberations."

This argument went on and on, and it felt tired and contrived at this final stage in the trial, even though the entire trial took a mere twelve hours. Burns went through the instructions Judge Ray had given, begging jurors to convict Bobbi on those instructions alone. He quoted from Bobbi's second statement again and again. He asked jurors to take Bobbi's second statement as gospel and line it up with those instructions and find her guilty of the crime of murder.

If there was one thing clear by the time both

sides concluded, it was that this case, maybe more than any other in recent history, embodied the protection a defendant is given within the law of reasonable doubt. Because by the time a juror or a court watcher finished listening to all of this nonsense, there were so many varying stories of this murder narrative, there was no way any reasonable jury member, following the law and jury instructions, could convict. It didn't seem possible.

CHAPTER 64

INSIDE THE JURY deliberation room, according to a source inside the courthouse that day, jurors went toe-to-toe. The noise coming from the room was quite loud. At one point, a bailiff walked over and put his ear to the door, his hand on the doorknob, and walked in. It sounded as if jurors were at each other's throats.

Intense arguments had turned heated. Jurors were going back and forth, passionately discussing the case. As it turned out, on two separate occasions, the bailiff had to step into the room to make sure jurors weren't physically fighting.

That summed up this case and how polarizing it had become.

In the end, however, it took only six hours—half the length of the court case—to seal Bobbi's fate and send her packing for a trip to Gatesville Prison.

How long?

Fifty years.

Five decades.

Bobbi was sick when she heard that guilty verdict announced.

Jim Matthews was surprised. He thought for certain reasonable doubt was going to set Bobbi Jo Smith free.

The three appeals court judges—not all in agreement—denied Bobbi Jo Smith.

"One of the judges ruled in my favor," Jim Matthews told me. But two others didn't. "What they ruled on was the way that the judge explained the law to jurors. . . . I felt that that was incorrect because the way the judge explained it to the jury left the door open to say that they could find Bobbi Jo guilty if Bobbi Jo gave Jennifer the pistol she used to kill Mr. Dow. That's not true, though. Because it has to be that Bobbi *knowingly* and *intentionally* knew that when she gave it to her that she wanted to use that particular weapon to kill Mr. Dow. That she *gave* it to Jennifer with the *intent* that she go murder him."

In Matthews's opinion, the court of appeals judges got it wrong.

"Look, if I go into a pawnshop and buy a shotgun and then go rob and kill a security guard somewhere, you can't go out an arrest and charge the pawnshop owner as an accessory to the crime."

Exactly.

And that was crux of the state's case, fundamentally speaking: Bobbi provided the weapon. The argument that she had convinced Jen to kill Bob didn't hold up. Where's the evidence for that? The state provided zero.

Matthews had not filed a motion to change venues, he told me, even though Judge Ray said he was surprised he hadn't.

"I didn't, simply because I knew where he would have moved the trial to—a neighboring county."

The fear for Matthews was that this neighboring county, being ultraconservative, would have held it against Bobbi "even worse" for being homosexual. Palo Pinto County was by far one of the more liberal counties in the region; and although Matthews believed there was certainly some bias against Bobbi's sexual preference, he didn't feel it would gravely affect the outcome of the trial.

"The people of Palo Pinto County are openminded enough," Matthews told me, "to put things aside. I've gotten a lot of not guilty verdicts in that county that were kind of surprising to me. . . . I've seen all white juries acquit my black defendants."

Then there's the issue of that *Texas Monthly* article being published weeks before Bobbi's trial, giving potential jurors an opinion of the case from Jen's point of view, most of which Jen lied about.

No one involved in this case I spoke to seemed to think it was a big deal.

* * *

Look, I don't want to be accused of condoning Bobbi Jo Smith's behavior during those years, her drug use and alcoholism, luring girls to Bob's, et cetera. Or not sympathizing with Bob Dow as a murder victim. But questions began for me as I looked into this case.

Bobbi is not guilty of the crime she was charged with. That realization is as clear to me as anything in this case.

EPILOGUE

DURING JEN'S SENTENCING HEARING, she made an observation (which I covered in the narrative, but becomes a statement that deserves further scrutiny here): "Well, first, we would—we would get—we would do drugs to get inside that state of mind. And then after that, we would just sit there and read each other's minds. We would just talk to each other without saying a word, you know, verbally. And it's—it's kind of, like, you know—you and someone say something at the same time. You know, y'all's minds are thinking alike."

One has to wonder, was Jen under this "Wiccan" influence when she purportedly heard Bobbi tell her that Bob Dow needed to die in order for them to be together? Did she actually believe later, after becoming "sober" while in prison, that Bobbi could control her mind? Or was this just another lie in a long list to cover those of which she told all along?

At another point during court proceedings, Jen made this claim: "I felt like I was afraid of losing her [Bobbi]."

That's an important piece of information in the scope of this case.

Jen was referring to how she felt near the time of the murder. Remember, Kathy caught Bobbi in bed with another chick shortly before and told Jen about it. Jen said she didn't believe it. And so here was Bobbi—another lover whom Jen felt slipping away from her. We know how Jen felt about her past loves and losses because she wrote about it in her journal. We also know from that journal that Jen could not hold down relationships. Losing a lover was traumatic to Jen—always. Loss was something she began to comprehend and, truthfully, expect as far back as when Kathy started going to prison. Loss was something Jen sensed coming. But with Bobbi, Jen was obsessed. There's clear evidence of that obsession. She had never been obsessed with a lover before this. And then later, talking about this moment in her life, Jen admitted what?

"I felt like I was afraid of losing her."

To me, that statement was such a vital piece of this puzzle.

Think about it: *I felt like I was afraid of losing her.*

One of the most profound statements Jen ever

made was in the form of a journal entry: *I'm just a . . . girl with only a broken heart and no one to fix it.*

Bobbi was the fixer. But Jen was beginning to realize that Bobbi was not exclusive, and Bobbi was not in love with her, like she wanted her to be.

This statement, all by itself, said so much about Jen's psyche, her character, and her skewed mentality at the time she met Bobbi. When I look at all of the available evidence, it's certainly obvious to me that Jen was jealous of Bob Dow and Bobbi's relationship. When I put that up against the three main motivations for murder—love, money, and revenge (with several subcategories bracketing off those)—and a narrative comes into focus. I would have liked to have seen a more thorough questioning of Jen by police: her life, her loves, her crimes, her passions, her thoughts about Bobbi and Bob.

But nobody asked those questions.

I had so many things to talk to Jen about. I assumed she'd step right up to the task. Hell, she had spoken to everyone else. So I pursued Jen with dogged determination (through Audrey, Kathy, and several letters of my own). I wanted her story. My aim was to see if it would change again. I wrote. Audrey said she wrote to her on my behalf. And for a time there, I heard nothing other than Jen was gravely ill, cancer or some sort of benign tumor (I heard later it was her liver), and she had spent a better part of a year in the infirmary. There were even some who thought she might die.

As I mentioned in the narrative, in early May

2012, a letter from Jen arrived. It was brief. She sounded bitter and frustrated. She described a "lack of interest" in telling me "anything" about her life "then or now." She went on to say I should not send her anything. She wrote how she didn't *wish to see how my ex-beloved and unfavorable sister have added their foolishness to my present state of being.* She claimed to be sorry for an "unwillingness to help" me "write a great story."

Jen is obviously afraid of the truth—and may not even know at this point what that *truth* is. She openly and shamelessly lied to Katy Vine and *Texas Monthly* after pleading out her case, weeks before Bobbi's trial. I believe this was part of a carefully thought-out design to bury Bobbi for turning on her. Look at those incredible tales of meeting Bobbi under a tree out on the library green, the road trip, and what happened with Bob, which Jen had told Katy Vine (whom I later spoke to about this case).

There comes a time in a series of lies when the liar needs to stop talking. How could Jen keep track of it all? Her story fell apart each time she told it. If she laid out *another* version to me, it would only add to the disaster that turned out to be her life during those days before and after she murdered Bob Dow.

Scary numbers appear when the facts surrounding the imprisonment of women in this country are studied. According to The Sentencing Project: Research and Advocacy for Reform in Washington, DC, the numbers are staggering: *Women in state prison . . . were more likely to report using drugs at the time of their offense than men (40% vs. 32%), and nearly one-third reported that they had committed their offense to obtain money to buy drugs.* One out of every three women is serving time in prison because of drugs. *More than half (57%) of women incarcerated under state jurisdiction reported that they had experienced either sexual or physical abuse before their admission to prison. Nearly three-quarters (73.1%) of women in state prison in 2005 had a mental health problem, compared to 55% of men in prison. Women in prison are considerably more likely than men to have been diagnosed with a mental illness. In state prisons . . . 23.6% of women were identified as mentally ill, compared to 15.8% of men, while in federal prisons the proportions were 12.5% of women and 7% of men.*

These numbers play a role in this case.

As I researched the fact that a good portion of the females in our prison system are a product of abuse, I came across some rather disturbing information that played directly into the Jennifer Jones/Bobbi Jo Smith story. According to the American Academy of Child & Adolescent Psychiatry, *Childhood trauma darkens the child's vision of the future as well as her attitudes about people. Young people who have been traumatized will voice cautious, one-day-at-a-time attitudes. They may say that you can't count on anyone. Sexually traumatized girls may shrink from men (using avoidance to cope with the trauma) or approach them with overly friendly sexual advances (in an attempt to master the trauma by trying to relive it). Traumatized children tend to recognize the profound vulnerability in all people, especially themselves.*

That same article went on to say, these *trauma-related fears often persist into adulthood.*

What I found most compelling when I compared this research to the girls was: *Within the traumatized child, internal changes may occur which can affect her later in life, surfacing in adolescence or early adulthood.* The key here is that without the proper treatment, *some childhood traumas can result in later problems [characterized] by violent behavior, extremes of passivity and re-victimization (people who were raped or incestuously abused as children often fail to protect themselves from rape), self-mutilation, suicidal or self-endangering behavior, and anxiety disturbances.*

After finishing this book, readers, how do the girls match up to this research?

"I think it was a combination of them both and the things that were going on in their lives at that point," Brian Boetz later told me when I expressed the opinion of not categorizing Bobbi as a cold-blooded killer. Both girls were amped up on dope. Both had come from hard-core backgrounds and grew up without a sense of direction. Their view of right and wrong was skewed.

On top of it all, as well, Bob Dow did not help

his own cause. What he did to Bobbi and Jen (along with scores of other women he used) was immoral and sadistic. He took advantage of these girls as much as he possibly could. I'm never one to bash the victim of a homicide, and that's not what I mean here. I only say this to point out how the girls' lives turned out was, partly, manifested by the adults around them. Both of the girls were, arguably, adults by age. But we would have to ask: Were they adults emotionally?

This story is not over. I am going to pursue— and I have no idea why; after all, I could just let Bobbi go and let her do this on her own—the idea of getting Bobbi someone who will listen to the facts of her case. I am going to try and convince someone that this woman has been overprosecuted, at the least, and deserves a new trial.

I also have to wonder: Was Bobbi punished for the disgust those closely connected to this case felt for Bob Dow, along with the rather ugly relationship Bobbi and Bob had?

In one of the last letters she wrote to me regarding this book, Bobbi did not have good things to say about her attorney, Jim Matthews.

I never believed he was for me, she said.

As my own relationship with Matthews continued, I began to agree with Bobbi. Matthews repeatedly promised me documentation he never delivered, including Bobbi's entire court file, which she had given written permission for him to send. He had repeatedly said he wanted to help Bobbi, believed in her innocence, and wanted to see that she got a new trial. Yet, time and again, Jim Matthews did not do what he told me he would.

In the end, Bobbi was quite a different person than when I first met her. She was no longer defensive and bitter and continually on guard. She said she did want to meet me "face-to-face" at some point, adding, "I thank God that you've come along. I pray in hopes for a second chance with my son. I want to take him to his baseball games. I want to be there for his first crush. I'll admit I've learned a lot being trapped within these walls. I use my lessons for positive motivation now, and I will not make the same mistakes twice. I am a woman. I am a mother. . . . I refuse to give up.

Look, I could be entirely wrong about Bobbi— as I'm sure there will be some who read this book and disbelieve her. What's most important to me, always, are facts. Personally, I'd need a *hell* of a lot more than what was presented in court to send a nineteen-year-old away for fifty years. There were too many lies told, too many variables. I couldn't convict on twelve hours' worth of testimony—half of which was Jennifer Jones lying under oath. I think a major part of this case revolves around the repulsion some felt when they looked at the photographs left behind. Did Bobbi's extremely graphic and revolting sexual acts on film condemn her? Did the fact that she had sex with Bob and was promiscuous with females turn into a terrible loathing that convicted her? Was Bobbi punished for Bob Dow's reprehensible behavior? Was she shown bias because of her sexuality? We live in a society today where these questions become relevant.

I've never questioned a jury's decision before. And I hesitated to do it here. But sometimes, well . . . sometimes juries just get it wrong.

AFTERWORD

ANY READER of my twenty-plus books about murder will know that I hold little back when going after guilty parties. I often chastise female murderers, in particular, as the narrative chugs along, providing all the supplementary evidence to back up my opinions. As I started working on this case during the summer of 2011, it seemed to be another one of those familiar, tragic stories: Two girls, who happen to be lovers, get high, look for action, and electrify their already violent tendencies, conspiring together to whack a guy they viewed as sleazy and disposable. I assumed I'd run into the same psychological makeup I had seen in just about all of the prior female murder cases I've covered, save for a few female serial-killer stories (a different psychological makeup altogether). As I read through the prosecution's case and the police reports, it seemed a pretty open-and-shut case. It was easy (then) to see how both girls had been arrested and charged and sentenced. Some of my first calls were to law enforcement, which began to back up this general feeling I had.

As I dug deeply into the case, however, studying it more closely (and objectively), interviewing people involved, long before I ever spoke to Bobbi Jo Smith, for the first time in my long career I found myself wondering what the hell happened inside that Texas courtroom during the *one and a half* days of Bobbi's trial. Reading through the trial transcripts, I was amazed at the lack of evidence that convicted this woman. I put myself in her place. The mendacious tales and outright lies that Jennifer Jones told were so enormous and all-encompassing and repetitive and incredibly hard to believe, there can be absolutely no way any right-minded juror should have taken one word out of Jen's mouth as fact.

Remember, to convict Bobbi, a person would have to sign off on the notion that Jen was telling the truth when she claimed Bobbi gave her the gun (a fact that Jen herself disputed in her second statement) *and* asked her to kill Bob Dow, plying her with the "He'll never allow us to be together" argument. Or, one better, a juror would have to believe that Bobbi gave Jen the gun with the malicious *intention* of Jen killing Bob. You'd also have to believe Bobbi's statements, both of which she said were contrived lies she and Jen had cooked up to protect each other and get out of it all. (It's important to note when Bobbi gave those statements: all within a week after being arrested.) After having read those statements, I saw clearly all of the fantasy and Hollywood elements of what the girls were telling the police. Jim Matthews told me he saw that scene—the one where Jen was holding the gun and Bobbi supposedly walked in the room and said, "You look sexy"—in a film.

In my opinion, as soon as police (men and women I have a tremendous amount of respect for—my career, my readers, and my friends in law enforcement can easily back up this statement) got the story that matched the case they wanted to present to the prosecutor, they stopped investigating. Look, I don't think this was done out of malfeasance or a deep-seated desire to condemn Bobbi. I don't believe that for a minute. These cops are good cops. I know that. Boetz and Judd were following orders from the top. Their integrity was never in question for me; that's not what I am saying here in this book. I think it's more out of ignorance and lack of experience in investigating this sort of complicated murder. Police and prosecutors believed the girls when it fit the scenario they had wanted (and needed) to close the case. It happens. I've seen this sort of blinders mentality in several cases. And what's more, I feel Mike Burns got stuck on his "he needed killin'" theme and believed the girls acted in this manner. Burns and Boetz told me several times that, to them, it seemed the girls figured nothing would happen to them legally because they had killed a scumbag. The girls, however, had never said this outright.

I don't believe this is true.

Also, the fact that the judge fast-tracked this case and a change of venue was never discussed—even after that *Texas Monthly* article condemning Bobbi was published weeks before her trial—is overwhelmingly and unmistakably unfair to the defendant. Then, when Bobbi's lawyer asked for some extra time to give his final argument, this during a murder trial that lasted all of twelve hours to begin with, the judge denied it.

Those three circumstances alone boggle the mind.

Jen's testimony should have been tossed from the record as soon as deliberations began. And if Jen's testimony was scratched, all the state had left was Bobbi's second statement, weakly implicating herself in the "I gave Jennifer the gun" argument. Here was a second statement, it should be pointed out, that did nothing to prove Bobbi gave Jen that gun, knowing she would kill Bob Dow with it. None of the state's witnesses added *any* evidence to the state's contention that Bobbi told or convinced Jen to kill Bob Dow, and then *provided* her with the means to commit that horrible crime.

I've read it maybe a hundred times before: *Mr. Phelps, I'm innocent. I didn't do it. You have to help me.*

I get letters from the convicted (and their friends and family members) with those exact words (I'll get even more once this book is published). I get e-mails from loved ones writing on behalf of those they believe were wrongly convicted.

In those cases where I looked into a defendant claiming innocence, as I continued investigating the case, the claim was repeatedly and quickly disproven by the *evidence*. When I looked at this case early on, in fact, and had heard that Bobbi (who did not want to talk to me until months after I began) had made this same claim, I thought, *Yeah, right . . . here we go again.*

Yet, as I dug through the case, I was overwhelmed by the lack of evidence that convicted Bobbi. *Jennifer Jones is all that convicted this woman?* I asked myself time and again. *Bobbi Jo's own statements, in which she clearly lied and admitted as much later on, were the only corroborating pieces of evidence against her? Bobbi telling her grandmother that she killed Bob, after Jen said she killed Bob, is enough to convict a woman of murder and sentence her to fifty years?*

Bobbi Jo Smith, if nothing else, was grossly—*grossly*—overcharged.

I was told by Mike Burns that the law is different in Texas. Somebody murders someone in your presence and you somehow knew about it beforehand and provided the means (he was talking about his Bobbi Jo theory), you're just as guilty. You will be convicted and sentenced in the same way as the person who pulled the trigger.

Looking at this case, even from Burns's perspective, I was amazed that this sort of failure of justice could take place in the United States. And I can only guess that had Bobbi the means to hire herself a hotshot, high-profile attorney, she would have walked out of that courtroom, or been able to plead her case to a far lesser charge and sentence.

From there, readers, you'd have to ask yourself: *How in the hell did those first statements by the girls ever become part of the record? And why would a jury cherry-pick certain pieces of a statement, believe them as fact, but not believe other parts of the same statements? Also, why didn't Bobbi's lawyer argue to have the statements tossed out of her trial?*

In a recent New York Court of Appeals ruling, four judges ordered a new trial for a woman "facing murder and assault charges," finding that her lawyer "should have moved to suppress statements she made to police during a lengthy interrogation." In a four-to-one decision, the Appellate Division, Third Judicial Department, found that the defendant's admission that she had helped her husband plan to kill two people turned out to be "the crucial evidence" in her case and should have been challenged by her lawyer. Remember, that one sentence in the second statement by Bobbi, according to Mike Burns, is the reason why the jury had to convict her.

Look, I realize New York and Texas have vastly different ways (the most respectable word I can come up with here) of interpreting the law and how each of their courts (liberal vs. conservative) should be run. But again, all of this flies in the face of simple common sense and—at the *very* least—reasonable doubt.

Even Jen's sister believed this. Jen's story of what happened "kept changing," Audrey explained during a phone call. "She told me that she went inside [Bob's house] and they had both decided to go back over there. . . . They broke into the house. Bob wasn't there. They waited until Bob got back. She [Jen] had [the gun] behind her back in her pants. She told Bob that they decided that they wanted to move back in and that she wanted to have sex with him. So she took Bob to the bedroom, he got undressed, and she told him to put something over his head so she could make believe it was Bobbi Jo. And she shot him." Audrey said Jen never clarified if she was "doing him at the time" she murdered him, or that she "was fixin' to do him. But I know he was lying on the bed naked."

Not once did Audrey ever tell me that Jen said Bobbi coerced her into committing this crime, gave her the gun, or was with her. Audrey, in fact, gave the indication that Jen did it all on her own.

The first time Jen told Audrey about the murder: "She told me that she was the only one that shot him and that she freaked out. Then she changed it up the second time. All the other stuff was the same. But that she had shot him twice, got off of him, and then Bobbi Jo came into the room, picked up the gun off the floor, and that Bob was shaking and asking them for help. . . . So that after [Jen] shot him, [Jen] went over there and choked him and then he died."

There were no bruises on Bob Dow's neck that would indicate strangulation. This was simply more of Jen telling erroneous lies to either make herself look more badass gangsta, or because lying for Jen was just another one of her many emotions—something she did, I believe, without thinking, at will.

I asked Bobbi why she believed Jen killed Bob. If Bobbi was to be believed, then Jen committed this crime for her own reasons, on her own.

"I don't know . . . why would *anyone* do this? If I had to say, I'd say she did it for Kathy," Bobbi said. "Kathy wanted to go back to the house and rob Robert as soon as [we] went over there [to the Spanish Trace apartment]. They were all packed and ready to run when we got there. . . ."

What's clear to me was that Bobbi took the brunt and burden of Jen's entire life of loss, emotional pain, and dysfunction. As someone who has studied for his profession the minds of female murderers, I can see clearly that as Jen grew, she developed what I'll coin as a "soft conscience"— she was systematically able to commit crimes, lie to those she loved, sleep around, do drugs, drink excessively, even change her sexuality to feel accepted and loved, and it all became easier for her as time went on. She began to feel normal while involved in abnormal behaviors. She was comforted by her own psychological fall. Lying became a way for Jen to feel right.

If Jen's journal was read in its entirety, a clear picture would emerge of a girl hardened by her surroundings, growing increasingly angrier by the day, nurturing a volcanic rage, which would need to be released at some point. Jen was a pressure cooker. She was a woman who, when the right moment came around, would feel the need to deal with her anger issues in a violent manner. That was Jennifer Jones. The end result and facts of her life support it.

In one of her last letters, Bobbi made a valid point when she wrote, *I came into this with you by my own choice. I've kept my mouth and my mind closed down and shut out—and at times all of this overwhelms me. It makes me remember things I hid deep down. . . . Regardless what happens, I know I've been able to tell the truth.*

She thanked me for that opportunity.

ACKNOWLEDGMENTS

I WOULD LIKE to thank the usual suspects (you know who you are). It gets kind of redundant naming the same list of people at the end of every book. So I will just say here that my family and friends, colleagues, and those working for me are the foundation of what I do, and I could not continue my work without any one of them. When it comes to my readers, moreover, I am always at a loss for words when trying to address all of you and express my gratitude to your continued support. You are the most important part of my work.

I am also profoundly grateful to each one of my *Dark Minds,* Investigation Discovery viewers. Thank you for allowing me to do what I love.

I am honored and humbled by both my readers and viewers and their dedication and willingness to spend the time they do with me.

It feels weird for me to thank Bobbi Jo, and there's really no reason to. Moreover, she wouldn't want me to thank her. We had a love/hate relationship. Bobbi understands she has issues that need dealing with and she is working toward the goal of getting the help she needs. I greatly respect that. Sobriety is a wonderful thing, a gift. In 2013, I celebrate eighteen years of sobriety myself.

I do want to thank Kathy Jones, Tamey Hurley, and Audrey Sawyer for opening up to me. Tamey, especially, was brutally honest, as was Kathy Jones. Tamey shared many personal bits of her life, which I chose not to include in this book. Tamey is a tortured soul, like her daughter. They need time to reconcile. Time to love again. I'm told they are beginning anew.

For Kathy and Audrey, I wish them the best. There is love in their hearts. Jennifer should have trusted Audrey more.

There was one person, Shauntá Weston, a friend of Bobbi's, who initiated a dialogue with me. Miss Weston was very helpful. She believes in Bobbi. Thank you, Shauntá, for your help.

Brian Boetz was helpful in responding to my queries in a timely fashion and I thank him for that. Mike Burns, mostly, as well. Boetz and Burns were sincere in their responses to me. I appreciate that. Both believe in justice and that they did the right thing here—and who says they didn't.

I would not have heard of this story or written this book if it had not been for my good friend Chip Selby. A freelance television producer by day, Chip told me about this story, took some photos, and was a great source early on. I want to extend a big thanks to Chip for turning me on to this great true-crime tale. And perhaps, most important,

M2 Pictures researcher Joanne Taylor, who originally found this story. This one hovered under everyone's radar, but Joanne plucked it out. For that, I am thankful to her.

I would like to extend my sincere appreciation to everyone at Investigation Discovery and Beyond Productions involved in making *Dark Minds* the best (nonfiction) crime show on television: Andrew "Fazz" Farrell, Alex Barry, Colette "Coco" Sandstedt, John Mavety, Peter Heap, Mark Middis, Toby Prior, Peter Coleman, Derek Ichilcik, Jared "Jars" Transfield, Jo Telfer, Claire Westerman, Milena Gozzo, Cameron Power, Katie Ryerson, Inneke Smit, Pele Hehea, Jeremy Peek, Jeremy Adair, Geri Berman, Nadine Terens, Samantha Hertz, Lale Teoman, Hayden Anderson, Savino (from Onyx Sound Lab in Manchester, CT), David O'Brien, Ra-ey Saleh, Nathan Brand, Rebecca Clare, Anthony Toy, Mark Wheeler, Mandy Chapman, Jenny O'shea, Jen Longhurst, Anita Bezjak, Geoff Fitzpatrick, John Luscombe, Debbie Gottschalk, Eugenie Vink, Sucheta Sachdev, Sara Kozak, Kevin Bennett, Jane Latman, and Henry Schleiff.

As you can see, it takes an army to make a television show.

I also need to extend my deepest gratitude to the families of my *Dark Minds* road crew, as well as my own, for allowing us to take the time we need on the road to shoot *Dark Minds*. It's a lot of time away from home and I realize the sacrifice all of you make on my behalf, especially the children: India, Ivo and April—and, of course, our spouses, Bates and Regina.

Cara at Inspirations—thanks.

Lastly, my publisher, Laurie Parkin, and the entire team at Kensington Publishing Corp., all of whom continue to believe in me and make great things possible. I want to extend a big, huge thanks to all of you. Likewise, I need to thank Kensington CEO Steve Zacharius, editorial director Audrey LeFehr, and Karen Auerbach, publicity director. My longtime editor, Michaela Hamilton, has been an instrumental part of my career for well over a decade now, and also a great friend. We've done nearly twenty books together and Michaela's passion for what I do continues to grow with each book. I am indebted and thankful, not to mention amazed by, Michaela's desire to see me succeed. There is a ton of work that goes on behind the scenes of each book, and I want to point out to the Kensington team that I realize how hard you all work on my behalf—and I'm very grateful for that.

**Keep reading to enjoy an exclusive preview of
M. William Phelps's next true-crime book!**

Obsessed

Coming from Pinnacle Books in 2014

CHAPTER 1

SUSAN RAYMUNDO WAS used to her daughter calling her Florida winter home at least twice a day. Anna Lisa was good that way. She liked to stay in touch with her parents, even if it was just to say hello.

"She was a very thoughtful daughter," Anna's father, Renato, later said. "She was a perfect daughter . . . an excellent human being."

Smart too: Anna Lisa held degrees from Harvard and Columbia.

On November 8, 2002, Susan, a retired pediatrician, was at a local hospital near her Florida home with her mother, who was undergoing a routine procedure. When she returned to the house, Susan noticed the light on the answering machine blinking.

Tossing her keys on the counter, putting her handbag down, Susan hit the button and listened. She knew who it was.

Anna . . .

"Hi, Mom and Dad. I just want you to know what's going on. I know you're busy with Grandma, but I'll talk to you sometime."

It was 10:34 A.M., Susan noticed, when the message came in.

After she got herself situated, Susan called Anna Lisa back. The line rang several times, but there was no answer.

It was odd, Susan supposed, because her daughter worked from home. She was there all the time, especially during the day, during the week. Susan and her husband had purchased the Connecticut condo for Anna Lisa, closing the deal on March 15, 2000.

I'll try again later, Susan told herself, perhaps sensing—if only in a subtle, mother's intuition way—that something was amiss.

CHAPTER 2

THE WOMAN SOUNDED FRANTIC. She was in a terrible hurry. Inhaling and exhaling heavily, as if out of breath. Yet, strangely enough, she cleared her throat before speaking for the first time.

"Yes, hello," she said after the Stamford, Connecticut, 911 police dispatcher beckoned the caller to speak up. "Yes . . . the guy . . . the . . . He attacked my neighbor."

"You mean someone attacked your neighbor?" dispatch asked as the caller blew two deeply dramatic breaths into the phone receiver: *Whoosh, whoosh.*

"Yes, yes . . . ," the caller said sheepishly.

"When did this happen?" dispatch asked.

It sounded as if the caller said: "I saw a guy go into the apartment at One-Two-Six Harbor View. . . ."

Dispatch noted the address. Then: "One twenty-six Harbor View—"

But the caller corrected her angrily, yelling over the dispatcher's voice: "One twenty-*three* Harbor View!"

"Okay," dispatch said. "Don't yell, because I cannot understand you."

Almost in tears now, the seemingly frantic caller spoke over dispatch: "One twenty-*three* Harbor View."

"Listen to me . . . one-two-three Harbor View . . . what is your friend's name?"

"I don't know her name, but she's my neighbor and she lives in apartment one-oh-five."

"She lives in apartment one-oh-five?"

"Right! And the guy was in there, and he . . ."

"He what?"

"He *attacked* her."

"Okay, can you tell me what the guy looks like?"

"I just don't know. I heard yelling. I heard yelling."

There was a clicking sound next.

"Hello?" dispatch said. "Hello? Hello?"

The line was dead. The call, in its entirety, lasted about one minute, thirty seconds.

He had just finished eating lunch. It was near 12:30 in the afternoon, November 8, 2002, a Friday. The weather was rather mild for this time of the year near the Connecticut shoreline,

the temperature ranging from 46 to 57 degrees
Fahrenheit. The air was dry and sharp; a slight
breeze of winds, around six miles per hour, rolled
off the Atlantic Ocean. The sun was bright. There
was a waxing crescent moon (7/8 full) out, nearly
visible in the luminous blue skies. By all accounts,
a picture-perfect late fall day in one of Connecticut's more prominent, seaside communities.

The cop drove a marked police car. He was
dressed in full uniform. The area that twenty-two-
year-veteran officer David Sileo patrolled was
indeed exclusive. Officers called it "District Three."
Stamford had seen a sharp economic resurgence,
its downtown area revitalized and energized with
excitement and shoppers and business. The bubble
all around them might have been bursting, but
Stamford was hopping. This region where Sileo was
headed was known to locals as "Cove/Shippan,"
located just south of Interstate 95, in between
Cummings Park and Cove Island Park.

Yachts. Fishing and houseboats. Money, status,
and exclusivity.

Sitting in an inlet, a cove, southwest of West
Beach, just across the waterway from Dyke Park,
was 123 Harbor Drive. People walked dogs down
here. Docked their massive sailboats and Bayliners
and Sea Rays and cruise liners. Men and women
jogged in their expensive sweat suits, earbuds
booming, minding their own business. Families
had picnics and tossed Frisbees. They lay out in
the sun. Stamford, Connecticut, by and large, is

a wealthy region of this small state of 3,500,000 residents; it is the sister to the more select, more expensive Greenwich. By big-city standards, Stamford boasts a small population of about 120,000. Median income holds steady at $75,000. Taxes are high. The streets are clean. Crime rates in certain areas are low. Housing prices not too shabby. Stamford is often named one of the top ten places to live in the country.

Officer Sileo was dispatched to 123 Harbor View Drive, unit 105, specifically, after a rather strange 911 call had come in minutes before, whereby an anonymous woman had maintained that a neighbor of hers—someone she apparently knew—was being attacked by a man.

When Sileo arrived, another officer was just pulling up behind him to the same scene. They agreed to knock on the door. See what the hell was going on inside the condo.

The unit at 105 Harbor Drive sat on top of a three-car garage. A visitor would have to walk up several steps to the front door.

The officer who had arrived as Sileo pulled up knocked on the screen door. With no answer, he opened it and knocked on the interior door, looking in all directions to see if anyone was around.

When no one answered, the patrol officer tried the handle.

It was unlocked.

Sileo watched as his colleague opened the door

"a few inches," took a quick peek inside, and then yelled, "Stamford Police . . . is anyone home?"

No response. It was eerily quiet. Especially for a domestic, which was called into 911.

Pushing the door fully open, Sileo's colleague spied a ghastly sight, which immediately prompted him to draw his weapon.

Officer Sileo hurried up behind, hand on his sidearm. They made eye contact and agreed to enter the condo slowly, barrels of their weapons leading the way.

CHAPTER 3

IN SEPTEMBER 2000, NELSON SESSLER WAS hired by Stamford-based Purdue Pharma, a major player in the pharmaceutical world of developing medications. Purdue Pharma boasts of being the industry leader in pain management. For Sessler, who held a doctorate in pharmacy from the Massachusetts College of Pharmacy and Health Sciences, Purdue was the ideal company to work for. He could pursue his passion for researching and developing new medications, and ultimately carve out a career that he could excel in and, at the same rate, be proud of the work he was doing.

At thirty-five years old, Sessler had hit his prime. He was a good-looking man, tall and handsome. He took care of himself, working out and working hard. Purdue was one of those companies so big, with an employee list of so many diverse individuals, cliques kicked up within the group an employee worked for. Sessler had no trouble making friends. And in December 2000, merely months after he started with the company, he met and started dating a fellow employee, thirty-two-year-old Anna Lisa Raymundo. Anna Lisa was bright and from a family of well-educated high achievers working within the medical field. Filipino by descent, Anna Lisa had beautifully dark, shiny skin, eyes to match, a cheerful demeanor, and a smile so large it was hard not to like the woman and feel her magnetic charm the moment she was introduced. With a master's in public health, Anna Lisa had been working at Purdue for several years. She liked Nelson Sessler the moment she met him. They hit it off.

Nelson shared an apartment in town with several men, about three miles away from Anna Lisa's Harbor Drive unit. By November 2002, however, as their relationship had hit its stride, going from its highest and lowest points, Nelson had been spending most of his time over at Anna Lisa's condo.

"Five to seven [days]," Sessler said later. "The majority of the week."

In February 2002, Anna Lisa left Purdue Pharma and went to work for a New Jersey company, Farmacia. There was a time when Anna Lisa was actually commuting back and forth to New Jersey from her Stamford condo, spending four hours per day on the road. By November, though, Anna Lisa had worked it out with Farmacia that she would work from home and head into the office for meetings on an as-needed basis.

Nelson Sessler was the first to admit later on that by November 2002 his relationship with Anna Lisa had nearly run its course. They had hit a stride, sure, but it was more or less lined with complacency as he, anyway, was simply going through the motions. As long as Nelson had known Anna Lisa, he had not given up his room at the apartment across town he shared with three other men. And that alone said something about how he felt.

There was that feeling of going through the motions with Anna Lisa and, well, this secret Nelson had been keeping from Anna: He was sneaking around, sleeping with one of his coworkers at Purdue Pharma, a rather elegant, highly intelligent, dark-skinned woman, born in Iran, who had long, flowing, curly tar black hair. Nelson had met her at the local bar that the Purdue Pharma employees hung out at in town. Nelson had been having a fling with the thirty-two-year-old woman since the summer of 2001, almost a year by then. Their relationship was hot and cold. Nelson couldn't really see his concubine too often because, he later explained, she "had a handicapped brother—a mentally challenged or retarded brother that she took care of, and elderly parents, and volleyball. And that those three items took up most of her weekends. . . ."

So, for Nelson and his lover, they could only see each other sporadically, at various times during the week, in the evenings. This worked out well when

Anna Lisa was going down to New Jersey to work;
but the affair had become more difficult to contain
as soon as Anna started working from home.
Nelson would have to make excuses.

He'd have to lie.

CHAPTER 4

JUST BEYOND THE DOOR inside that Harbor Drive condo that Stamford police officers had been summoned to on the afternoon of November 2, 2002, Officer Sileo and his colleague immediately entered through the unlocked front door and stumbled onto a ghastly sight.

"The apartment was in disarray," Sileo said later. "There were signs of a violent struggle."

Indeed. The body of a young female was stretched out on the floor, her legs spread open, one leg propped up on a box, the other on the floor. There was blood all over, smears and smudges on the white tile underneath her body, the walls, the carpeting, heading toward the bathroom, on her jeans, on her bare feet. She was fully clothed, but her white shirt (a sweater) had been pulled up to her breasts (not sexually, but amid some sort of struggle for life). By her foot on the wood floor was a barbell, a ten-pound chunk of steel, essentially. Next to that was a plant, its dirt out of the pot, spread all around during the deadly skirmish. They found her adjacent to the stairs heading up to a second level inside the home and the front door. A laundry basket was tipped over, as were other pieces of furniture. There were boxes and everyday items found in any home scattered around as though there had been a terribly violent, extended scuffle. The smudges of blood on the floor told a story these officers were immediately familiar with: There had been a terrific fight *after* blood was present.

Another officer was on his way to the scene when he heard a superior over the radio notify dispatch that BCI was needed at the Harbor Drive scene. The Bureau of Criminal Investigation, the officer knew, was called out only when there was serious trouble.

"We got a ten-one," the superior announced over the radio.

And the officer knew: *10-1 equals homicide.*

The troops were on their way. Scores of officers were then dispatched to the scene.

As the officer headed toward Harbor Drive himself, he was called off.

"We need you to head out to the Duchess Restaurant to secure a pay phone there," dispatch intoned.

"Ten-four."

Seemed like a strange request, but the officer shifted his destination and went on his way.

Back at the Harbor Drive condo, it was immediately clear that the dead woman on the floor had been viciously attacked. No doubt about it. But what was also made clear by quickly analyzing the scene around the woman was that it had taken a while for her to be murdered. It wasn't fast. The scuffle had started in one place and finished in another. She put up one heck of a fight, too. That was obvious in the way in which things were tossed around and blood was spattered and smudged all over. It wasn't as if she had been murdered in the spot where an obvious argument took place. The fight—and that's what this was, for certain— started in a place and went throughout the home and ended where she had been found, lying on the floor.

Officer Sileo, gun in hand, eyes roaming the condo, his colleague covering him, reached down and checked the victim for vital signs.

There were none.

The wounds appear fresh, Sileo thought. The blood had not even had time to begin coagulation. Puddles of blood were shiny and wet.

Whatever had taken place inside this home had perhaps happened within the hour. A few hours, maybe.

The officers knew what to do next. They had

been trained and had been in this circumstance before. The first thing an officer should do upon entering a residence with a dead body (DB) is clear the remainder of the home. Make sure there were no additional victims or a perp hiding out, waiting on them.

After a cursory search of the home, Sileo was confident they were alone with one victim.

Now, all Sileo and his colleague could do was seal off the front door, not allow anyone in, and greet the team of investigators on their way, and begin the process of finding out what in the name of God happened to this woman and, more important, who was responsible.